WITHDRAWN

30/-

£1.50

D1485412

SALINGER

SALINGER

A CRITICAL AND PERSONAL PORTRAIT
INTRODUCED AND EDITED BY

Henry Anatole Grunwald

PETER OWEN · LONDON

PETER OWEN LIMITED
50 Old Brompton Road London SW7

*

First British Commonwealth edition 1964
© 1962 by Henry Anatole Grunwald
Printed in Great Britain
by Lowe & Brydone (Printers) Limited, London

Contents

Acknowledgments

The editor is grateful for permission to reprint material that originally appeared in the following publications: *American Quarterly, American Speech, The Atlantic, Chicago Review, Commonweal, Harper's Magazine, National Review, New Leader, New Republic, New World Writing, New York Times Book Review, Partisan Review, Saturday Review, Time, Twentieth Century, Washington Post, Western Humanities Review;* and in the following books: *The Eye of Innocence,* copyright 1960 by Leslie Fiedler, by permission of Beacon Press; *American Modern,* copyright 1958 by Maxwell Geismar, by permission of Hill and Wang Inc.; *The Fiction of J. D. Salinger,* copyright 1958 by Frederick Gywnn and Joseph Blotner, by permission of University of Pittsburgh Press; *A Mirror for Anglo-Saxons,* copyright 1960 by Martin Green, by permission of Harper & Brothers; *Radical Innocence,* copyright 1961 by Ihab Hassan, by permission of Princeton University Press.

Special thanks to Wendy Kupsick for research assistance, and for invaluable help in assembling the material and obtaining the permissions that made this volume possible; to Pat Locke, Martha Murphy MacDowell, Joyce Haber and Marguerite Johnson for help with the manuscript; and to John Leggett of Harper & Brothers for unfailingly patient and sage advice.

Introduction

There is a feeling in many quarters that altogether too much fuss is being made about J. D. Salinger.

George Steiner expressed this irritation several years ago in the *Nation* when he castigated "the Salinger industry," and that was even before *Franny and Zooey* reached semipermanence atop the best-seller lists, or before the author's lean, somewhat horsy face appeared on the cover of *Time*. Of course Steiner is right in seeking to put Salinger in perspective and in suggesting that the creator of *The Catcher in the Rye* falls considerably short of Dostoevsky or Mark Twain. On the other hand, in accusing Salinger's audience of being "by any ordinary tokens largely illiterate," Steiner sounds ill-tempered and snobbish. While it is difficult to quarrel with his classification of Salinger as a "good minor writer," the extraordinary thing about Salinger is that somehow he will not stay classified. In his work, the sum of the parts adds up to more than the whole. He preoccupies us more than the equation of all his virtues and all his shortcomings would suggest. There are other "good minor" writers whose work may be better than Salinger's but who do not hold our imagination—or for that matter, irritate us—in nearly the same way.

This is true not only of Salinger's sympathetic critics; it is even truer of his unsympathetic ones. How many "minor writers" are there whom the critics feel called upon to put in their places? Alfred Kazin goes to considerable trouble to prove a charge of self-love against Salinger's Glass family; in bothering to do this, Kazin in effect concedes the Glasses' extraordinary degree of reality. The same applies to other, more hostile critics who indignantly point out the philosophical defects or the irritating manners of Salinger's characters.

The One-Armed Violinist

Frederick Gwynn and Joseph Blotner, two English professors writing in tandem, disapprove of the Glass stories, but they seem to believe in the family's existence to the point of writing biography rather than criticism. There is, for instance, the matter of the vaudeville team of Gallagher & Glass; is this really, they wonder, an echo of "the old team of Gallagher & Shean (Schoenberg)"? From there, Gwynn and Blotner (not a bad name for a vaudeville team itself) go on to note "that Al Shean was uncle to the five Marx brothers." What this fact may mean is not clear, but the sudden intrusion of the world of *Variety* into the world of *College English* gives the Glasses an even more lifelike air.

In short, if there is a Salinger cult, the hostile as well as the friendly critics are caught up in it. We have not yet reached the Baker Street stage. To the best of my knowledge, no organization known as the Riverside Drive Irregulars meets periodically over consecrated cups of chicken soup to discuss the contents of Bessie Glass's kimono pockets or to try to track down the telephone number of Seymour Glass. On the other hand, an English critic, David Leitch, reports that once in Venice he was called by a sober and serious-minded friend who insisted that he had just met Seymour Glass's brother-in-law in a bar.

But to say that a Salinger cult exists, even at times a ridiculous one, is not to dispose of Salinger or to diminish him. The fact merely illustrates the author's power to give reality to his creatures and to invent characters who, as Martin Green puts it, "act on the reader's capacity for self-creation"; in other words, characters who enter into the reader's mind and there assume a life of their own.

This is a fact despite all the cogent and expert strictures against Salinger's technique. Many critics, including Maxwell Geismar, complain that Salinger's characters exist in a sociological void and that they are not rounded fictional creations, with their environment, their friends and foes, their politics, their jobs, their psychological case histories, and their sex lives all in place. In a recent essay on

"Characters in Fiction," Mary McCarthy, whose literary bitchiness has long been a delight, complains that *"The Catcher in the Rye* compels admiration more as a feat than as a novel, like the performance of a one-armed violinist." Miss McCarthy's argument goes to the method of first-person narrative. She feels that such modern writers as Saul Bellow, Vladimir Nabokov, Salinger and Mary McCarthy, in such books as *The Adventures of Augie March, Lolita, The Catcher in the Rye* and *A Charmed Life,* are really attempting impersonations or "ventriloquial acts." (The same was true, of course, of the epistolary novelists; literary ventriloquism is not as modern as all that.) She feels that this device is too laborious and too private, that it robs the author of objectivity and the characters of reality, and that as a result "the common world that lies between the contemporary reader and the contemporary author remains unexplored, almost undescribed, just as queer and empty a place as Dickens' world would be if he had spent eight years recording the impressions of Fagin or the sensory data received by Uriah Heep on the slithery course of a morning's walk."

Undoubtedly too many interior monologues have been mumbled since Joyce. Undoubtedly literary ventriloquism can be a bore. The fact remains that, for our own time, Holden Caulfield is no less real than Fagin and Uriah Heep, and the world around him is not empty.

Dr. Eckleburg's Eyes

Whatever their differences, most Salinger critics have two things in common. First, they are at a loss when it comes to comparisons. The writers to whom Salinger is most frequently compared are Scott Fitzgerald and Ring Lardner, but in addition there is an almost frantic search for models, parallels, or at least echoes, and the search takes in everyone from Tolstoy to Kerouac. Surely this is at least in part tribute to Salinger's originality. Second, the critics all quote from Salinger at great and even tedious length. Obviously they do this not merely to pad out their reviews, nor are they necessarily lazy. It is simply that Salinger is not easily described. With a certain desperation, the critics seem to be pushing the reader up to the quoted passages, as if to say: "Here, see for yourself. This is what he's like." The method usually fails.

In Salinger's work, persons and objects, even when they are part
of the commonplace, assume a certain glow that cannot be con-
veyed in lengthy quotations out of context. It is this quality, among
all the many others enumerated, that most strongly links Salinger
to Fitzgerald.

In *The Great Gatsby*, Fitzgerald could take a very obvious and
theatrical device, the all-seeing eyes of Dr. T. J. Eckleburg, and
make it work. Similarly in "Zooey" Salinger employs the theatrical
trick of the telephone in the unused room and makes it work almost
as well. In *The Last Tycoon*, Fitzgerald managed to give stature,
dignity and reality to a motion-picture producer, a nearly impossible
accomplishment; there is an air of petty glamour and slightly false
shoptalk about theater or film people in fiction that usually keeps
them from appearing as believable characters. On a lesser scale,
Salinger is as successful in overcoming this handicap with Zooey,
the television actor, as Fitzgerald was with Monroe Stahr, the
soulful producer. Both Fitzgerald and Salinger seem to have an
inner conviction about their stories and their characters which is
comparable to the successful comedian's profound, contagious conviction that the joke he is telling is funny. Without this conviction,
the best joke fizzles; with it, even a poor joke can seem hilarious.
This is not merely a matter of technique; it is a matter of faith.
Alfred Kazin may have something like this in mind when he speaks
of an author's love for his characters; he sees this love in Fitzgerald
but, I think unjustly, fails to see it in Salinger.

The Lonely Crowd vs. the Beatitudes

Salinger criticism runs along a fairly clear ideological and philosophical spectrum, from left to right. On the left are the critics who
regard Salinger as a sociological writer whose theme is man *vs.*
society, the individual *vs.* conformity. Thus David Stevenson en-
titles an essay on Salinger "A Mirror of Crisis," meaning specifically
the crisis of mid-twentieth-century American life. Stevenson ap-
proves of Salinger, perhaps for the wrong reasons, but most other
sociology-minded critics disapprove. Salinger disappoints them.
Geismar sees in Holden Caulfield "the differential revolt of the lonesome rich child, the conspicuous display of leisure class emotions."
Obviously, one cannot get much mileage out of Salinger along these

lines. A particularly disgruntled critic, Isa Kapp, complains flatly: "You cannot find out much about society from Salinger." Thus he is often blamed for simply not being what critics would like him to be—a junior Marquand or, better still, an urban, Jewish, upper-middle-class, alienated (and, of course, differential) John O'Hara.

On the right, moving to the other extreme, are the critics who see Salinger as a religious novelist. Josephine Jacobsen probably carries this approach to its utmost and a little beyond when she discerns in Salinger the theme of "incarnation, the revelation through matter of spirit . . . the gift made flesh." The main Salinger theme, she feels, is "the human exchange of beatific signals." Such adulation threatens to turn Salinger into a sort of Dostoevsky of the nursery. On the whole, though, the critics on the right have the better of the argument. Salinger is simply not a sociological novelist. As Ihab Hassan puts it: "The Glasses tell us far more about the darkness of love and self-hate than about the conditions of an urban Jewish family in mid-century America." The extremes of Salinger criticism, Donald Barr suggests, thus range from the Lonely Crowd to the Beatitudes. The views of most critics fall somewhere in between, but few fail to see that what Salinger is up to is not a description of social life but an exploration of inner life, not the critique of a period or a particular situation but of the human condition, however narrowly observed. In short, he knows that the Lonely Crowd is mankind.

Beatnik Peter Pan vs. Ivan Karamazov

Like Huck Finn, with whom Holden Caulfield is constantly compared, the hero of The Catcher in the Rye is usually described as a rebel, either against the materialism and ugliness of "our society" or against the realities of the adult world. But he does not make a very satisfactory rebel because he is not for anything. Everybody knows that the well-adjusted, successful, "adult" rebel should have a positive program; otherwise, is he not merely an anarchist? Among the critics who know that Holden lacks a positive program is Phoebe Caulfield, his sister, who complains that he doesn't like anything that's happening. There have been some rather charming critical attempts to show that he is, after all, for some things—and the things add up to love. But love gets nowhere on the barricades; it is ideologically neutral and no substitute either for a plan of attack or for a program of reform. The alleged futility and immaturity of Holden's rebellion are most strikingly expressed by John Aldridge, who comes to the defense of the phonies, bores and deceivers whom Holden so dislikes. They "constitute a fair average of what the culture affords. They are part of the truth which Holden does not see and, as it turns out, is never able to see— that this is what one part of humanity *is;* the lies, the phoniness, the hypocrisy are the compromises which innocence is forced by the world to make. This is the reality on which Holden's illusion is finally broken, but no recognition follows, and no conversion. He remains at the end what he was at the beginning—cynical, defiant, and blind."

This passage seems to me almost dazzling in its obtuseness. It goes beyond the hostility which some other critics show toward Holden, who is a "sad little screwed-up" neurotic to Geismar, a "lout" to George Steiner—expressions of almost personal anger by grown men toward a juvenile hero which suggest that Holden is touching a nerve somewhere. (Amusingly enough, some of the critics are annoyed particularly by Holden's literary judgments, in which he encroaches, without proper qualifications, on their own field.) The Aldridge passage also goes somewhat beyond the basic case against Holden, made by Kazin and others, that he is immature and that his creator is confusing the familiar rebellion of the adolescent with something more profound. Aldridge views Holden as a boy who refuses to grow up, a beatnik Peter Pan, not only a retarded child but a moral idiot. Yet Aldridge's assertion that he fails to see as well as to learn seems utterly wrong. It is precisely because Holden does see the realities, precisely because he does recognize the phonies and perverts as a "fair average of what the culture affords" that he despairs. But he refuses to accept the situation. In other words, he is capable of "recognition" but not of "conversion."

Aldridge obviously feels that Holden should "grow up," accept the world for what it is, and live in it. This is a perfectly sound, conservative recommendation, somewhat startling in a book entitled *In Search of Heresy.* Taken seriously and logically, the advice would put romanticism out of business and abolish tragedy. It is the kind of advice that most of us, whose lives are neither romantic nor tragic, are forced to give sooner or later—and to take. But there are some who are simply not like most of us, who cannot accept the human condition for what it is, who cannot resign themselves to the existence of injustice, ugliness and pain—and who cannot accept the theological argument that suffering is a part of God's equation. One of those is Ivan Karamazov, who says: "If the suffering of children serves to complete the sum of suffering necessary for the acquisition of truth, I affirm from now onward that truth is not worth such a price." One may regard this attitude as childish, and futile, but it also contains the ultimate rebellion—against God. Huck is perhaps a little closer to that rebellion than Holden; Huck can say, "All right, then I'll *go* to hell," but Holden has no hell to go to, at least no hell as specific as Huck's. And yet Huck's rebellion is both more limited and resolute ("practical," as Edgar Branch says), while Holden's is more general and dreamlike; his sensitivity and compassion give him a faint odor of sanctity rather than the headier scent of defiance.

It may seem preposterous to apply such terms as sanctity, even with due qualifications, to this prep-school fugitive. But to call him saintly is really no more of an exaggeration than to call him blind and cynical. If we must exaggerate, let us exaggerate in the right categories.

The refusal to accept the status quo in the universe marks not only adolescents; it also marks the saints and, at times, the mad. The connection is not accidental but necessary and functional. The young have the clarity and newness of vision, the relentless but two-dimensional logic, and the almost unbearable sensitivity that often characterize the saintly and the insane. A saint as well as a madman may be an adolescent who has refused to "grow up," unable or unwilling to cover his soul with the calluses necessary for the ordinary life; the crucial difference being that the saint finds a protective armor in religion while the madman's only protection is flight. All three, in different ways, wage war with the-way-things-are; they are martyrs to the commonplace.

It is true that we sentimentalize childhood and youth. In their essay, Arthur Heiserman and James Miller have called this "childism." The phrase is awkward but accurate, as is its opposite, "adultism." But if some of us sentimentalize the child and innocence, surely others sentimentalize age (particularly middle age) and experience. If some of us are overemotional about the dewy freshness of the half-grown, surely others are equally emotional about the dry, grown-up courage that it takes to live life as it is. Compromise can be sentimentalized as much as courage, and resignation has its own lyricism, the kind that Prufrock serves with tea and stale crumpets.

If Holden falls considerably short of heroic stature, it is because the author has, after all, limited his range and chosen to tell, in speech, setting and incident, the story of an adolescent. The child or adolescent cannot be the hero of a tragedy, because his powers are not fully developed and his defeat or destruction, no matter how affecting, is not as pitiful or terrible as the downfall of a human being at the height of his power and glory. But the fact remains that Holden Caulfield, if he is a rebel at all, is a rebel against the human condition and as such he deserves his small share of nobility.

Freudian Puritanism

Leslie Fiedler ingeniously debunks the cult of the child and suggests that the Original Innocence we have come to worship is a reaction against Original Sin. The innocent child, in other words, is a myth like the noble savage—savage, perhaps, but not noble. Fiedler is particularly fascinating on this subject because, by applying Freudian theory, he winds up standing solidly alongside the orthodox theologian. Using the insights of depth psychology (surely scientific and enlightened?) he reaches conclusions considerably closer to St. Augustine or Calvin than to Freud. On examination, this is all quite logical. The orthodox theologian sees sin in the infant as well as in the adult; similarly the Freudian sees sex (which of course he does not call sin) in the infant as well as in the adult. They are thus allies, though they usually fail to recognize it, against the notion of childish innocence.

Those who hold that human nature is essentially good ("un-

fallen") and corrupted only by society regard the child as an unspoiled bundle of life which "goes wrong" mostly because of bad
things happening in the "environment." (Hence, as Fiedler points
out, the orgies of self-reproach on the part of modern parents.)
Freudian doctrine, of course, has an environmental explanation of
what shapes the human being, and certainly does not speak the
language of "guilt" or "innocence." But it cannot assert the essential
goodness of human nature with the serenity of the Enlightenment,
having discovered the dark and mysterious force of the unconscious.
With Original Sin replaced by the Original Id, Fiedler can gleefully
reassert the demonic nature of the child. As he demolishes the
liberals for their näiveté about the innocence of child witches, one
can almost see him casting a few stones in Salem. His essay suggests a new but little noticed force at work—Freudian Puritanism.

Yet debunking "childism" does not, in the end, dispose of the
child. It is surely no accident that in so many civilizations, the child,
like the fool, is assigned a special oracular authority. Nor can this
be dismissed simply as superstition. It is part of mankind's collective experience that out of the mouths of the young can come
truth and that in the eyes of the young, the world is new—that
youth, as Wordsworth said, is Nature's Priest. All of Salinger's work
is imbued with this belief, and it is only a matter of time before
a Ph.D. candidate points out that, in "A Perfect Day for Bananafish," Sibyl is really a sibyl. In cherishing the child we cherish
ourselves, or rather, the memory of ourselves in youth. We hug
what we once were, or think we were. Yet even this retroactive
narcissism (less obnoxious, perhaps, than the present-tense narcissism which worships our "maturity") cannot obscure the fact that
certain feelings, even devotions, toward the child are older than
the Enlightenment or the doctrine of Original Sin against which
the Enlightenment rebelled. One can be with Fiedler in his assertion that the view of unfallen human nature is shallow and illusory;
one can agree with him that we have made fools of ourselves in
the cult of the child and in its origin, which is really the cult of
man; and yet one can still feel that the child has a special place in
human emotions. It is a place ultimately linked to the woman's,
although Fiedler seems to think that the two are antagonistic.

One pleasure, incidentally, of which both the sentimentalizers and the psychologizers of the child deprive us is a certain kind of humor, exemplified by the jolly sadism of Hilaire Belloc's *Cautionary Tales*. Both factions suspect our motives in laughing at those little boys eaten by lions and those little girls trapped in burning houses. Fiedler would be more in sympathy with this sort of humor than Salinger, but he would find behind the laughter all kinds of hate, cruelty and perverted fantasies. For myself, I have long felt that Salinger's "Teddy" would have made a great little Belloc poem. Surely "Henry King, Who chewed bits of String, and was early cut off in Dreadful Agonies" and "George, Who played with a Dangerous Toy, and suffered a Catastrophe of considerable Dimensions" should welcome into their company "Teddy McArdle, Who had Strange Powers and was cut down to Size by his Sister." One can imagine the conclusion of the Belloc version:

> . . . And then (oh jealous Little Fool!)
> His Sister pushed him in the Pool,
> Succeeding with the first Attempt. He
> Was not Surprised to find it Empty.

> MORAL
> Bright Little Boys who play with Zen
> May not grow up to be Big Men.

Belloc would have done much better, of course. At any rate, *Cautionary Tales* is highly recommended after prolonged reading of either Salinger or Leslie Fiedler.

How Much Does God Love the Glasses?

A part of the charge of immaturity often brought against Salinger is the fact that he does not deal with mature love. The implication is that he "escapes" from sex. The absence of sex, except in suppressed and allegedly perverted forms that are apparent to Freudians, is certainly one of the striking facts about Salinger's work. It is an open question whether this absence is not one of the things that makes him so popular. The accepted formula for success on the best-seller lists is of course an abundance of sex. But it is entirely possible that, when we measure the phenomenon not only over the last few decades but over the last few centuries, a point of surfeit has been reached. "Mature love" between men and women has not always been at the center of the storytelling art. The great epics dealt more with the themes of war, nature and the gods. The novel has made the love story so much a part of our very atmosphere that we can scarcely imagine it otherwise, but "mature love" alone has rarely been sufficient to sustain fiction and it has almost always needed the admixture of the other, older themes. It is just possible that Salinger's sexless story comes as something of a relief.

Alfred Kazin brings the charge of immaturity against Salinger's characters in a more specific and damaging way than other critics. He accuses the Glasses of being cute (Fiedler earlier used the same word about Huck), and by cuteness Kazin means a deliberate and calculated prolongation of adolescent winsomeness into adult life. With the adolescent, he feels, this winsomeness is a legitimate weapon against a world that is too much for him; but in the adult it becomes an unfair advantage. Furthermore, he feels that the Glasses love only themselves and each other; for the rest of mankind, as Kazin puts it, there is only forgiveness, and the author is accused of abetting and blessing this cute little woolly nest of self-love by "'his extraordinary cherishing" of the Glasses. John Updike raises a similar objection. Franny and Zooey and the other young Glasses, he feels, "condemn the world only to condescend to it, to forgive it." And he too feels that Salinger is their accomplice by cherishing them too much, too exclusively: "Salinger loves the Glasses more than God loves them."

Quite a trick, of course, even for an author of Mr. Updike's considerable talent, to know just how much God loves the Glasses. What irritates Updike particularly is that Salinger not only loves his creatures but insists that the reader must love them too. He very shrewdly observes that "Salinger robs the reader of the initiative upon which love must be given." But the same could be said of Dickens. At any rate, it is likely that most readers are not so much irritated as exhilarated by the love which Salinger compels from them. To the receptive, he gives a sense of joy and *Gemütlichkeit* that is almost wholly absent from contemporary fiction. Perhaps only Dickens could provide a comparable sense of well-being, not only through his characters but through his treatment of life's humbler joys, notably food. Dickens' descriptions of the family gathered around the festive board evoke a cosmic coziness that resembles the extraordinary warmth generated in the sympathetic reader by the Glasses. The warmth is far less physical or sensuous; but precisely as one wants to be with the Dickens clan around the silver tureen, one longs to be part of a Glass family occasion—perhaps that extraordinary party where the junior vaudevillians put on their acts for Les and Bessie, or just going with Seymour to the barbershop down the street. David Leitch is right when he says, somewhat sarcastically, that the Glasses have been made to seem members of a "peculiarly intimate club, a club which Salinger readers are overtly invited to associate themselves with."

It is this clubbiness which provokes the objection that the Glasses love each other and themselves at the expense of others; the rest of the world is shut out. One does indeed get the feeling that there is an invisible barrier between the Glass living room and the rest of the universe. But what both Kazin and Updike do not fully acknowledge is that the Glass children themselves are very much aware of this. There is little the critics have said about them that they have not said about themselves.

The fact that, as Kazin charges, "they love certain people only" is surely known to Bessie when she accuses Zooey of being able to talk only to people he loves. When Zooey accuses himself and the others of being freaks, there is no reason to think that he does not mean it—or that Salinger does not mean it. Their clever, cute sensitivity irritates them quite as much as it irritates some critics: "If it makes them remarkable," says Arthur Mizener, "it is also a quite terrible burden [on themselves]." According to Kazin, the Glasses' feeling about society is "that they are too sensitive to live in it." Perhaps the opposite is true; perhaps they are too sensitive to ignore it, to look the other way, to withdraw, as well-adjusted, busy, adult people withdraw into their protective shells when faced with society's terrors. Like Holden, the Glasses simply cannot accept the injustices, the ugliness, the lovelessness and the egomania that surround them. It is true that Holden and the Glasses dislike phonies too much, are too perturbed by all the people who are in Franny's words "so tiny and meaningless and sad-making." But that is, after all, the very condition which Zooey is trying to cure in his sister—and in himself. That is the very spiritual fault which the parable of the Fat Lady is meant to correct. Almost all the critics concentrate on the Fat Lady as the ultimate meaning of *Franny and Zooey*, perhaps the ultimate message which Salinger has for the reader. According to their sympathies, they either take the Fat Lady as a moving and poetic testament to Christian love expressed in the vernacular, or as a rather shallow, sticky and unconvincing religious sentiment. To explore the question further, it is perhaps necessary to become personal.

Between Toy and Salvation

When I first read these stories, I was carried along by the marvelous and heady stream of talk. These two characters did not precisely remind me of anyone I ever knew, because the Glasses are obviously not, and are not meant to be, realistic portrayals. But they did evoke a memory here, a recognition there, of the kind of overarticulate, overemotional young people who excitedly theorize about the universe and themselves, who forever question what they are saying, and then question the question itself, who sound as if they knew it all (or felt it all) but who are vulnerable in their youth and lovable in their enthusiasm. When the Fat Lady made her first appearance, I winced. I could not help thinking for a few moments that this was parody, just as perhaps the admonition to "Be God's actress" was parody, as well as the story of Christ dropping into the Glass kitchen and asking for some orange juice. The whole thing stirred an echo of Holden talking about the sanctimonious undertaker: "He told us to think about Jesus as our buddy and all."

On reflection, of course, it could *not* be parody. Quite clearly Salinger was *with* the Glasses too much to laugh at them. Then must the reader accept the Fat Lady as Zooey's (and Salinger's) ultimate wisdom, and "God's actress" as the modern equivalent of the Juggler of Our Lady? Perhaps. Religious truth can reside in the obvious, even the simple-minded. Possibly the point is that man must humble his senses in loving even the ugly, and humble his intellect by finding truth even in the banal. The parable of the Fat Lady was slightly repulsive and slightly too simple, and Salinger, as he often does, seemed to be daring one to take it or leave it.

I think one can take it, but not necessarily at face value.

Standing by itself, the parable of the Fat Lady is faulted easily enough. To love everyone can mean loving no one. As Leitch puts it, there is a kind of "blanket love" that is simply a way of escaping commitments. It is love without responsibility (although there may be worse sins in a world that is full of responsibility without love). Similarly there is room for doubt about Zooey's version of Christ as a sort of saintly missionary with great executive abilities. It is perhaps unfair to compare this, as does Geismar, to the "religious fantasies" of Bruce Barton. It is much closer, for instance, to the muscular and practical view of Bernard Shaw in the preface to *Androcles and the Lion* in which he derides the nursery myth of "gentle Jesus meek and mild." But one can certainly have one's reservations about Zooey Glass, boy theologian.

What the friendly as well as the hostile critics have in common here is that they unhesitatingly attribute Zooey's views to the sponsor; for the most part, they fail to see that Zooey's views *are in character*. No matter how extraordinarily Salinger cherishes the Glasses, he does see some of their weaknesses, does allow Zooey to jeer at himself for the yay-team spirit with which he approaches Buddhism and does, however mildly, reproach Franny for the sentimentality of those tap shoes in the closet. These characters speak with perfect naturalness about someone having "a hell of a lot of karma." They are both serious and not serious about religion; to them it is somewhere between toy and salvation. Zooey is not a prophet but an intelligent, engaging, rather glib, frighteningly articulate young television actor trying first this approach, then that, always with just the touch of the spiritual con man about him, to snap his sister out of a spiritual funk. Seen in that light, to repeat, the parable of the Fat Lady is in character; it is precisely what Zooey Glass would come up with. Salinger is much too close to his characters to permit any obvious hint of satire, but is there not between them and him just enough space for irony? He does not laugh at them, because he loves them; but he does smile at them— because he loves them. He indulges them, but he does not fail to judge them. Fiedler seems to be the only critic to see this clearly: "It is with his [Salinger's] collaboration, we remind ourselves, that we are able to say of his hidden saints, when they become insufferably cute or clever or smug, 'The little bastards!' Surely this is Salinger's joke, not just one on him and on his world."

Perhaps Geismar feels something similar when in the Glass stories he finds a certain ambiguity, "where the artist both is and is not responsible for what he is saying." But to Geismar this ambiguity is a flaw, while actually it is the opening that admits the author's irony, his "joke" and his judgment. The ambiguity is strongest about Seymour, who is regarded by the surviving Glasses as something of a holy man. But there are hints in *Zooey* that coexistence with a saint, living or dead, can have its drawbacks and that his sainthood itself is open to question. Zooey senses quite clearly that Seymour has deformed them all, however lovingly, and that he has ultimately destroyed their peace through his suicide; why else would there be talk about having to forgive him? These hints of discord within the cozy Glass club become downright thunderous in "Seymour: An Introduction," a story remarkably little discussed by critics and, one may guess, widely misunderstood.

The Proscenium Destroyed

It is generally assumed that the title means what it says and that this is a story about Seymour, but it is as much, if not more, a story about the narrator, Buddy Glass. The story's overwhelming mannerisms, the convolutions, endless digressions and apologies, the narrator's asides to himself and to the reader, the ramblings toward and away from the subject, are usually dismissed as Salinger's self-indulgence of thought or sloppiness of style. But when Buddy Glass writes things like

"with a striking resemblance to—alley oop—myself,"
or, "I live alone (but catless I'd like everybody to know),"
or, "I would to God the reader had something terrible to tell me first (O you out there—with your enviable golden silence),"
or, "I privately say to you, old friend (unto you, really, I'm afraid), please accept from me this unpretentious bouquet of very early blooming parentheses: (((()))),"
or simply, in self-admonition: "(stop that now)"

Salinger is not speaking in his own voice but again *in character*. True, the style uncomfortably recalls Salinger's own self-consciousness in his jacket blurb to *Franny and Zooey* or in his rare, early magazine notes about himself; it sounds like a wild caricature of those things. But the story is an indirect character portrait of

Buddy Glass. In one of those "ventriloquial acts" which Miss Mc-
Carthy dislikes, Salinger is letting us see and guess the personality
of a weirdly, fantastically self-conscious and mannered writer on
the point of breaking down under the strain of living with Seymour's ghost. This is the climax to date of Salinger's nearly constant
and obsessive preoccupation with dead siblings.

There are hints not only that it was always difficult to live with
the near-saintly Seymour, but also that his saintliness as well as his
talent may have been exaggerated by his family. Along with
genuine love for the dead man there are hints of envy and of terror.
When Buddy exclaims: "Why does this exhaust me so? The hands
are sweating, the bowels churning," or, "This last little pentimento,
or whatever it is, has started me sweating literally from head to
foot," Salinger is forcing us to witness a crack-up far more severe
than Franny's and motivated far less simply. He is showing us that
the members of the Glass club may be paying stiff dues for that
cozy withdrawal from the world which earlier had seemed so
enviable and, to some, so cute.

The method of the telling is admittedly devious. The author
plays games with the reader and with reality when he makes Buddy
Glass sound like the author of *The Catcher in the Rye* and makes
Buddy the butt of the familiar rumors (the Buddhist monastery,
the sanatorium) that from time to time have circulated about J. D.
Salinger. All this may be an irritating private joke, but it also has
a literary purpose. In theatrical terms, Salinger is trying to destroy
the proscenium. Like a number of playwrights from Pirandello to
Jack Gelber, he is attempting to bring the audience completely into
the action, to make them forget what is real and what is not. The
same is true of the rambling, fussy style, the neurotic asides, the
clinical notes that ooze from the narrator. It may be argued that
this method does not work or that it is not worth the effort, but it
should at least be recognized that it *is* a method and not merely
self-indulgence and sloppiness. I for one feel that the method works
hair-raisingly well, though it should not and could not be attempted
often, and that "Seymour" is Salinger's most impressive story. The
case could hardly be put better than it has been by John Updike,
who, despite serious objections to Salinger's manner and technique,
says: "The willingness to risk excess on behalf of one's obsessions

is what distinguishes artists from entertainers." One might add, for Updike, that the willingness to recognize this fact is what distinguishes critics from reviewers.

In a curious way, the convulsions of "Seymour," the carefully built-up struggle between Salinger-Buddy and the subject matter, recall that old literary theme, the Revolt of the Puppets. If the story is a form of ventriloquism, the dummy seems to be taking over, recalling the film *Dead of Night* in which the ventriloquist, played by Michael Redgrave, was engaged in a schizoid and deadly struggle with the painted, wooden figure he used in this act and which gradually became a hostile incarnation of his own other self. Whether any of this reflects real problems the real Salinger may be having with his series about the Glasses is not known and is, perhaps, beside the point. As a work of fiction, "Seymour" is fascinating partly because it suggests a struggle on the edge of sanity, a rebellion of puppet against puppeteer.

The Aim Is Celebration

American literary criticism, in George Steiner's phrase, is a great machine constantly in need of raw material. It is, in fact, many machines; press the right button, pull the right lever, and off the conveyor belt will roll social consciousness, depth psychology, historical perspective, neatly stamped-out pedantry and, gratifyingly often, passion for literature. It is possible, as has been charged, that in this vast enterprise Salinger's importance has been overrated. But this concern seems already out of date. There are signs that the critics, far from overestimating Salinger, have begun to turn against him. It seems "in" these days to be anti-Salinger. Edmund Wilson suggested long ago that the critic's ego is flattered when he can champion a new, unknown writer; but that when the writer becomes successful, the same ego demands his being put down; there is nothing left for the critic of such a writer but "to try to make him ashamed of himself." Something like this is undoubtedly at work in Salinger's case, exacerbated by extravagant and even pious praise from some quarters. Best-sellerdom piled upon intimations of sainthood is clearly more than most critics can bear. The vast majority of critics, moreover, seem irritated by Salinger's connection with *The New Yorker*. In a strange display of literary guilt by association, they suggest that, as a *New Yorker* writer, he somehow carries an objectionable label. This is extraordinarily unfair, both to Salinger and to the magazine. *The New Yorker* certainly has its limitations and mannerisms, but it has performed great service in the development of American fiction over the past quarter century, from O'Hara to Updike. As for Salinger, he simply does not fit into the usual *New Yorker* mold, or molds. To all this must be added Salinger's personal inaccessibility, his total refusal to communicate with anyone in the world outside his family and close friends; if one resents the Glasses' fictional withdrawal from the world, one is likely to resent their creator's actual withdrawal even more. If there is a club centering around the Glasses, there is an even more exclusive club centering around Salinger himself, and it is considerably harder to join it than, say, the Union.

Yet this still does not account for all the critical attitudes toward Salinger; the praise is not fully explained by Steiner's theory of the machine's hunger for raw material, nor the condemnation by Wilson's observations about the critical ego. One of the extraordinary things about Salinger is the range of responses he evokes. All critics find themselves in the author they review, and read their own philosophy into his; but Salinger seems to allow a far greater variety of interpretation than almost any other contemporary writer. As we have seen, critics by turns identify his themes as faith, conformity *vs.* society, love of various kinds, the psychology of youth *vs.* age, the sentimentalization of the child, the dream of unfallen man, the repressed and perverted sex instinct, the emotional excess of the idle rich. One critic, Hugh McClean, in a discussion of several American writers, has found in *Catcher in the Rye* "a terrifying picture of the conservative's plight today," while others see Holden Caulfield as an intense, slightly confused liberal, while still others, among them Kenneth Tynan, treat him as an exponent of the Angry Young Men's revolt against all politics. These and many other shades of interpretation will be found in this volume, and the book's purpose, finally, is not merely to add another product to the Salinger Industry, but to illustrate the range of meaning our society can find in the work of one "minor" but magical writer. He apparently touches something very deep in us. If some dwell a little too emphatically on Holden's sainthood or Salinger's knight-

hood, it must be because we are badly in need of saints and
knights. If others grow shrill about the Glasses' antisocial traits
and the intellectual softness of their religion, it must be because
we feel the need for powerful community and strong, clear ideas.
And if the young, in particular, have made Salinger their laureate,
it must be not only because he speaks their language and expresses
some of their discontents but because he meets their needs. One
inevitably recalls the era of nineteenth-century romanticism. Then,
too, a great, revolutionary, utopian promise had disappeared in
blood and disillusion; then, too, the younger generation escaped
into the personal search for truth and beauty. The phrase "truth
and beauty" may be a little too rich, too self-conscious for the contemporary young, but it is really the same as their Holdenesque
search for something that is not phony, even if this search often
seems remarkably negative. It is intriguing to note that "phony" has
no exact contrary; "wrong" has "right," "square" has "hip," "out" has
"in," but "phony"—bypassing "sincere," "true," "real," none of which
quite fit—has only the vague and awkward "nonphony" as its affirmative opposite.

Today Byron going forth to fight in Greece might still be applauded, but his drinking wine from a skull would surely be
dismissed as phony. The nineteenth century's young romantics,
for all their infatuation with death, were more vigorous, more
eccentric, more public; the romanticism of the present American
generation is more private, more limited, more given to intro-
spection than to the dream, marked by the small gesture rather than
the large escapade. In a sense, Salinger fits into that mood. But
the mood is not wholly new. The American young have always
been less adventurous than the young of other civilizations and
certainly less concerned with politics. For centuries, and to this
day, the European student has taken his place on the barricades.
To this day "student riots" are a familiar and significant factor in
European politics. The phenomenon has no equivalent in the United
States. With some oversimplification, it might be said that in Europe
revolutions are made by the young, in America by the middle-aged.

The revolutionary, political and social literature of the twenties
and thirties was in part written by young men but it was not really
treasured by youth. The writers who truly stirred young readers

were always the romantics, the nonsocial, nonpolitical ones from
Cooper to Hemingway to Fitzgerald. After decades of the political,
the social and the psychological novel, the young could only feel
relief when they met Salinger. For Salinger is a romantic. His adventures may be small, his battles all interior, but the gleam in his
eye is unmistakable.

This great variety of meaning the critics find in Salinger illustrates his power to compel our imagination, but it also means that
we may ideologize him to death. The peril is just as great as the
possibility that we will footnote him to death; one thinks of such
academic exercises as Messrs. Gwynn and Blotner's discovery of
eight—no more, no less—themes in "Zooey," or the scholarly examination of Holden Caulfield's language, which catalogues all the
four-letter words as if they were rare butterflies. Such work has
its place and its usefulness for anyone who cares about the craft
of writing, but it should not keep us from reading, or from savoring
what we read.

"Delight" is not a proper critical term, but delight is what Salinger
has to offer the halfway sympathetic reader. Martin Green remarks
that Salinger is not so much a writer who depicts life as one who
celebrates it. This is an accurate characterization of the humor and
the love in his work, if not of the darker patches in "Seymour."
Ultimately the most serious charge against him is that his output
is too small, that his Songs of Innocence do not reach us often
enough. What we need is more Salinger fiction, not only to feed
that critical machine, not only to judge him more precisely,
but to start a few more celebrations.

NOTE

Wherever possible, the pieces in this collection are presented un-
cut. In a few instances, some abridgment was necessary; these cuts
were made with the authors' approval and are indicated either in
the text or in the notes. In addition, some deletions or changes were
made to eliminate obvious errors and outdated information.

Many of the contributors retell the plots of Salinger stories, often
using the same quotations. The famous "Fat Lady" passage, for example, appears a number of times. It would have been possible to
edit out these repetitions, but it is doubtful whether she (or he?)
would have forgiven such a move. The contributors themselves
certainly would have objected, and with good reason, for each brings
to the Fat Lady, and even to the plot summaries, his own special
emphasis and understanding.

SALINGER

1. The Invisible Man: A Biographical Collage

J. D. Salinger's isolation from the world is a unique accomplishment in American life. He certainly is "the boy/ who can enjoy/ invisibility," and he enjoys it with more grim determination than anyone else who is not confined in a high-security prison or a monastery of the strictest rule. Yet Salinger need not stay in his remote country home to be out of sight. Because his friends protect him with almost fanatical devotion, his invisibility follows him everywhere; he wears it like the *Tarnkappe* of Germanic legend. It is literally true that the Chairman of the Council of Ministers of the Union of Soviet Socialist Republics, or any monarch in the world, or the Pope, or anyone else who comes to mind can be interviewed by a newspaperman; but not J. D. Salinger. Except for the fact that he *is* occasionally seen, J. D. Salinger might be thought not to exist; he might be a syndicate, slowly spinning out Glass installments in the New Hampshire woods. This feat is a great joke on our time, perhaps a solitary protest against an age in which publicity, not punctuality, is the politeness of kings.

But the feat is not universally applauded. One critic angrily calls Salinger's attitude an affectation, and another refers to him as the Greta Garbo of American Letters. One of his early editors feels that a writer is a public person, no more entitled to privacy than a legislator. The point is debatable. The reason for Salinger's behavior may be a simple and forgivable fear of being distracted from his already slow labors, a feeling that giving interviews, delivering lectures, signing autographs and advising Ph.D. candidates may make a man evaporate until he is vaguely seen by everyone, invisible only to himself. But whatever his motives, Salinger's elusiveness adds a special element to his fiction. He plays with it, and on it. He works unmistakable facts about himself into his stories, and grins at the resulting confusion when, in his jacket notes to *Franny and Zooey*, he refers to Buddy Glass as his "alter-ego and collaborator." In short, he teases, and curiosity about his life is therefore even more natural, more legitimate, than in the case of other artists. The serious critics experience it as much as any reader of a Salinger paperback. "Very likely these stories represent the writer's search for his lost origins," Maxwell Geismar has written, "[and] the failure of the writer to understand his own, true, life experience and to fulfill himself." Since practically no one knows anything about J. D. Salinger's own, true, life experience, this statement —however perspicacious it may be—in effect is literary gossip. It is the equivalent of "Which best-selling author has been seen holding hands with which fascinating Persona?"

No one can really blame the critics or the public for entertaining such gossip; the provocation is immense. What is all the more remarkable is that Salinger, who has never talked back to the critics, apparently follows them carefully. It seems incredible, but all the elaborate effort to withdraw has not really allowed him to shut out the world. A popular monthly not long ago decided to publish some material about Salinger. Representations were made, and the magazine dropped the project. The reason given was that anything appearing in print about Salinger slows him down for weeks and even months. In short, there is a spy hole in the wall. He is not seen, but he sees. One recalls John Keats, whose death, it is said, was hastened by bad reviews, prompting Byron to remark in *Don Juan:*

> 'Tis strange the mind, that very fiery
>   particle,
> Should let itself be snuffed out by an
>   article.

The only solid and sizable body of biographical material about Salinger to date was assembled by *Time* magazine, for its cover story on the author, which appeared when *Franny and Zooey* came out in book form. The article, being the closest thing to a Salinger biography in existence, follows. It is, of course, the work of "the editors of *Time*," but in particular of a highly talented young writer and critic, John Skow. Information was gathered by several reporters, mainly Art Seidenbaum, Robert Jones, William Smith and Martha Murphy McDowell. The article includes not only biography but criticism, not only the Salinger story but the Glass story; it is nevertheless presented in its entirety, under the heading of biography, because Salinger's life (or what we know of it) and his work cast such intriguing shadows upon each other.

SONNY: AN INTRODUCTION

I thought what I'd do was, I'd pretend I was one of those deaf-mutes. That way I wouldn't have to have any goddam stupid useless conversations with anybody. If anybody wanted to tell me something, they'd have to write it on a piece of paper and shove it over to me. I'd build me a little cabin somewhere with the dough I made. I'd build it right near the woods, but not right *in* them, because I'd want it to be sunny as hell all the time.

—The Catcher in the Rye

It is sunny at the edge of the woods, but the tall man's face is drawn and white. When he came to Cornish, New Hampshire, nine years ago, he was friendly and talkative; now when he jeeps to town, he speaks only the few words necessary to buy food or newspapers. Outsiders trying to reach him are, in fact, reduced to passing notes or letters, to which there is usually no reply. Only a small group of friends has ever been inside his hilltop house. Not long ago, when he and his family were away, a couple of neighbors could stand it no longer, put on dungarees and climbed over the six-and-one-half-foot fence to take a look around.

What they saw behind a cluster of birches was a simple, one-story New England house painted barn-red, a modest vegetable garden, and—a hundred yards and across a stream from the house—a little concrete cell with a skylight. The cell contains a fireplace, a long table with a typewriter, books and a filing cabinet. Here the pale man usually sits, sometimes writing quickly, other times throwing logs into the fire for hours and making long lists of words until he finds the right one. The writer is Jerome David Salinger, and almost all his fictional characters seem more real, more plausible, than he.

In twenty-one years as a professional writer, he has produced only one novel, one collection entitled *Nine Stories*, and twenty other stories in magazines. And Salinger's tempo is slowing: since 1953, he has published only four stories, though three of these are as long as short novels. He promises "some new material soon or Soon." Despite the meagerness of his output, Salinger has spoken with more magic, particularly to the young, than any other U.S. writer since World War II. The appearance of his book, *Franny and Zooey*, actually two long, related stories that originally ran in *The New Yorker*, was not just a literary event but, to countless fans, an epiphany. Weeks before the official publication date, Salinger's followers queued up, and bookstores sold out their first supplies. To a large extent, the excitement was fueled by memories of Salinger's most famous work. A decade after first publication, the book still sells 250,000 copies a year in the U.S. Of all the characters set to paper by American authors since the war, only Holden Caulfield, the gallant scatologer of *The Catcher in the Rye*, has taken flesh permanently, as George F. Babbitt, Jay Gatsby, Lieutenant Henry and Eugene Gant took flesh in the twenties and thirties.

A generation or two of high school and college students, particularly those who have at least a sneering acquaintance with the Ivy League, still see in *Catcher* their hymn, their epic, their Treasury of Humor, and their manifesto against the world. Sociologist David Riesman assigns *Catcher* in his Harvard course on Character and Social Structure in the U.S., perhaps because every campus has its lonely crowd of imitation Holdens—doomed wearers of raincoats-in-December, who rehearse faithfully their Caulfield hyperbole ("It was the last game of the year, and you were supposed to commit suicide or something if old Pencey didn't win"). Holden is not merely a sort of Penrod of the *Angst* age. He is more nearly a modern and urban Huckleberry Finn. Both Huck and Holden are in the same lineage of what Critic Leslie Fiedler calls the Good Bad Boys of American literature. Like Huck, Holden longs to be out of civilization and back in innocent nature. Like Huck, speaking the superbly authentic dialect of his age and his place, Holden is a runaway from respectability, the possessor of a fierce sense of justice, the arbiter of his own morality. If one fact more than any other links *Catcher* to its generation, it is that for Holden—as presumably for his creator—the ultimate condemnation is summed up in the word phony. A whole, vague system of ethics centers around that word, and Holden Caulfield is its Kant.

But Holden is not a rebel, though he is usually called that. He longs to do good in a dream world. When he broods about dirty words on the walls where little children can see them, or feels compassion for a prostitute, he is not protesting against "the system" or the adult order; he is merely suffering from the way things are, always and everywhere, in a world of insufficient love. He is a self-conscious and sometimes absurd adolescent, but he is also a doomed human being of special sensitivity—not merely special, as Salinger might say, but Special. As such, he sets the theme for almost everything Salinger has written since *Catcher*. Most men know how to ignore, suppress or outwit the occasional suspicion that the world is really not to be borne—but the young, the mad and the saints do not know the trick. To varying degrees, most Salinger characters, including those in *Franny and Zooey*, belong in these three categories.

Strangely enough, the young, slightly mad saints are also full of laughter.

The characters of Salinger's most astonishing legend belong to a gaudy and eccentric family named Glass. The chronicle of the clan's fortunes is far from finished (the Glasses have so far made their appearance only in "Franny," "Zooey," and five other stories), but it is already one of the indelible family sagas to appear in the U.S.

The elder Glasses are Irish-Jewish vaudevillians now retired to a life of comfortable reminiscence. Les Glass and Bessie Gallagher, professionally known as Gallagher & Glass, achieved "more than

just passing notability on the old Pantages and Orpheum circuits."
They are descended from "an astonishingly long and motley double-
file of professional entertainers"; Les's grandfather, for instance, was
"a quite famous Polish-Jewish carnival clown named Zozo, who had
a penchant—right up to the end, one necessarily gathers—for
diving from immense heights into small containers of water." The
seven children, too, have been professionals; they were all prodigies,
and they all appeared, at one time or another, on a radio kiddy-
quiz called, slyly enough, "It's a Wise Child."

Any author who promises board and room to seven fictional child
prodigies would seem to be diving into a container of water that is
very small indeed. The Glass children, moreover, are brave, clean,
reverent and overwhelmingly lovable. Yet they never become the
seven deadly siblings (at least they are never all deadly at the
same time). The Irish strain makes them formidably talkative and
occasionally fey. The Jewish strain lends family warmth as well as
a talent for Talmudic brooding. The vaudeville heritage provides
theatricality.

The new book concerns a religious-emotional crisis in the life of
Franny Glass, youngest member of the clan, and tells how her
brother Zooey argues, browbeats and jollies her out of it. Franny
is first seen during a football weekend being met at the station by
a young man named Lane Coutell. The train pulls in: "Then, like
so many people, who, perhaps, ought to be issued only a very pro-
bational pass to meet trains, he tried to empty his face of all expression that might quite simply, perhaps even beautifully, reveal how
he felt about the arriving person." This is the sort of bull's-eye at
which Salinger is unmatched. It is felt by the flesh as much as by
the mind; for an instant, the reader's cheeks sag as he remembers,
with ridiculous guilt, the last time he met a train.

During lunch (at a French restaurant, naturally; Lane is no steak
man), the young man turns out to be insufferable. Salinger destroys
him mercilessly as he shows Lane smugly explaining some choice
portions of his latest A paper. Gradually it becomes clear what is
troubling Franny; she suffers, like Holden Caulfield, from an intense weariness of all that is phony, from an oversensitivity to the
world. She is sick of all the egos madly dancing around her—at
school, in her summer theater, at the luncheon table at which Lane

Coutell is dissecting Flaubert along with his frogs' legs. To escape, Franny has seized on a religious classic called *The Way of a Pilgrim*, in which an anonymous Russian peasant tells how he roamed the land first learning, and then teaching, the Jesus Prayer. "'Lord Jesus Christ, have mercy on me.' I mean that's what it is," Franny explains with careful casualness. ". . . if you keep saying that prayer over and over again—you only have to just do it with your lips at first—then eventually what happens, the prayer becomes self-active. Something *happens* after a while. I don't know what, but something happens, and the words get synchronized with the person's heartbeats. . . ."

Lane, bored, listens just closely enough to be able to dismiss the whole thing: "I mean I think all those religious experiences have a very obvious psychological background." He is supposedly talking as a realist, but he obviously knows nothing about reality. Franny, on the contrary—weak, overwrought, muttering mysticism—has about her the luminous common sense and the clear eye for life that mark all the memorable Salinger girls of whatever age, from Phoebe Caulfield on. Eventually Franny faints. When the story first appeared, co-ed readers, earthy creatures all, ignored Salinger's mysticism and decided that she was pregnant. (So did their mothers, who telephoned by the dozens to say not on any account to go to Dartmouth the next weekend.) But Franny is not pregnant. When she comes back to consciousness, she stares at the ceiling, then begins to move her lips soundlessly over and over again in the Jesus Prayer.

In "Zooey" (which is as long and discursive as "Franny" is tightly and conventionally constructed), she has come back from the weekend and has taken to the couch in the Glass living room, clutching *The Way of a Pilgrim*, and petting her cat, Bloomberg. About her hover her actor brother Zooey (Zachary on the TV credits) and her mother Bessie. Zooey is a brilliant, funny and frighteningly eloquent "verbal stunt pilot" who, in the words of another member of the family, looks like "the blue-eyed Jewish-Irish Mohican scout who died in your arms at the roulette table at Monte Carlo." Bessie, vainly offering restorative cups of chicken soup to her daughter, is a fading Irish rose, looking touchingly marsupial in her blue kimono equipped with huge auxiliary pockets, whose contents

Salinger, a master list maker, thoughtfully assays.

Early in "Zooey" she invades the bathroom occupied by her son to start a 71-page dialogue that leaves broad hints, for those who care to take them, that Salinger has set himself to writing an American *Remembrance of Things Past*. From this scene of high family comedy—Zooey in the tub with the shower curtain drawn for decency, affectionately insolent and fighting for a little privacy, Bessie philosophical and unbudgeable on the toilet seat, brooding over her family's fate—the reader learns that these two are not the only characters surrounding Franny in her crisis.

One of the others, the central but still shadowy character of the whole Glass legend, is Seymour, both family ghost and family guru, of whom little is said in the present book beyond the fact that he killed himself almost seven years before, that he was (at least in the eyes of his family) both a genius and a near saint, and that he relentlessly haunts all the surviving Glasses. It was Seymour who forced the other, younger Glass children to swallow an indigestible mass of Eastern mysticism and Western philosophy so that now they somehow give the impression of having collected quotations from Epictetus rather than baseball cards, of having played catch with some West Side reincarnation of Buddha. It is Salinger's special triumph that the wondrous and weird, the trivial and homey, coexist with complete naturalness—and humor—in the Glass world.

It is in this atmosphere that Zooey attempts to bring Franny out of her obsession with the Jesus Prayer, mostly by seeking to show her that in her withdrawal from the people around her, by her spurning "cups of consecrated chicken soup" ("which is the only kind . . . Bessie ever brings to anybody around this madhouse"), she is being egotistical. He fails, but much later, at the climax of the story, Zooey enters an unused bedroom in the huge apartment. It once belonged to Seymour, and it still contains a private phone listed in Seymour's name. Zooey sits for nearly an hour in a near trance, a pocket handkerchief on his head—this is the sort of touch that hooks itself permanently in the minds of Salinger readers—and then picks up the phone. A role is played, an identity shuffled (why and how involves complications that defy summary but seem perfectly plausible in the Salinger vaudeville) and finally Zooey talks Franny around by invoking, of course, the dead brother.

When they were child prodigies on radio, Zooey reminds her, Seymour always insisted that they shine their shoes "for the Fat Lady" —for all the lonely, unlovely, unseen but very real people "out there." Zooey's monologue soars: "Are you listening to me? *There isn't anyone out there who isn't Seymour's Fat Lady.* Don't you know that? Don't you know that goddam secret yet? And don't you know—*listen to me, now—don't you know who that Fat Lady really is?* . . . Ah, buddy. Ah, buddy. It's Christ Himself. Christ Himself, buddy."

Franny listens, smiles and peacefully goes to sleep.

The reader may almost feel sorry that she has exchanged the mystic's mad glint for the calm smile of a mere lover of humanity. And the parable of the Fat Lady may seem intellectually underweight. But Zooey's lyric rant is not a seminarian's thesis; it is a gift of love received from Seymour and transmitted to a distraught, prayer-drunk, twenty-year-old girl. Apart from questioning the depth of this message, critics—notably Alfred Kazin, who apologizes solemnly for having to say it—have suggested that the Glass children are too cute and too possessed by self-love. The charge is unjust. They are too clearly shadowed by death, even in their woolliest, most kittenish moments, to be cute, and they are too seriously worried about the very danger of self-love to be true egotists.

Some readers also object to the book's italicized talkiness. But the talk, like the book itself, is dazzling, joyous and satisfying. Holden Caulfield was a gentle heart who lacked the strength to survive; Zooey and his sister in the end are harried but whole. Above all, by sheer force of eye and ear—rather than by psychologizing, which he detests—Salinger has given them, like Holden, an astonishing degree of life, a stunning and detailed air of presence. So real are the Glasses in fact that readers feel sure that the stories must be autobiographical. But Salinger has done his superhuman best to keep that matter dark.

As nearly as is possible in an age in which all relations are public, J. D. Salinger lives the life of a recluse. He says that he needs this isolation to keep his creativity intact, that he must not be interrupted "during working years." But the effort of evading the world must by now be almost more tiring than a certain amount of normal sociability would be. One critic and fellow novelist, Harvey Swados, has in fact suggested, pettishly, that Salinger's reputation is in part a consequence of his "tantalizing physical inaccessibility."

He has only once answered a reporter's questions; she was a sixteen-year-old Windsor, Vermont, high school girl who wrote an article for her school paper in 1953. He will turn and run if addressed on the street by a stranger, and his picture has not appeared on a dust jacket since the first two printings of *Catcher* (it was yanked off the third edition at his request). He has refused offers from at least three book clubs for *Franny and Zooey*, and has not sold anything to the movies since Hollywood made a Susan Hayward Kleenex-dampener of his "Uncle Wiggily in Connecticut" in 1949.

Salinger's family and friends respect his hermitage and protect him like Swiss pikemen. For some of them, the conspiracy of silence is wearing; Author Peter De Vries clams as loyally as anyone, but admits that knowing Salinger makes him feel like a TV gangster: "You go skulking around not talking."

Salinger fans have filled the resultant vacuum with splendid imagination. The author apparently listens now and then behind his locked door, because in "Seymour, An Introduction," his fictional alter-ego refers to "poignant get-well-soon notes from old readers of mine who have somewhere picked up the bogus information that I spend six months of the year in a Buddhist monastery and the other six in a mental institution." One source of bogus information is the author himself; in the jacket blurb for *Franny and Zooey*, which he wrote himself, he says with coy fraudulence that "I live in Westport with my dog." The dark facts are that he has not lived in Westport or had a dog for years. But to disprove such rumors and humors involves infiltrating a distant-early-warning system equipped to detect journalists half a continent away.

Some of the Glass legend, of course, parallels fact. All the Glass brothers sometimes sound like Salinger—introspective, sensitive, obsessed with words, hating what seems phony, dabbling in mysticism—and incidents in the author's life turn up later in his fiction. Like the Glass children, Salinger was born in New York to a Jewish father and a Christian mother. To soothe her in-laws-to-be, Scotch-Irish Marie Jillich changed her name to Miriam when she married

Sol Salinger. But Sol was, and is, a prosperous importer of hams and cheeses, and any connection he or Miriam ever had with show business is well hidden by the Salinger counter-intelligence apparatus.

Sonny, as he was then called, a solemn, polite child who liked to take long walks by himself, had no brothers and only one sister, Doris, who was eight years older than he. Salinger once said that Seymour and Holden were modeled after a dead school friend, so reporters and Ph.D. candidates are forever searching for him. At least two of the author's prep school acquaintances died young, one of them a boy of great brilliance. But intensive detective work shows that Salinger, like a lonely child inventing brothers and sisters, has drawn most of his characters out of his own rare imagination.

Unlike Zooey and the rest, Sonny was anything but a Quiz Kid. His grades at public schools in Manhattan's Upper West Side were mostly B's, but arithmetic baffled him. His IQ test score was merely average at 104, and his deportment was sometimes poor. The tall, skinny boy had a better time of it at Camp Wigwam in Harrison, Maine, where, at eleven, he played a fair game of tennis, made friends readily, and was voted "the most popular actor of 1930."

Concerned about his studies, Sonny's parents enrolled him in Manhattan's highly rated McBurney School when he was thirteen; at the enrollment interview, he said he was interested in dramatics and tropical fish. He flunked out a year later. A friend who knew Sonny then recalled that "he wanted to do unconventional things. For hours, no one in the family knew where he was or what he was doing; he just showed up for meals. He was a nice boy, but he was the kind of kid who, if you wanted to have a card game, wouldn't join in."

When he was fifteen, Sonny was banished to Valley Forge Military Academy, a seat of learning heavily fortified with boxwood hedges and Revolutionary War cannon against dangers lurking in the Pennsylvania hills. Although the school is a recognizable model for Pencey Prep, the neurosis farm in *Catcher*, young Salinger—who talked of grabbing the big loot as a Hollywood writer-producer—was no Holden Caulfield. Classmate Alton McCloskey, first sergeant in Corporal Salinger's B Company and now a retired milk dealer in Lock Haven, Pennsylvania, remembers crawling through the fence with Salinger after lights out to poach local beer taps, but he is sure that Salinger never went A.W.O.L., as Holden did, and practiced only accepted sorts of nonconformism.

In June, 1936, Valley Forge gave him his only diploma. As literary editor of the yearbook, Salinger presented to the school a damply magnificent floral arrangement, since set to music and still sung at Last Parade:

> Hide not thy tears on this last day
> Your sorrow has no shame;
> To march no more midst lines of gray;
> No longer play the game.
> Four years have passed in joyful ways—
> Wouldst stay these old times dear?
> Then cherish now these fleeting days,
> The few while you are here.
>
> The last parade; our hearts sink low;
> Before us we survey—
> Cadets to be, where we are now
> And soon will come their day;
> Though distant now, yet not so far,
> Their years are but a few.
> Aye, soon they'll know why misty are
> Our eyes at last review.
>
> The lights are dimmed, the bugle sounds
> The notes we'll ne'er forget.
> And now a group of smiling lads;
> We part with much regret.
> Goodbyes are said; we march ahead,
> Success we go to find.
> Our forms are gone from Valley Forge;
> Our hearts are left behind.*

At night, tenting a blanket over his head to hide his flashlight beam from the Valley Forge duty officer, Salinger (by now called

---

* Some of Salinger's friends have denied that he wrote these lyrics. J. D. Salinger, however, is listed as their author in the Valley Forge yearbook.—ED.

Jerry) had written his first short stories. But if he told his family that he intended to be an author, he did not convince Papa Sol. In 1937, after Jerry spent a few unproductive weeks at New York University, the two Salingers set out for Vienna. "I was supposed to apprentice myself to the Polish ham business," Salinger wrote in a 1944 issue of *Story* magazine. "They finally dragged me off to Bydgoszcz for a couple of months, where I slaughtered pigs, wagoned through the snow with the big slaughter-master. Came back to America and tried college for half a semester, but quit like a quitter."

Salinger's last brush with institutional wisdom came at Columbia, where he signed up for a short-story course given by Whit Burnett, editor of *Story*. In 1942 the author was drafted and used his weekend passes to hole up in hotel rooms with his typewriter. Typical of his output then was an earnest piece for *Story*, and a weepy lament in the *Saturday Evening Post* about a sensitive young man who dies before he has time to finish the world's greatest novel, but whose brother, in penitence for his sins, abandons his own career as the world's greatest song writer to finish the book.

By 1944 the author was stationed in Tiverton, Devonshire, training with a small counter-intelligence detachment of the 4th Infantry Division—almost exactly the situation of Sergeant X, the tormented hero of the warmest and best of the *Nine Stories*, "For Esmé—with Love and Squalor" (the author, like Sergeant X, passed the time by listening to choir practice at a Methodist church in Tiverton).

On June 6, five hours after the first assault forces hit Utah Beach, Salinger landed with the 4th in Normandy, stayed with the division through the Battle of the Bulge. He was an aloof, solitary soldier whose job was to discover Gestapo agents by interviewing French civilians and captured Germans. In France, Staff Sergeant Salinger had an audience with War Correspondent Ernest Hemingway, who read Salinger's work and, possibly in appreciation of it ("Jesus, he has a helluva talent"), took out his Luger and shot the head off a chicken. Salinger used a similar incident in "Esmé."

With a swagger, the prospering young author in 1944 sent Burnett a two-hundred-dollar check to help other young writers, and added: "Am still writing whenever I can find the time and an unoccupied foxhole." He carried a typewriter around in his Jeep, and an army acquaintance remembers him typing away, crouching under a table, while his area was under attack. Salinger's stories were improving, although his dialogue still had the kind of workmanlike falsity taught in writing classes. In one of his *Post* stories, Salinger introduced Sergeant Vincent Caulfield, who "has a kid brother in the Army who flunked out of a lot of schools" and who is apparently killed in action in the Pacific. The story shows Salinger's fictional preoccupation with dead brothers, and his bent for starting his legends by killing off his main character. (The Glass legend similarly began with Seymour's suicide, in "A Perfect Day for Bananafish," in 1948.)

Salinger in 1946 was back in New York, rid not only of soldiering but of a brief, unsuccessful marriage to a European woman physician. Though the two were obviously incompatible, he later insisted that they had a telepathic link, were aware of the same events happening at the same time. He lived with his parents on Park Avenue and spent his nights in Greenwich Village. Gentle and humorous, he loved arguing about grammar and augmented his skinny frame with bar bells. Although this was years before Buddhism was peddled in supermarkets, he eagerly studied Zen, gave reading lists on the subject to his dates. He brought an astonishing collection of girls to the Village, bagged with unobtrusive efficiency at a drugstore in Manhattan's chaste Barbizon Hotel for Women. Friends could almost see him storing up dialogue. The Barrymore of Camp Wigwam fended off too curious Barbizonians with elaborate leg-pulls; one girl returned to the real world convinced that he was a goalie for the Montreal Canadiens.

Soon Salinger was much too absorbed with writing to need the Village, and he began a series of withdrawals. The first took him to a cottage twenty-four miles away, in Tarrytown. Friends apparently found his address, because he hid out in a sweatbox near the Third Avenue el for his three-week push to finish *Catcher*. He decided to move again, and in one of the notable failures of Zen archery, hit on Westport. The artsy-ginsy exurb was no place for Salinger. "A writer's worst enemy is another writer," he remarked ungraciously and accurately somewhat later.

There were no writers in Cornish, New Hampshire, and no plumbing or furnace in the gambrel-roofed cottage Salinger bought on a ninety-acre hillside tract overlooking the Connecticut River. That winter he happily carried water from his stream and cut wood with a chain saw. For company he hiked across the river to Windsor, Vermont, and passed the time with teenagers in a juke joint called Nap's Lunch. The kids loved him, but mothers worried that the tall, solemn writer fellow from New York would put their children in a book.

In 1953, at a party in Manchester, Vermont, Salinger met Claire Douglas, an English-born Radcliffe student. She was unimpeachably right looking, extraordinarily pretty, not too categorically cashmere sweater and flannel skirt. Claire was fascinated by the intense, thirty-four-year-old author, and visited him several times in Cornish. She soothed her family with a story that showed close attention to the master's style: Salinger lived, she said, with his mother, sister, fifteen Buddhist monks, and a yogi who stood on his head. The girl discovered mysticism. "She was hung on the Jesus Prayer," recalls her brother Gavin, a wandering movie photographer. "Jerry is very good at hanging people on things."

Abruptly, Claire broke off with Salinger and married a young blue-suit from the Harvard Business School. Just as abruptly, she ended the marriage after several months and returned to Cornish. She and Salinger were married in 1955. His wedding present to his bride was "Franny," whose heroine has Claire's looks, mannerisms and—the sort of private salute that amuses the author—Claire's blue suitcase.

Uncharacteristically, Salinger threw a party to celebrate his marriage. It was attended by his mother and his sister (about whom little is known except that she is a dress buyer at Bloomingdale's and has been divorced twice). Claire's first husband was also present. A little later, at the Cornish town meeting, pranksters elected Salinger Town Hargreave—an honorary office unseriously given to the most recently married man; he is supposed to round up pigs whenever they get loose. Salinger was unamused.

He had begun another of his withdrawals; he no longer spoke to the teenagers with whom he had talked for hours in Nap's Lunch, cut off his widely spaced visits with Cornish neighbors. Occasionally he was seen at work in the nearby Dartmouth library, wearing, as a friend described it at the time, a checked wool shirt and "Genghis Khan beard." His working habits have not changed: Salinger takes a packed lunch to his cement-block cell, and works from 8:30 A.M. to 5:30 P.M. He can be reached there by phone—but, says a relative, "the house had damn well better be burning down." When he is not working, Salinger watches TV as avidly as any Fat Lady.

The author's most recent withdrawal may mean merely that his social needs are met by a wife and two children (Matthew, born on February 13, 1960, and Margaret Ann, born December 10, 1955). But Salinger is at work on his first really large body of fiction. The Glass family story cycle is already far longer than Catcher, and clearly it is nowhere near completion—a friend reports that Salinger intends to write a Glass trilogy. Since his marriage, the author has exhausted himself, and his supply of sociability, in a protracted effort to give his legend structure and direction, to deal with characters who speak his own most shadowed thoughts, and to solve the snarls caused by piecemeal publication. His face, after six years of struggle, shows the pain of an artistic battle whose outcome still cannot be seen. The battle almost certainly involves the matter of Seymour's sainthood and suicide.

Once there was a man (so goes an ancient Taoist legend) who was so expert at judging horses that he ignored such trivialities as color and sex, looking as he did into the very essence of the beasts. Such a man, gifted with the eye for the core of reality, was Seymour —at least in the estimation of his family. His oldest surviving brother, Buddy Glass, remarks: "I haven't been able to think of anybody whom I'd care to send out to look for horses in his stead."

The evolution of Seymour into this being of almost supersensory perception is one of the more fascinating parts of J. D. Salinger's history. Seymour first appeared in the limpid, shattering, 1948 short story, "A Perfect Day for Bananafish," in which he goes swimming with a little girl on a Florida beach and, overcome by her innocence, swallows too much sublimity (or, one guesses later, too much despair). He returns to his hotel room, where his wife has been gabbling on the phone to her mother, and shoots himself through the head. Reasons for the cryptic suicide were suggested in a superb story written seven years later, "Raise High the Roof Beam, Car-

penters," in which Seymour's wedding day is recalled; it shows a
sensitive, gentle, somewhat weak man about to tie himself to a
mass of hair nets, deodorant bottles and parroted psychiatric un-
truths.

But not until Salinger's latest (1959), most convoluted and runic
story, "Seymour: An Introduction," in which the character is traced
even farther back, does Seymour appear as a saint and major poet
(although almost the only poetic evidence given is a verse Seymour
wrote when he was eight: "John Keats,/ John Keats,/ John,/ Please
put your scarf on"). The account was ostensibly set down by Buddy
as a memorial, and the neurotically involved style, the endless self-
conscious asides to the reader,° the masses of parentheses suggest
brilliantly that the narrator is cracking under the strain of having to
live with the ever-growing memory of a loved but envied dead
man. "Seymour: An Introduction" is one of the masterly seriocomic
performances of recent literature. But in it, Seymour's suicide no
longer makes sense. Saints may be martyred, but they do not shoot
themselves. If the suicide in the hotel room was the act of a man
weakened to insanity, then the whole legend is meaningless; Seymour supposedly was the sanest and strongest of men. If it was the
departure of a holy man from an unworthy world, it was out of
character; Seymour taught his six disciples not only to love and
forgive the world but also, one judges from Zooey, to play their
parts in the world wholeheartedly. The suicide was wrong, and, as
Buddy now explains him, Seymour was not capable of a wrong act.

Can Salinger write his way back to the suicide and make his myth
whole? If he brings it off, what he will have is anybody's guess. But
it is certain that the Glass legend's landscape will be largely interior; there will be little of the panoramic sweep of the social novel.
But whatever its form, it will express the essence of Salinger's time,
embodied in the only theme Salinger has ever written about—the

° Buddy's style reflects Salinger's own most delicate apostrophes, such as
this dedication of *Franny and Zooey:* "As nearly as possible in the spirit of
Matthew Salinger, age one, urging a luncheon companion to accept a cool
lima bean, I urge my editor, mentor, and (heaven help him) closest friend,
William Shawn, *genius domus* of *The New Yorker*, lover of the long shot, protector of the unprolific, defender of the hopelessly flamboyant, most unreason-
ably modest of born great artist-editors, to accept this pretty skimpy-looking
book."

predicament of the good, sensitive man in a private world of love and death. It is his rare skill to make even goodness credible. He is a sentimentalist, but his sentiment is counterweighted by a colloquial, ironic style, and it has not impaired his judgment. More important, he is one of today's few serious authors who write about their characters—about man—with hope.

Salinger is clearly an original, the kind whose shadow is seen not in the writers who precede him but in those who follow. If he were to stop writing now, *The Catcher in the Rye* would be judged a small masterpiece—say about the size of *The Red Badge of Courage* —the *Nine Stories* a collection unmatched since Hemingway's *In Our Time*, and *Franny and Zooey* a glowing minor work. This much is a certainty: there is no one writing now who could be sent to look for horses in his stead.

*   *   *

Thus, the *Time* account. Some biographical detail can be added. One of the more fascinating pastimes among Salinger students and fans is to try to trace parallels between his life and his work. Thus it could be noted that, in his schooldays, he managed the fencing team, like Holden Caulfield, though it is not known whether he lost the equipment in the subway. Like Seymour, he has written haiku and used to be an expert pool player. Like various Glasses, he used to have a penchant for reading his stories to friends or relatives, and his interest in Oriental religion sounds genuine enough. During the early stages of his marriage, it is reported that no living thing was ever killed in the Salinger household, presumably not even insects. If this is true, the situation has changed, for more recently, the Salingers were engaged in a furious campaign against woodchucks.

One of the difficulties faced by any Salinger biographer is the lingering effect of his practical jokes and legpulls. He once told someone, for instance, that when he was a child, the Marx brothers were always in and out of his parents' home. This information should interest Messrs. Gwynn and Blotner, who, as noted in the introduction, have found a connection between Gallagher & Glass, Gallagher & Shean, and the Marxes. An exciting clue, no doubt, but the Marx brothers disclaim any knowledge of the Salingers (one is almost tempted to say, of the Glasses). Perhaps Salinger was merely fibbing; and yet again, perhaps not.

Certain facts or semifacts can be ascertained in the fog. One of Salinger's fellow cadets at his military academy did commit suicide by jumping from a window, like James Castle in *Catcher in the Rye*. Another was expelled, and later apparently wound up in a West Coast mental institution. In Florida, Salinger once did befriend a girl much younger than he (Sibyl?), and apparently went on seeing her until she was in college. In a new biography of Eugene O'Neill, Arthur and Barbara Gelb tell a rather engaging story of O'Neill's daughter Oona and her friend, Carol Grace, who was then seventeen and engaged to the thirty-five-year-old William Saroyan. The author was in basic training at Sacramento, and Carol promised to write him daily. As she now recalls it:

Oona was receiving a letter almost every day from a boy named Jerry in New York. Some of the letters were fifteen pages long, and they were very witty, comments about all kinds of things. I told Oona I was afraid that if I wrote to Bill, he'd find out what an idiot I was, and decide not to marry me, so she marked the clever passages in her letters from Jerry and let me copy them, as my own, in my letters to Bill.

When Bill's two-week training period was up and I went to see him at camp, he was terribly surly. I asked him what was the matter, and he told me he'd changed his mind about marrying me. He said he had thought I was a sweet girl, but that "those lousy, glib letters" I'd been sending him had made him wonder. I was very upset, and told Oona about it, and she said we'd have to tell Bill the truth about the letters. But I knew that Bill hated liars more than anything else, so I didn't tell him.

The writer of the letters, of course, was J. D. Salinger. (Saroyan has since expressed intense admiration for him.)

Such is the small change of the Salinger legend; it becomes interesting only because there are so few big bills. Old friends eagerly recall his Greenwich Village days, and how he refused to take money from his family while trying to support himself through his writing; how he seemed warm toward his parents, and yet distant; how he wrote on an artist's drafting board, wore tweed jackets with leather elbow patches and (one can hear Buddy interjecting, "Stop that now!") loved dogs. Stories about his wife are even rarer and equally cherished as collector's items. There is, for instance, the occasion when Salinger was meeting an English publisher at the Stork Club, and Claire and a friend sat at a nearby table, pretending to be tarts. Or the time, after "Franny" was published, when friends would come upon Salinger and Claire, their lips moving silently. It was a private charade, acting out the near-final lines in the story: "Her lips began to move, forming soundless words. . . ."

Amid all this, Salinger's own words remain largely soundless. Occasionally he does materialize. When *Cosmopolitan* was getting ready to reprint "The Inverted Forest," an early Salinger story which the magazine owned but which Salinger would like to disown, one of the editors was astounded one evening to have the author call on him; he pleaded, politely and pleasantly, that the story should not be published. (As it happened, it was.) Attempts to unearth his old stories often seem to irritate him. When an overly ambitious acquaintance asked permission to include one in an anthology, Salinger declined curtly; reprimanded for his attitude, Salinger unbent and wrote back jovially to the effect that things had got to a pretty pass when he couldn't tell an old friend to —— his anthology. In general, Salinger letters are charming but rare. It is said, however (another legpull?), that he carries on a regular correspondence with a prisoner in Sing Sing.

One of the most intriguing Salinger stories concerns the time the finished manuscript of *Catcher in the Rye* had been submitted to a publisher. The book was accepted, a contract was signed and Salinger went to have a talk with his prospective editor. Some time later, he called his literary agent and insisted, close to tears, that the book must be taken away from the publishing firm in question. The agent wanted to know why. Salinger merely insisted that this was his wish. When the agent persisted, Salinger finally explained that he could not possibly deal with his prospective editor. "Why," said Salinger, "the man thought Holden is crazy."

The book was published elsewhere.

In the old days, Salinger occasionally permitted biographical notes about himself. One of them, written by William Shawn of *The New Yorker* for the Book-of-the-Month Club at the time *Catcher* appeared, quotes Salinger as describing a visit to a Sarah Lawrence short-story class. The combination of the Book-of-the-Month Club,

Sarah Lawrence *and* a short-story class seems, for the present Salinger, wildly unlikely; at the time he said:

> I enjoyed the day, but it isn't something I'd ever want to do again. I got very oracular and literary. I found myself labelling all the writers I respect. . . . A writer, when he's asked to discuss his craft, ought to get up and call out in a loud voice just the *names* of the writers he *loves*. I love Kafka, Flaubert, Tolstoy, Chekhov, Dostoevsky, Proust, O'Casey, Rilke, Lorca, Keats, Rimbaud, Burns, E. Brontë, Jane Austen, Henry James, Blake, Coleridge. I won't name any living writers. I don't think it's right.

In 1949, when *Harper's* published "Down at the Dinghy," he contributed the following statement about himself:

> In the first place, if I owned a magazine I would never publish a column full of contributors' biographical notes. I seldom care to know a writer's birthplace, his children's names, his working schedule, the date of his arrest for smuggling guns (the gallant rogue!) during the Irish Rebellion. The writer who tells you these things is also very likely to have his picture taken wearing an open-collared shirt—and he's sure to be looking three-quarter-profile and tragic. He can also be counted on to refer to his wife as a swell gal or a grand person.
>
> I've written biographical notes for a few magazines, and I doubt if I ever said anything honest in them. This time, though, I think I'm a little too far out of my Emily Brontë period to work myself into a Heathcliff. (All writers—no matter how many rebellions they actively support—go to their graves half-Oliver Twist and half-Mary, Mary, Quite Contrary.) This time I'm going to make it short and go straight home.
>
> I've been writing seriously for over ten years. Being modest almost to a fault, I won't say I'm a born writer, but I'm certainly a born professional. I don't think I ever *selected* writing as a career. I just started to write when I was eighteen or so and never stopped. (Maybe that isn't quite true. Maybe I *did* select writing as a profession. I don't really remember—I got into it so quickly—and finally.)
>
> I was with the Fourth Division during the war.
>
> I almost always write about very young people.

And that is where one must leave the matter, unless one happens to be one of those very young people, or a prisoner in Sing Sing.

II. The Good American

The two essays in this section see Salinger's work as essentially concerned with the American scene, and with what both critics regard as a peculiarly American problem—the conflict between the individual and society. To Arthur Mizener, it is the problem of the Good American trying to be, as it were, good to himself as well as good to society; to develop his own possibilities to the fullest, but not at the expense of the community around him. This may seem like a somewhat dry way of talking about Holden's yearning for goodness or Franny's disgust with sham, but Mizener makes quite clear that this is an emotional more than a social problem, that "conformity" and "nonconformity" can be another way of describing the pull of opposing loves. Unlike such critics as Alfred Kazin and John Updike, Mizener is not disturbed by the Glass children's exclusivity, by their inability to feel close to those they do not love, or to love those to whom they are not close. He sees this as part of their nature and their burden.

"Their alienation," David Stevenson would say, for that is his term for Salinger's theme. He pushes Mizener's view several steps closer to a purely sociological interpretation, and seems more concerned with the lonely crowd than with the lonely individual. In a later section, an essay by Donald Barr takes specific issue with this approach, and I think correctly so. The crisis Salinger writes about is deeper, and more permanent, than one afflicting "upper middle-class, mid-century America."

Among incidental benefits, it might be noted that Mizener's piece provides a good introduction to Salinger's early work and to the complexities of the Glass family; while Stevenson provides the neatest one-sentence definition on record of the *New Yorker* short story.

THE LOVE SONG OF J. D. SALINGER

by ARTHUR MIZENER

Some time ago I gave a lecture in the Middle West, on Scott Fitzgerald, before about as intelligent an undergraduate audience as you are likely to find. When I finished, the first question from the floor was about J. D. Salinger. This humbling non-sequitur is too familiar to be any surprise, for Salinger is probably the most avidly read author of any serious pretensions in his generation. There are good reasons why he should be, for though his work has certain limitations—both of subject matter and of technique—it is, within these limitations, the most interesting fiction that has come along for some me.

Salinger has been writing since he was fifteen and is evidently a dedicated—not to say obsessed—writer, but the relatively small amount of work he has produced in a career of nearly twenty years suggests that he has a hard time writing. Moreover, there is in his work a very high incidence of emotional collapse and even violent death. One of the sharpest implications of his work, in short, is that perceptive people have difficulty remaining operative, or even surviving, in our world; a great deal of his most brilliant wit, like so much of James Thurber's, is close to desperation. There are good and even historical reasons in American culture for this state of mind, as I shall try to suggest, but they make the difficulty Salinger himself apparently faces no less disturbing to contemplate.

His immediate appeal is that he speaks our language, or, to be exact, makes a kind of poetry out of the raw materials of our speech. His ear picks up with stunning exactness the speech of many kinds of people: of the brutally conventional—"But my *gosh*. Honestly! I just can't stand to see somebody get away with absolute murder. It makes my blood boil"; of the earnestly ignorant—"They got their *pores* open the whole time. That's their *nature,* for Chrissake. See what I mean?"; of the army—"This here's officers' quarters, Mac." His people are wholly present, in devastating dramatic immediacy, in everything they say.

What is more, Salinger uses with great skill the very American device of conveying meaning by describing object, gesture, action. He can create this kind of poetry on the simplest occasion, as for instance when an ordinary girl is waiting for a long-distance telephone call:

> She read an article in a women's pocket-size magazine, called "Sex Is Fun—or Hell." She washed her comb and brush. She took the spot out of the skirt of her beige suit. She moved the button on her Saks blouse. She tweezed out two freshly surfaced hairs in her mole. When the operator finally rang her room, she was sitting on the window seat and had almost finished putting lacquer on the nails of her left hand.

But if Salinger is a poet in this sense, he is also a poet in the only sense that he himself would probably take seriously: he's a man with his own special insight into the meaning of experience. "A good horse," as his characters the Glass children learned from Lo Po, "can be picked out by its general build and appearance. But the superlative horse—one that raises no dust and leaves no tracks—is something evanescent and fleeting, elusive as thin air."

An inescapable, intense awareness of this "poetry that flows through things, all things," marks every one of Salinger's significant characters. As Vincent Caulfield in "This Sandwich Has No Mayonnaise" (1945) remarks of his brother Holden, such people cannot "do anything but listen hectically to the maladjusted little apparatus [they wear] for a heart." That is what makes Holden worry all through *The Catcher in the Rye* about what the Central Park ducks do in the winter and constantly recall with delight that, when they played checkers, old Jane would never move her kings out of the back row.

Obviously Salinger did not burst on the world with these powers of observation and this sense of experience fully developed. He had, in fact, rather more trouble than most writers in discovering his own way of feeling and the best mode of expression for it. His first published stories, which appeared mainly in the *Saturday Evening*

Post and *Collier's* in the early forties, will quickly destroy any romantic notions one may have had about the value of the unpublished stories he wrote even earlier, by flashlight under the bedclothes after "Lights," when he was a student at Valley Forge Military Academy. The first published stories deal, in a mechanical and overingenious way, with the superficial interests of magazine readers of the time. In "The Hang of It" (1941), for example, a father tells us about his comically inept soldier son who keeps insisting that he will get the hang of soldiering. At the end we find out that the speaker is also the boy's commanding officer. This is intended to make what had at first appeared the boy's stupidity seem pathetic anxiety, but the events of the story are almost entirely farce and do not support the intention.

These trivial stories are nevertheless interesting. They show us Salinger's preoccupation with close personal relations, particularly family relations. They make clear his marked preference for first-person narration and interior monologue. And they show the related difficulty he has in saying what he wants to and at the same time constructing a "well-made" plot. In 1945 he was saying, "I am a dash man and not a miler, and it is probable that I will never write a novel."

Perhaps that judgment was right, for *The Catcher in the Rye*, despite its brillance of observation and the virtuosity with which Salinger keeps Holden Caulfield's monologue going for the length of a novel, is primarily concerned neither with the working out of a plot nor the development of a character. It is a lyric monologue in which the complex feelings of an essentially static character are gradually revealed. For all Salinger's skill, *The Catcher in the Rye* has a claustrophobic and, at the same time, random quality.

The second stage of Salinger's career runs from 1943, when he published his first mature story, "The Varioni Brothers," in the *Post*, to about 1948. In this period his powers of observation became much sharper and he began to understand much better what he wanted to say. His plots, if they still cramped him, were not completely irrelevant, though it was still true—as it is today—that he was at his best in meditations like "Boy in France" (1945) and in the monologues of plotted stories like "Last Day of the Last Furlough" (1944). His material was still a little conventional—the vicissitudes of Gershwinlike song writers, cruise-ship romances, soldiers going overseas. But his characteristic feelings about experience were beginning to come through. They are there in the beautifully revealed devotion of the letter from Babe Gladwaller's sister Mattie, age ten, that Babe reads in his foxhole in "Boy in France." They are there when Sonny Varioni, the talented, bored, ambitious song writer, realizes that he hears the music for the first time in his life when he reads his dead brother's book.

The best work of his second period is the group of independent but related stories about the Gladwaller and the Caulfield families, who are closely connected by the friendship of Babe Gladwaller and Vincent Caulfield. These stories appeared in four different magazines over a period of three years. The first four of them are mainly concerned with Babe and Vincent. Then, beginning in late 1945 with "I'm Crazy," Salinger began to focus on Holden Caulfield. Much of the family detail from the first four stories is kept in the two stories about Holden, but there are important changes, and, with only slight revisions, these two stories became chapters in *The Catcher in the Rye.* I think it is a fairly good guess that, after writing *The Catcher in the Rye*, which was published in 1951, Salinger decided that most of the things he had been working out in the Gladwaller-Caulfield stories could be more clearly realized if he started afresh without some of the awkward commitments of these stories.

In any event, in 1948 he began the third period of his career with the publication of "A Perfect Day for Bananafish" in *The New Yorker.* This is, in order of publication anyway, the first of his stories about the Glass family. It is anybody's guess, of course, whether Salinger had the whole, still unfinished history of the Glass family in mind when he wrote "A Perfect Day for Bananafish," but my guess is that, much as William Faulkner has apparently always had at least the main outlines of the McCaslin family history in mind, Salinger has known about all the Glasses from the beginning. For one thing, the order in which the stories have appeared (and probably were written) has little relation to the chronological order of events in the family history, yet all the minute particulars of the Glass family history are consistent. What we are told about Seymour Glass in 1948 in the first story fits precisely, both in fact and in implication, with what we have learned about him and the rest of the family since. Salinger's conception of the Glass children's situation has become richer during these nine years, but neither the facts nor the essential nature of that situation has changed.

Because the details about the Glass family are scattered and because a resonable knowledge of them is necessary for an understanding of Salinger's best work, it may help to set down in outline what we so far know about them. The parents, Les Glass (Jewish) and Bessie Gallagher Glass (a fat Irish Rose, her youngest son lovingly calls her), were successful Pantages Circuit vaudevillians in the twenties. By the forties Les Glass was "hustling talent for a motion picture studio in Los Angeles." In the fifties they are living with their two youngest children in New York, in "an old but, categorically, not unfashionable apartment house in the East Seventies." They have had seven children.

The oldest, Seymour, was born in February, 1917, entered Columbia at the age of fifteen and took a Ph.D. in English. In 1940 he and his brother Buddy reluctantly gave up the room they had shared in the Glasses' apartment since 1929 and moved into an apartment of their own near Seventy-ninth and Madison. Seymour taught English for a year or two before entering the service. While he was stationed at Forth Monmouth, he met a girl named Muriel Fedder, whom he married on June 4, 1942. When he returned from the service, he was—as he had promised Muriel and her mother he would be—psychoanalyzed, presumably by what Buddy calls one of those "summa-cum-laude Thinker[s] and intellectual men's-room attendant[s]" so greatly admired by people like Muriel's mother. Possibly as a result, Seymour one day deliberately drove the Fedder's car into a tree, and it was decided that he and Muriel should take a vacation in Florida, at the place where they had spent their honeymoon. There, in Room 507 of a fashionable beach hotel, on the afternoon of March 18, 1948, Seymour made his second, successful attempt to commit suicide, by putting a bullet from an Ortgies caliber 7.65 through his right temple.

The second child, Buddy (whose given name is, I think, Webb), was born in 1919, as was Jerome David Salinger. Buddy is the writer of the family, and it is sometimes difficult to distinguish his voice from Salinger's. *"The Great Gatsby,"* he says, ". . . was my 'Tom Sawyer' when I was twelve." Buddy never finished college (nor did Salinger, who tried three). He entered the service early in 1942 and, when he got out, became "a writer in residence." In 1955 he was teaching "at a girl's junior college in upper New York state, where he lived alone, in a small, unwinterized, unelectrified house about a quarter of a mile away from a rather popular ski run."

The next child and first girl in the family is Boo Boo Glass. "Her joke of a name aside, her general unprettiness aside, she is—in terms of permanently memorable, immoderately perceptive, small-area faces—a stunning and final girl." She appears to be—we do not know a great deal about her yet—more successfully reconciled to the world than the rest of the Glass children. Boo Boo was a Wave, stationed in Brooklyn. During the war she met "a very resolute-looking young man" named Tannenbaum, whom she later married. The Tannenbaums live in Tuckahoe and have a summer place in New England. By 1955 they had three children, the oldest of whom is Lionel, the central character in "Down at the Dinghy," which was published in *Harper's* in 1949.

Boo Boo was followed by twins, Waker and Walt. Waker spent the war in a conscientious objector's camp in Maryland and by 1955 had become a Catholic priest: "If you tell Waker it looks like *rain,* his eyes all fill up." Walt entered the service in the spring of 1941 and by May of 1942 was in the Pacific. In Japan, late in the autumn of 1945, a Japanese stove he was packing as a souvenir for his commanding officer exploded and killed him.

The sixth child, Zachary Martin Glass, known in the family as Zooey, was born in 1929. Zooey's face is close to being "a wholly beautiful face" or, as Boo Boo says, he looks like "the blue-eyed Jewish-Irish Mohican scout who died in your arms at the roulette table at Monte Carlo." After college he became a television actor, though his mother very much wanted him to take his Ph.D. in Mathematics or Greek, as he easily could have. By 1952 he was playing leads.

The youngest child is a girl named Frances, born in 1934. Like Zooey she is extraordinarily beautiful. In the summer of 1954, between her junior and senior years in college, she played summer

stock. Zooey, an enthusiastically unrelenting critic, says she was
very good, and Franny clearly loves the theater. In her junior year
she became interested in a boy named Lane Coutell—interested
enough to sleep with him. But in November of 1955 she was plunged
into a spiritual crisis—"I'm sick of ego, ego, ego. My own and
everybody else's. I'm sick of everybody that wants to get somewhere, do something distinguished and all, be somebody interesting.
It's disgusting—it is, it *is*. I don't care what anybody says." After
three difficult days at home, she is saved from collapse by her
brother Zooey, who possibly saves himself at the same time.

Over a period of nearly eighteen years, beginning in 1927, one or
more of the Glass children were performing, under the name of
Black, on a famous radio quiz show known—"with perhaps typical
Coast-to-Coast irony"—as "It's a Wise Child." Their educations
were paid for by these performances.

This is the barest outline of what we know about the Glass family.
Even so, the fullness of these details and their exactness are striking
evidence of the imaginative intensity with which they have been
conceived. They also make it possible for Salinger, for the first time,
to use consistently the technique he is most happy with and to
convey directly the feelings he cares most about.

For example, they provide the fullest opportunity for the kind of
surprise an author can get from delayed or implied explanation,
which writers of monologues like Salinger and Faulkner usually
substitute for narrative suspense—an awkward and artificial device
in a monologue. In Faulkner, one has to reconstruct the genealogy
of the McCaslin family from dozens of scattered allusions before
one fully understands any particular McCaslin story. In the same
way one has to reconstruct the history of the Glass family.

Salinger uses suspended explanation much less extravagantly
than Faulkner, but he has nonetheless confused some readers. Some
of them, for instance, seem to have thought (until the matter was
fully explained in "Zooey" in 1957) that the heroine of "Franny"
(1955) was so badly upset during her football weekend with Lane
Coutell not because she was in a spiritual crisis but because she
was pregnant. There is no real reason for a careful reader to make
this mistake about "Franny." In that story, Franny describes at

length the idea of prayer in *The Way of a Pilgrim*, the little book she carries with her everywhere; and at the end of the story her lips are moving in the Jesus Prayer the Pilgrim recommends. Nevertheless, a good many readers apparently did misunderstand "Franny." Some even seem to have doubts about who pushed whom into the empty swimming pool at the end of "Teddy," where, for much the same dramatic reasons that are at work in "Franny," Salinger depends on our understanding of Teddy's attitude to make us understand that it is Teddy who dies.

This kind of surprise is one of the most effective devices available to a writer like Salinger, and he uses it with great skill. He always plays fair; any careful reader knows what is going on. But we are frequently astonished and delighted when we catch our first glimpse of the precise connections between what had before seemed unconnected events. It must be some time, for instance, before a reader discovers that the Walt whom the drunken Eloise is talking about in "Uncle Wiggily in Connecticut" (1948) is Walt Glass, whose family connections did not begin to emerge in any detail until "Raise High the Roof Beam, Carpenters" (1955). But when the reader makes this discovery, a fascinating and important aspect of the Glass family falls into place for him. Walt was Bessie Glass's "only truly lighthearted son"; as such he shows us an important aspect of Salinger's sense of human possibilities.

The fact that the Glass family is large and closely knit is also important to the feelings Salinger cares most about. The essential reality for him subsists in personal relations, when people, however agonizingly, love one another. "I say," remarks Buddy Glass as he begins to tell us the story "Zooey," "that my current offering isn't a mystical story, or a religiously mystifying story, at all. *I* say it is a compound, or multiple, love story, pure and complicated."

This is true of all Salinger's mature stories. Their subject is the power to love, pure and—in children and the childlike— simple, but in aware people, pure and complicated. Salinger's constant allusions to the Bhagavad-Gita, Sri Ramakrishna, Chuang-tzu, and the rest are only efforts to find alternate ways of expressing what his stories are about. This power to love can be realized— and represented—most fully in complicated personal relations like those of the Glasses.

Salinger's conception of these relations is an impressive—and certainly unconscious—evidence of the way he fits into a major tradition of American literature, what might be called the effort to define the Good American. For this tradition, American experience creates a dilemma by encouraging the individual man to cultivate his perception to the limit according to his own lights and at the same time committing him to a society on which the majority has firmly imposed a well-meaning but imperceptive and uniform attitude. People in this tradition of our cultural history have a highly developed, personal sense of their experience. At the same time, they have a strong conviction—even if a bitter conviction like Henry Adams'—that no man can survive in isolation and that the only community they have to love is the American community to which they have been committed by a lifetime's involvement. Such people cannot escape knowing that the Good American must be a member of a particularly demanding and not very perceptive community and simultaneously a supremely aware man, because they themselves live partly in the world of ordinary American experience and partly in what may perhaps fairly be called the transcendental world of extraordinary American experience.

The Glass children stand in this way at the center of our dilemma as, with less clarity of perception and less intensity of feeling, large numbers of Americans do. Like Thoreau and Henry Adams, Huck Finn and Ike McCaslin, Ishmael and Jay Gatsby, the Glass children are well aware of where they stand—committed, involved, torn.

"I'd enjoy [doing a movie in France], yes," says Zooey. "*God*, yes. But I'd hate like hell to leave New York. If you must know, I hate any kind of so-called creative type who gets on any kind of ship. I don't give a goddam what his reasons are. I was *born* here. I went to *school* here. I've been *run over* here—*twice*, and on the same damn *street*. I have no business acting in Europe, for God's sake."

This sounds like the speaker in Allen Tate's "Ode to the Confederate Dead," except that the voice is wholly Northern and urban and is—for all its desperateness—less despairing.

It is the effort to convey their full sense of this situation that leads the Glass children to talk the way they do. For this extra dimension of understanding they use the everyday urban speech Salinger has been listening to all his life. The Glass children must speak the language of the place where they were born, went to school, were run over; it is their native language, the only one wholly theirs, just as the place itself is. But they need to express in this language an understanding of their experience which, if possessed to some degree by many Americans, is wholly clear to only a few of them.

An effort to resolve a similar conflict of feelings affects most of the writers of this tradition, with the result that they too develop odd, brilliant styles. Salinger's style most obviously resembles that of Mark Twain, Lardner and Hemingway, who prided themselves on using homely American speech with great accuracy, but were saying things with it that few homely Americans are wholly conscious of.

Like Twain and Lardner, Salinger depends more than most prose writers on the fine shading of his style to convey his meaning. That is why he is at his best when one of his characters is speaking. When Buddy Glass writes his brother Zooey about Zooey's unprofitable love of Greek, he says, "Of course, you can go to Athens. Sunny *old* Athens." When Zooey wants to get out of the bathtub, he says to his mother, "I'm getting out of here in about three seconds, Bessie! I'm giving you fair warning. Let's not wear out our welcome, buddy." Each of these clichés is made absurd by the special quality of the Glass child's feeling, but it is at the same time what holds him, for all his special insight, in contact with the perception of ordinary people.

This perception is at its purest in children, whose wonderful directness fascinates Salinger. But he respects it wherever he finds it, whether in "the very corny boy" who gave Franny the gold swizzle stick she cannot bear to throw away, or in Zooey's producer LeSage, who delights in scripts that are down-to-earth, simple and untrue, but believes with beautiful innocence that his "tired, bosomy, Persian-looking blonde [wife is] a dead ringer [for] the late Carole Lombard, in the movies." As Bill Gorton in *The Sun Also Rises* says of Cohn, "The funny thing is, he's nice, too. I like him. But he's just so awful."

The Glass family's most treasured jokes hover close to this reluctant sympathy with people like LeSage. For instance, at the end of Buddy's trip to Florida after Seymour's suicide, when he had wept nearly all the way, he heard a woman back of him in the plane saying, "with all of Back Bay Boston and most of Harvard Square in her voice, '. . . and the *next morning*, mind you, they took a pint of pus out of that lovely young body of hers.'" As a result, when he got off the plane and Muriel "the Bereaved Widow came toward me all in Bergdorf Goodman black, I had the Wrong Expression on my face. I was grinning." It is this delicately balanced perception that gives the Glass children their special quality.

But if it makes them remarkable, it is also a quite terrible burden. "Smart men," as Dick Diver said a long time ago about Abe North in *Tender Is the Night*, "play close to the line because they have to—some of them can't stand it, so they quit." Like Abe North, Seymour, the most gifted of the Glass children, kills himself. He knows that, in spite of—because of—the unusual depth and intensity of his perception of experience, he needs to be a part of the daily life of the ordinary world. He tries, by psychoanalysis and marriage, to become part of Muriel Fedder's world. This commitment is not merely an intellectual need; it is a desperate emotional necessity for him: "How I love and need her undiscriminating heart," he says of Muriel. But Seymour finds it impossible to love simultaneously the life of his own discriminating heart and Muriel's life, with its "primal urge to play house permanently . . . to go up to the desk clerk in some very posh hotel and ask if her Husband has picked up the mail yet . . . to shop for maternity clothes . . . [to have] her own Christmas-tree ornaments to unbox annually." He is torn apart by two incompatible worlds of feeling.

This, then, is the hard thing—not to find out "what it [is] all about," which the Glass children have known from very early, but "how to live it." Knowing what it is all about, in fact, is the burden.

"Those two bastards," says Zooey of Seymour and Buddy, who had taught Franny and him what wisdom is, "got us nice and early and made us into freaks with freakish standards, that's all. We're the Tattooed Lady, and we're never going to have a minute's peace, the rest of our lives, till everybody else is tattooed, too. . . . The minute I'm in a room with somebody who has the usual number of ears, I either turn into a goddam *seer* or a human hatpin. The Prince of Bores."

This, Zooey knows, is not a failure of love—he would not be concerned with his own freakishness if love failed—but a distortion of it. As his mother says to him:

"If you [take to somebody] then you do all the talking and nobody can even get a word in edgewise. If you *don't* like somebody —which is most of the time—then you just sit around like death it*self* and let the person talk themself into a hole. I've seen you do it. . . . You do," she said, without accusation in her voice. "Neither you nor Buddy knows how to talk to people you don't like." She thought it over. "Don't love, really," she amended.

"Which is most of the time" because, apart from children and the occasionally simple adult, the world is made up of people who are innocently imperceptive and emotionally dead.

Of the drastic limitations of such people, Salinger has a terrifyingly lucid perception. His stories are filled with undergraduates "giving the impression of having at least three lighted cigarettes in each hand"; young teachers "who come . . . in, in [their] little button-down-collar shirt[s] and striped tie[s], and start . . . knocking Turgenev for about half an hour . . . [and] if you get into an argument with them, all they do is get this terribly *benign* expression"; parents who say, "I'll exquisite day *you*, buddy, if you don't get down off that bag this minute. And I mean it." Such people, as Teddy, in the story which bears his name, says of his parents, "love their reasons for loving us almost as much as they love us, and most of the time more."

Nevertheless the power to love can exist in unimaginative people, and when it does, as the Glass children know they ought to know, nothing else really counts. Bessie Glass "often seem[s] to be an impenetrable mass of prejudices, clichés, and bromides"; these are a continual irritation to her children: Franny is driven nearly frantic by Bessie's insistence on nice cups of chicken soup when Franny is suffering something like a crisis of the soul. But Zooey is right when he points out to her that she is "missing out on every single goddam religious action that's going on around this house. You don't even have sense enough to *drink* when somebody brings you a cup of consecrated chicken soup—which is the only kind of chicken soup Bessie ever brings anybody around this mad-house."

Even if the acts of such people are not consecrated by love, they must not be hated. "What I don't like," Zooey says to Franny, ". . . is the way you talk about all these people. I mean you don't just despise what they represent—you despise them. It's too damned personal, Franny."

What Zooey knows he must learn to do in order to survive is to love even what he calls the "fishy" people—because they are all the Fat Lady for whom Seymour told him to shine his shoes before going on the air, even though the audience could not see his feet.

"This terribly clear, clear picture of the Fat Lady formed in my mind," he tells Franny. "I had her sitting on this porch all day, swatting flies, with her radio going full-blast from morning till night. I figured the heat was terrible, and she probably had cancer and—I don't know. Anyway, it seemed goddam clear why Seymour wanted me to shine my shoes when I went on the air. It made *sense*."

It makes sense because the highest standard of performance a man's own understanding can set for him must ultimately be embodied—however mystically—in the ordinary, suffering members of the community of his fellows. Otherwise there can be no solution to the dilemma the Glass children are caught in. Zooey puts this conviction in the highest possible terms:

"But I'll tell you a terrible secret [he says to Franny]—Are you listening to me? *There isn't anyone out there who isn't Seymour's Fat Lady. . . .* Don't you know that? Don't you know that goddam secret yet? And don't you know—*listen* to me, now—*don't you know who that Fat Lady really is?* . . . Ah, buddy. Ah, buddy. It's Christ Himself. Christ Himself, buddy."

What Salinger has seen in American life is the extraordinary tension it sets up between our passion to understand and evaluate our experience for ourselves, and our need to belong to a community that is unusually energetic in imposing its understanding and values on its individual members. Whatever one may think of Salinger's answer to the problem, this view of American life is important; it has a long and distinguished history. But Salinger's achievement is not that he has grasped an abstract idea of American experience, important as that idea may be in itself; it is that he has seen this idea working in the actual life of our times, in our habitual activities, in the very turns of our speech, and has found a way to make us see it there, too.

THE MIRROR OF CRISIS

by DAVID L. STEVENSON

J. D. Salinger has never been an artist in residence at a summer session. He has published no critical treatise in a literary quarterly on the mythic symbolism in Faulkner, no "thoughts" on the conversion of Edith Sitwell or on Wimsatt's theory of the intentional fallacy. He is not a proper man of letters who occasionally publishes a short story or a novel; he is that rare thing among contemporary writers who' take their craft seriously, a complete professional.

Because of this diffidence to things dedicatedly literary, Salinger is usually identified by book reviewers, and properly, as a *New Yorker* writer, implying thereby both city wit and surface brilliance in his use of prose and stylized irony of situation in his use of plot. Such an identification suggests that his published work is meant to satisfy the reading tastes of a fairly heterogeneous audience, composed more of the highly literate men and women of the upper middle-class than of the "avant garde" or of the peer group of the quarterlies. Such an identification means also that any attempt to define the nature of his excellence as a writer and the serious but elusive sense of commitment in his work must take into account his use of the design and structure of the *New Yorker* story itself.

Salinger is surely one of the most skillful practitioners of the *New Yorker* short story or sketch. And, invidious critics aside, his sketches show it to be, at its best, one of the truly distinctive and definable fictional types of mid-century American letters. This kind of story contains no more than two or three characters, seen always at a moment of crisis in one of their lives. The concentration is on the crisis: the relationships which have led to it are indistinct, only suggested by the tone of the dialogue, by characters' momentary actions and gestures. The Salinger-*New Yorker* story is always a kind of closet scene between Hamlet and his mother with the rest of the play left out. It accomplishes its shock of surprise, and it evokes our emotions, by a frugal underplaying of plot and event, by its very minimizing of narrative. The reader is usually not projected into the problems of its characters because he is not given enough of the fabric of their lives to make such projection possible.

What a Salinger story *does* involve the reader in is something quite different. It is his awareness that the crisis of the sketch is a generic one of our time and place. The crisis of the usual *New Yorker* story may be fairly casual, and we have come to expect a Salinger story to be more stern in its implications because its roots are stronger and probe more deeply. But its crisis runs true to form. Salinger does not take you out of yourself into a living, substantial world of fiction. He throws you back into your own problems, or into an awareness of them in your contemporaries. His characters do not exist in a rich narrative, in a detailed setting, so that they become wholly separable, fictional beings. Rather they give us a feeling of our own sensitivity to compensate for their lack of created density.

One can best illustrate this quality of a Salinger story by comparing his *New Yorker* sketch "Pretty Mouth and Green My Eyes" with Hemingway's "The Short Happy Life of Francis Macomber." The two stories offer the same basic character relationships: passively suffering husband, aggressively lustful wife, and casual, opportunistic lover. In Hemingway's version, however, the characters are embedded in a full, complex plot in which motive and event are made inexorably overt. The tensions of the characters are in open balance for the reader, and the husband's declared failure of nerve is what provokes his wife's ruthless retaliation in taking a lover. The Macombers exist in the round as "created" individuals in a self-contained narrative which could be translated into Mandarin and remain comprehensible.

Part of the virtue of "Pretty Mouth and Green My Eyes," on the other hand, is that it is not a self-contained narrative. We know of the characters only that they are apartment dwellers in New York. They exist as voices on a telephone to illustrate the desperate irony of a husband calling his wife's latest lover, after a party the three of them have attended, at the moment when the lover is in bed with the wife. The tearing crisis of the story is the husband's slow realization, as he complains in hideously maudlin, drunken terms of his wife's infidelities, that he has put his own self-respect beyond the point of salvage. Salinger's characters, here, come alive *New Yorker* fashion through the skillful verisimilitude of their conversation. But, like E. B. White's famous figure in "The Door" (also translatable into Mandarin), they have social rather than narrative roots. They are important to us in direct proportion to our recognition of them as generic sketches of our urban, childless, apartmented men and women, alienated by the hectic nature of their lives from all quiet interflow of love and affection.

One significant element in the structure of a Salinger story, then, and a source of his power over us, is that his characters come alive in our recognition of them. In complementary fashion, an equally significant element is the effect on us of the special kind of crisis he asks us to identify. As in "Pretty Mouth and Green My Eyes," it is a crisis in a character's life or personality peculiar to upper-middle-class, mid-century America. It is related to our sense of the heightened vulnerability of men and women to emotional disaster.

I am not prepared to argue that the Salinger species of crisis is unique, and that other ages did not feel themselves alienated from inner security and outward affection. *Hamlet* alone would suffice. I should only assert that in our time and place the individual estranged from his fellows seems peculiarly understandable and therefore touching to us. If one needs outside documentation, I cite the fact that no age but our own has found a partial picture of itself in such a sociological study of estrangement as David Riesman's *The Lonely Crowd*. It is not that we, as a generation, are defeated, or without will. Perhaps it is merely that our religion, our family ties, our cultural traditions now give us a lighter armor than our predecessors wore.

At any rate, Salinger's fiction convicts us, as readers, of being deeply aware of a haunting inconclusiveness in our own, and in contemporary, emotional relationships—members all of the lonely crowd. His characters exist outside the charmed circle of the well-adjusted, and their thin cries for love and understanding go unheard. They are men, women and adolescents, not trapped by outside fate, but by their own frightened, and sometimes tragicomic, awareness of the uncrossable gulf between their need for love and the futility of trying to achieve it on any foreseeable terms.

Salinger's short stories are all variations on the theme of emotional estrangement. In "Down at the Dinghy," a small boy runs away when he overhears his father referred to as a "kike." In "Uncle Wiggily in Connecticut," two women, unsuccessful adventurers in love, let a Connecticut afternoon drift away on highballs and reminiscences, while the timid child of one of them retreats farther and farther into compensatory fantasy as the two women get progressively more sodden. In "A Perfect Day for Bananafish," a young soldier released from an army hospital confronts his wife's complicated indifference during their first reunion. When he is forced to weigh a small child's warm, intuitive sympathy against his wife's society prettiness, he shoots himself. The actions of the characters in all these stories could seem arbitrary, judged by the sketchiness of Salinger's narrative. In fact, however, the actions seem real and shocking because they are the kind of thing we can anticipate from the needs and stresses we share at least in part with the characters.

Salinger's most ambitious presentation of aspects of contemporary alienation, and his most successful capture of an American audience, is in his novel *The Catcher in the Rye.* It is the brief chronicle of Holden Caulfield, a sixteen-year-old boy who escapes to New York after flunking out of his third prep school. The novel is written as the boy's comment, half-humorous, half-agonizing, concerning his attempt to recapture his identity and his hopes for belonging by playing a man-about-town for a lost, partially tragic, certainly frenetic weekend. *The Catcher in the Rye* is a full-length novel, and yet gives much the effect of his shorter pieces. Its dimensional depth is extrinsic to the narrative, and is measured by the reader's response to the dialogue, and the background of city America. It is supplied by one's recognition that Holden Caulfield, sensitive, perceptive, is too aware of the discrepancies between the surface intentions and the submerged motives of himself and of his acquaintances to feel at ease in any world. Through him, Salinger has evoked the reader's consciousness of indefinable rejections and rebellions that are part of the malaise of our times.

As we have come to expect from Salinger's other work, the main devices of characterization in *The Catcher in the Rye* are an apparently effortless verisimilitude of dialogue and an unerring sense of the appropriate in details of gesture, of bodily movement. There is a further fictional device, used elsewhere in his short stories but of paramount importance in his novel in creating a hold on the reader. It is his use of almost Chaplinlike incidents and dialogue, half-amusing, half-desperate, to keep his story always hovering in ambivalence between comedy and tragedy. Whenever a character approaches hopelessness in a Salinger sketch, he is getting there by the route of the comic. It is usually both the character's way of holding on for a moment longer (as when the husband in "A Perfect Day for Bananafish" goes out of his way to insult a proper dowager just before he kills himself) and, at its sharpest, a way of dramatic irony, a way of heightening the intensity of a character's predicament (as when Holden attempts to be bored with sex to get rid of a prostitute). But no single scene from his novel completely demonstrates this peculiar strain of comedy in Salinger: it pervades, seeps into, almost every incident.

When one is reading Salinger, one accepts his carefully placed *New Yorker*ish style and tone, and surrenders one's mind almost completely. It is only when you put the story aside and turn to other contemporary writers and to other fictional methods and techniques that you begin to wonder whether the immediacy and vividness of Salinger might be limited in power. Nowhere in Salinger do we find ourselves plunged into the emotional coiling and recoiling provoked by passages from Styron's novel *Lie Down in Darkness*. Nowhere in Salinger is a character moved against the murky intensity-in-depth of a Nelson Algren Chicago scene in *The Man with the Golden Arm*. Nowhere is a character revealed by the great clots of heterogeneous detail yoked together in single crowded sentences, as by Saul Bellow in *The Adventures of Augie March*.

But despite the temptations of comparison there remains one's conviction that Salinger is deeply and seriously committed in his fiction. Further, a little research into the Salinger canon reveals that two of his major creations, Holden Caulfield and Seymour Glass, the young husband of "A Perfect Day for Bananafish," have deep roots in Salinger's own imagination. His novel, in its way, is as much a final version of "work in progress" as are the novels of his more literary contemporaries, pulled together from fragmentary excursions as short stories in *Partisan Review*, in *Hudson Review*, in *New World Writing*. Only with Salinger, the professional, early sketches of Holden Caulfield occur in a series of stories published in *The Saturday Evening Post, Collier's,* and in *The New Yorker,* in the years 1944-1946.

This extrinsic information helps verify one's feeling that there is actually more weight to his explorations of human alienation than his bright dialogue and his frugal use of background and event might suggest. Moreover, Salinger's nonliterary status leaves him, as a serious writer, almost unique as a wholly free agent, unhampered by the commitments of his more dedicated contemporaries to one or another school of critics. One might guess that this is Salinger's most precious asset. Rather than wishing quarterly significance or "greatness" on him, we can be content to take him for what he is: a beautifully deft, professional performer who gives us a chance to catch quick, half-amused, half-frightened glimpses of ourselves and our contemporaries, as he confronts us with his brilliant mirror images.

III. Is "Cute" the Word?

A quality of sympathetic and reluctant disapproval, more-in-sorrow-than-in-anger, joins the opinions in this section. The Alfred Kazin piece, discussed at some length in the introduction, is one of the most interesting and already one of the most influential contributions to the growing stack of Salinger criticism. His argument, in part, is that the Glass family is too cute to bear; that their cuteness is not redeemed by love, because (this is only suggested) love may be overrated anyway as a means of fictional salvation, and more importantly because the Glasses' love is too self-centered. One can disagree with this view and argue that Kazin misses the point, as well as the humor, of the Glasses. But his essay is bound to shape the discussion for a long time to come. And one must particularly cheer certain of his observations, notably his reminder that writers today are bored by too many things.

John Updike's review of *Franny and Zooey* reflects many of Kazin's opinions, with the great added interest that it is the work of an excellent writer of fiction who speaks of Salinger as one professional about another. When he points out the discrepancies in mood and tone between the two stories; or notes the strange impression of a "second male" being present at Franny's lunch with Lane; or wonders why her ample religious indoctrination from the crib on did not prepare her for her spiritual crisis, Updike is talking shop like the expert craftsman he is. His objection to the "vehement editorializing of the obvious" is particularly well-taken; a minor but irritating flaw in Salinger has always been his eagerness to attack unworthy targets, such as cigarette commercials or TV scripts. But amid all of Updike's

42

superb expertise, and despite his evident sympathy and fairness, one wonders whether something about Salinger does not elude him.

Leslie Fiedler says at the outset that he is not sure why he rather dislikes *Franny and Zooey*, and his review suggests that he has not found an answer; it is never quite certain whether his observations indicate praise, blame or merely interest. But even in this uncharacteristically short piece (a longer one appears elsewhere in this volume) he once again shows himself to be perhaps the most fascinating American critic now at work, and he makes several notable points about Salinger. He is one of the few to see that madness is one of Salinger's themes, and that it acts as a temptation, a longed-for refuge; he is the only critic, it would seem, who recognizes the fact that, while the Glasses are Salinger's joy, they are also, at times, his joke; and he is certainly the only critic intrepid enough to call "Esmé" a tear-jerker. Altogether, a very refreshing performance.

"EVERYBODY'S FAVORITE"

by ALFRED KAZIN

The publication of his two well-known stories from *The New Yorker* in book form, *Franny and Zooey*, brings home the fact that, for one reason or another, J. D. Salinger now figures in American writing as a special case. After all, there are not many writers who could bring out a book composed of two stories—both of which have already been read and argued over and analyzed to death by that enormous public of sophisticated people which radiates from *The New Yorker* to every English department in the land.

In one form or another, as a fellow novelist commented unlovingly, Salinger is "everybody's favorite." He is certainly a favorite of *The New Yorker*, which in 1959 published another long story around the Glass family called "Seymour: An Introduction" (almost 30,000 words), and thus gave the impression of stretching and remaking itself to Salinger's latest stories, which have been appearing, like visits from outer space, at two-year intervals. But above all, he is a favorite with that audience of students, student intellectuals, instructors and generally literary, sensitive and sophisticated young people who respond to him with a consciousness that he speaks for them and virtually *to* them, in a language that is peculiarly honest and their own, with a vision of things that captures their most secret judgments of the world. The only thing that Salinger does not do for this audience is to meet with them. Holden Caulfield said in *The Catcher in the Rye* that "What really knocks me out is a book that, when you're all done reading it, you wish the author that wrote it was a terrific friend of yours and you could call him up on the phone whenever you felt like it." It is well for him that all the people in this country who now regard J. D. Salinger as a "terrific friend" do not call him up and reach him.

A fundamental reason for Salinger's appeal (like that of Hemingway in the short stories that made *him* famous) is that he has exciting professional mastery of a peculiarly charged and dramatic medium, the American short story. At a time when so much American fiction has been discursive in tone, careless in language, lacking in edge and force—when else would it have been possible for crudities like the Beat novelists to be taken seriously?—Salinger has done an honest and stimulating professional job in a medium which, when it is expertly handled, projects emotion like a cry from the stage and in form can be as intense as a lyric poem. A short story which is not handled with necessary concentration and wit is like a play which does not engage its audience; a story does not exist unless it hits its mark with terrific impact. It is a constant projection of meanings at an audience, and it is a performance minutely made up of the only possible language, as a poem is. In America, at least, where, on the whole, the best stories are the most professional stories and so are published in the most famous magazines, second-rate stories belong in the same limbo with unsuccessful musical comedies; unless you hit the bull's-eye, you don't score.

This does not mean that the best-known stories are first-rate pieces of literature any more than that so many triumphant musical comedies are additions to the world's drama; it means only that a story has communicated itself with entire vividness to its editor and its audience. The profundity that may exist in a short story by Chekhov or Tolstoy also depends upon the author's immediate success in conveying his purpose. Even in the medieval tale, which Tolstoy in his greatest stories seems to recapture in tone and spirit, the final comment on human existence follows from the deliberate artlessness of tone that the author has managed to capture like a speech in a play.

What makes Salinger's stories particularly exciting is his intense, his almost compulsive need to fill in each inch of his canvas, each moment of his scene. Many great novels owe their grandeur to a leisurely sense of suggestion, to the imitation of life as a boundless road or flowing river, to the very relaxation of that intensity which Poe thought was the aesthetic perfection of a poem or a story. But whatever the professional superficiality of the short story in American hands, which have molded and polished it so as to reach, dazzle and on occasion deceive the reader, a writer like Salinger, by working so hard to keep his tiny scene alive, keeps everything humming.

Someday there will be learned theses on *The Use of the Ashtray in J. D. Salinger's Stories*; no other writer has made so much of Americans lighting up, reaching for the ashtray, setting up the ashtray with one hand while with the other they reach for a ringing telephone. Ours is a society complicated with many appliances, and Salinger always tells you what his characters are doing with each of their hands. In one long stretch of "Zooey," he describes that young man sitting in a bathtub, reading a long letter from his brother and smoking; he manages to describe every exertion made and every sensation felt in that bathtub by the young man whose knees made "dry islands." Then the young man's mother comes into the bathroom; he draws the shower curtains around the tub, she rearranges the medicine cabinet, and while they talk (in full), everything they do is described. Everything, that is, within Salinger's purpose in getting at such detail, which is not the loose, shuffling catalogue of the old-fashioned naturalists, who had the illusion of reproducing the whole world, but the tension of a dramatist or theater director making a fuss about a character's walking just so.

For Salinger, the expert performer and director (brother Buddy Glass, who is supposed to be narrating "Zooey," speaks of "directing" it and calls the story itself a "prose home movie"), gesture is the essence of the medium. A short story does not offer room enough for the development of character; it can present only character itself, by gesture. And Salinger is remarkable, I would say he is almost frenetically proficient, in getting us, at the opening of "Franny," to *see* college boys waiting on a train platform to greet their dates arriving for a big football weekend. They rush out to the train, "most of them giving the impression of having at least three lighted cigarettes in each hand." He knows exactly how Franny Glass would be greeted by Lane Coutell: "It was a station-platform kiss—spontaneous enough to begin with, but rather inhibited in the follow-through, and with something of a forehead-bumping aspect."

And even better is his description of the boy at a good restaurant, taking a first sip of his martini and then looking "around the room with an almost palpable sense of well-being at finding himself (he must have been sure no one could dispute) in the right place with an unimpeachably right-looking girl." Salinger knows how to prepare us with this gesture for the later insensitivity of a boy who is exactly one of those elaborately up-to-date and anxiously sophisticated people whom Franny Glass, pure in heart, must learn to tolerate, and even to love, in what she regards as an unbearably shallow culture.

But apart from this, which is the theme of *Franny and Zooey,* the gesture itself is recognized by the reader not only as a compliment to himself but as a sign that Salinger is working all the time, not merely working to get the reader to see, but working to make his scene itself hum with life and creative observation. I don't know how much this appearance of intensity on the part of Salinger, of constant as well as full coverage, is due to *New Yorker* editorial nudging, since its famous alertness to repetitions of words and vagueness of diction tends to give an external look of freshness and movement to prose. Salinger not only works very hard indeed over each story, but he obviously writes to and for some particular editorial mind he identifies with *The New Yorker*; look up the stories he used to write for the *Saturday Evening Post* and *Cosmopolitan,* and you will see that just as married people get to look alike by reproducing each other's facial expressions, so a story by Salinger and a passage of commentary in *The New Yorker* now tend to resemble each other.

But whatever the enormous influence of any magazine on those who write regularly for it, Salinger's emphasis of certain words and syllables in American speech and his own compulsiveness in bearing down hard on certain details (almost as if he wanted to make the furniture, like the gestures of certain people, tell *everything* about the people who use them) do give his stories the intensity of observation that is fundamental to his success. Lane Coutell, sitting in that restaurant with Franny and talking about a college paper on Flaubert he is horribly well satisfied with, says, "I think the emphasis I put on *why* he was so neurotically attached to the *mot juste* wasn't too bad. I mean in the light of what we know today. Not just psychoanalysis and all that crap, but certainly to a certain extent. You know what I mean. I'm no Freudian man or anything like that, but certain things you can't just pass over as capital-F Freudian and let them go at that. I mean to a certain extent I think I was perfectly justified to point out that none of the really good boys—Tolstoy, Dostoevski, *Shakes*peare, for Chrissake—were such goddam word-squeezers. They just *wrote*. Know what I mean?" What strikes me about this mimicry is not merely that it is so clever, but that it is also so relentless. In everything that this sophisticated ass, Lane Coutell, says, one recognizes that he is and will be wrong. Salinger disapproves of him in the deepest possible way; he is a spiritual enemy.

Of course, it is a vision of things that lies behind Salinger's expert manner. There is always one behind every manner. The language of fiction, whatever it may accomplish as representation, ultimately conveys an author's imitation of things; makes us hear, not in a statement, but in the ensemble of his realized efforts, his quintessential commentary on the nature of existence. However, the more deliberate the language of the writer, as it must be in a short story, the more the writer must convey his judgment of things in one highlighted dramatic action, as is done on the stage.

At the end of "Franny," the young girl collapses in the ladies' room of the restaurant where she has been lunching with her cool boy friend. This conveys her spiritual desperation in his company, for Lane typifies a society where "Everything everybody does is so—I don't know—not *wrong*, or even mean, or even stupid necessarily. But just so tiny and meaningless and—sad-making." Her brother Zooey (Zachary Glass), at the end of the long second story, calls her up from another telephone number in the same apartment and somehow reaches to the heart of her problem and gives her peace by reminding her that the "Fat Lady" they used to picture somnolently listening to them when they were quiz kids on the radio—the ugly, lazy, even disgusting-looking Fat Lady, who more and more typifies unattractive and selfish humanity in our day—can be loved after all, for she, too, is Jesus Christ.

In each story, the climax bears a burden of meaning that it would not have to bear in a novel; besides being stagy, the stories are related in a way that connects both of them into a single chronicle. This, to quote the title of a little religious pamphlet often mentioned in it, might be called *The Way of a Pilgrim*. Both Franny and Zooey Glass are, indeed, pilgrims seeking their way in a society typified by the Fat Lady, and even by Lane Coutell's meaningless patter of sophistication. No wonder Franny cries out to her unhearing escort: "I'm sick of just liking people. I wish to God I could meet somebody I could respect." The Glasses (mother Irish, father Jewish) are ex-vaudevillians whose children were all, as infant prodigies, performers on a radio quiz program called "It's a Wise Child." Now, though engaged in normally sophisticated enterprises (Franny goes to a fashionable women's college, Zooey is a television actor, Buddy a college instructor), they have retained their intellectual precocity —and, indeed, their precocious charm—and have translated, as it were, their awareness of themselves as special beings into a conviction that they alone can do justice to their search for the true way.

The eldest and most brilliant of the children, Seymour, shot himself in 1948 in Florida; this was the climax of Salinger's perhaps most famous story, "A Perfect Day for Bananafish." And it is from Seymour's old room in the Glass apartment that Zooey calls up his sister, Franny, on a phone that is normally never used, that is still listed in the name of Seymour Glass, and that has been kept up by Buddy (who does not want a phone in his own country retreat) and by Zooey in order to perpetuate Seymour's name and to symbolize his continuing influence on them as a teacher and guide. It is from reading over again, in Seymour's old room, various religious sayings from the world's literature that Seymour had copied out on a piece of beaverboard nailed to the back of a door that Zooey is inspired to make the phone call to Franny that ends with the revelation that the horrible Fat Lady is really Jesus Christ.

This final episode, both in the cuteness of its invention and in the cuteness of speech so often attributed to Seymour, who is regarded in his own family as a kind of guru, or sage, helps us to understand Salinger's wide popularity. I am sorry to have to use the word "cute" in respect to Salinger, but there is absolutely no other word that for me so accurately typifies the self-conscious charm and prankishness of his own writing and his extraordinary cherishing of his favorite Glass characters.

Holden Caulfield is also cute in *The Catcher in the Rye*, cute in his little-boy suffering for his dead brother, Allie, and cute in his tenderness for his sister, "old Phoebe." But we expect that boys of that age may be cute—that is, consciously appealing and consciously clever. To be these things is almost their only resource in a world where parents and schoolmasters have all the power and the experience. Cuteness, for an adolescent, is to turn the normal self-pity of children, which arises from their relative weakness, into a relative advantage vis-à-vis the adult world. It becomes a role boys can play in the absence of other advantages, and *The Catcher in the Rye* is so full of Holden's cute speech and cute innocence and cute lovingness for his own family that one must be an absolute monster not to like it.

And on a higher level, but with the same conscious winsomeness, the same conscious mournfulness and intellectual loneliness and lovingness (though not for his wife), Seymour Glass is cute when he sits on the beach with a little girl telling her a parable of "bananafish"—ordinary-looking fish when "they swim into a hole where there's a lot of bananas," but "after that they're so fat they can't get out of the hole again. . . . They die." His wife, meanwhile busy in their room on the long-distance phone to her mother in New York, makes it abundantly clear in the hilariously accurate cadences and substance of her conversation why her husband finds it more natural to talk to a four-year-old girl on the beach than to her. Among other things, Seymour expects not to be understood outside the Glass family. But agonizing as this situation is, the brilliantly entertaining texture of "A Perfect Day for Bananafish" depends on Seymour Glass's conscious cleverness as well as on his conscious suffering— even his conscious cleverness *about* the suffering of "ordinary-looking" fish who get so bloated eating too many bananas in a "hole" they shouldn't have been attracted to in the first place.

In the same way, not only does the entertaining surface of *Franny and Zooey* depend on the conscious appealingness and youthfulness and generosity and sensitivity of Seymour's brother and sister, but Salinger himself, in describing these two, so obviously feels such boundless affection for them that you finally get the sense of all these child prodigies and child entertainers being tied round and round with veils of self-love in a culture which they—and Salinger— just despise. Despise, above all, for its intellectual pretentiousness. Yet this is the society, typified by the Fat Lady (symbolically, they pictured her as their audience), whom they must now force them- selves to think of as Jesus Christ, and whom, as Christ Himself, they can now at last learn to love.

For myself, I must confess that the spiritual transformation that so many people associate with the very sight of the word "love" on the printed page does not move me as it should. In what has been considered Salinger's best story, "For Esmé—with Love and Squalor," Sergeant X in the American Army of Occupation in Germany is saved from a hopeless breakdown by the beautiful magnanimity and remembrance of an aristocratic young English girl. We are prepared for this climax or visitation by an earlier scene in which the sergeant comes upon a book by Goebbels in which a Nazi woman had writ- ten, "Dear God, life is hell." Under this, persuaded at last of his common suffering even with a Nazi, X writes down, from *The Brothers Karamazov*: "Fathers and teachers, I ponder 'What is hell?' I maintain that it is the suffering of being unable to love."

But the love that Father Zossima in Dostoevsky's novel speaks for is surely love for the world, for God's creation itself, for all that pre- cedes us and supports us, that will outlast us and that alone helps us to explain ourselves to ourselves. It is the love that D. H. Law- rence, another religious novelist, spoke of as "the sympathetic bond" and that in one form or another lies behind all the great novels as a primary interest in everyone and everything alive with us on this common earth. The love that Salinger's horribly precocious Glass characters speak of is love for certain people only—forgiveness is for the rest; finally, through Seymour Glass's indoctrination of his brothers and sisters in so many different (and pretentiously assembled) religious teachings, it is love of certain ideas. So what is ultimate in their love is the love of their own moral and intellectual excellence, of their chastity and purity in a world full of bananafish swollen with too much food. It is the love that they have for themselves as an idea.

The worst they can say about our society is that they are too sensitive to live in it. They are the special case in whose name society is condemned. And what makes them so is that they are young, precocious, sensitive, different. In Salinger's work, the two estates—the world and the cutely sensitive young—never really touch at all. Holden Caulfield condemns parents and schools because he knows that they are incapable of understanding him; Zooey and Franny and Buddy (like Seymour before them) know that the great mass of prosperous spiritual savages in our society will never understand them.

This may be true, but to think so can lead to a violation of art. Huckleberry Finn, so often cited as a parallel to the hero of *The Catcher in the Rye,* was two years younger than Holden, but the reason he was not afraid of an adult's world is that he had respect for it. He had never even seen very much of it until he got on that raft with a runaway Negro slave he came to love and was able to save. It was still all God's creation, and inspired him with wonder. But Holden and, even more, the Glass children are beaten before they start; beaten in order not to start. They do not trust anything or anyone but themselves and their great idea. And what troubles me about this is not what it reflects of their theology but what it does to Salinger's art.

Frank O'Connor once said of this special métier, the short story, that it is "the art form that deals with the individual when there is no longer a society to absorb him, and when he is compelled to exist, as it were, by his own inner light." This is the condition on which Salinger's work rests, and I should be sorry to seem unsympathetic toward it. It is an American fact, as one can see from the relative lack in our literature of the ripe and fully developed social novel in which the individual and society are in concrete and constant relationship with each other. But whatever this lack, which in one sense is as marked in the novels of Scott Fitzgerald as it is in Salinger's emphasis upon the short story, it is a fact that when Fitzgerald describes a character's voice, it is because he really loves—in the creative sense, is fully interested in—this character. When Salinger describes a character's voice, it is to tell us that the man is a phony. He has, to borrow a phrase from his own work, a "categorical aversion" to whole classes and types of our society. The "sympathetic bond" that Lawrence spoke of has been broken. People stink in our nostrils. We are mad with captious observation of one another. As a friend of mine once said about the novels of Mary McCarthy, trying to say with absolute justice what it was that shocked her so much in them, "The heroine is always right and everyone else is wrong." Salinger is a far more accomplished and objective writer of fiction than Mary McCarthy, but I would say that in his work the Glass children alone are right and everyone else is wrong.

And it is finally this condition, not just the famous alienation of Americans from a society like our own, that explains the popularity of Salinger's work. Salinger's vast public, I am convinced, is based not merely on the vast number of young people who recognize their emotional problems in his fiction and their frustrated rebellions in the sophisticated language he manipulates so skillfully. It is based perhaps even more on the vast numbers who have been released by our society to think of themselves as endlessly sensitive, spiritually alone, gifted, and whose suffering lies in the narrowing of their consciousness to themselves, in the withdrawal of their curiosity from a society which they think they understand all too well, in the drying up of their hope, their trust, and their wonder at the great world itself. The worst of American sophistication today is that it is so bored, so full of categorical aversion to things that writers should never take for granted and never close their eyes to.

The fact that Salinger's work is particularly directed against the "well-fed sunburned" people at the summer theater, at the "section men" in colleges parroting the latest fashionable literary formulas, at the "three-martini" men—this, indeed, is what is wrong. He hates them. They are no longer people, but symbols, like the Fat Lady. No wonder that Zooey tells his sister: Love them, love them all, love them anyway! But the problem is not one of spiritual pride or of guilt; it is that in the tearing of the "sympathetic bond" it is not love that goes, but the deepest possbilities of literary art.

FRANNY AND ZOOEY
by JOHN UPDIKE

Quite suddenly, as things go in the middle period of J. D. Salinger, his later, longer stories are descending from the clouds of old *New Yorkers* and assuming incarnations between hard covers. "Raise High the Roof Beam, Carpenters" became available in *Stories from The New Yorker 1950–1960*, and now "Franny" and "Zooey" have a book to themselves. These two stories—the first medium-short, the second novella-length—are contiguous in time, and have as their common subject Franny's spiritual crisis.

In the first story, she arrives by train from a Smithlike college to spend the weekend of the Yale game at what must be Princeton. She and her date, Lane Coutell, go to a restaurant where it develops that she is not only unenthusiastic but downright ill. She attempts to explain herself while her friend brags about a superbly obnoxious term paper and eats frogs' legs. Finally, she faints, and is last seen lying in the manager's office silently praying at the ceiling.

In the second story, Franny has returned to her home, a large apartment in the East Seventies. It is the Monday following her unhappy Saturday. Only Franny's mother, Bessie, and her youngest brother, Zooey, are home. While Franny lies sleeplessly on the living-room sofa, her mother communicates, in an interminably rendered conversation, her concern and affection to Zooey, who then, after an even longer conversation with Franny, manages to gather from the haunted atmosphere of the apartment the crucial word of consolation. Franny, "as if all of what little or much wisdom there is in the world were suddenly hers," smiles at the ceiling and falls asleep.

Few writers since Joyce would risk such a wealth of words upon events that are purely internal and deeds that are purely talk. We live in a world, however, where the decisive deed may invite the holocaust, and Salinger's conviction that our inner lives greatly matter peculiarly qualifies him to sing of an America where, for most of us, there seems little to do but to feel. Introversion, perhaps, has been forced upon history; an age of nuance, of ambiguous gestures and psychological jockeying on a national and private scale, is upon us, and Salinger's intense attention to gesture and intonation help make him, among the contemporaries, a uniquely pertinent literary artist. As Hemingway sought the words for things in motion, Salinger seeks the words for things transmuted into human subjectivity. His fiction, in its rather grim bravado, its humor, its morbidity, its wry but persistent hopefulness, matches the shape and tint of present American life. It pays the price, however, of becoming dangerously convoluted and static. A sense of composition is not among Salinger's strengths, and even these two stories, so apparently complementary, distinctly jangle as components of one book.

The Franny of "Franny" and the Franny of "Zooey" are not the same person. The heroine of "Franny" is a pretty college girl passing through a plausible moment of disgust. She has discovered —one feels rather recently—a certain ugliness in the hungry human ego and a certain fatuity in her college environment. She is attempting to find her way out with the help of a religious book, *The Way of a Pilgrim,* which was mentioned by a professor. She got the book out of the college library. Her family, glimpsed briefly in the P.S. of a letter she has written, appear to be standard upper-middle gentry. Their name is nowhere given as Glass, though some "brothers" are mentioned—once—in passing. Her boy friend is crass and self-centered but not entirely unsympathetic; he clumsily does try to "get through" to Franny, with a love whose physical bias has become painfully inappropriate. Finally, there is a suggestion—perhaps inadvertent—that the girl may be pregnant.

The Franny of "Zooey," on the other hand, is Franny Glass, the youngest of the seven famous Glass children, all of whom have been in turn wondrously brilliant performers on a radio quiz program, "It's a Wise Child." Their parents, a distinctly unstandard combination of Jewish and Irish, are an old vaudeville team. From infancy on, Franny has been saturated by her two oldest brothers, Seymour and Buddy, in the religious wisdom of the East. *The Way of a Pilgrim,* far from being newly encountered at college, comes from Seymour's desk, where it has been for years.

One wonders how a girl raised in a home where Buddhism and

crisis theology were table talk could have postponed her own crisis so long and, when it came, be so disarmed by it. At any rate, there is no question of her being pregnant; the very idea seems a violation of the awesome Glass ethereality. Lane Coutell, who for all his faults was at least a considerable man in the first Franny's universe, is now just one of the remote millions coarse and foolish enough to be born outside the Glass family.

The more Salinger writes about them, the more the seven Glass children melt indistinguishably together in an impossible radiance of personal beauty and intelligence. Franny is described thus: "Her skin was lovely, and her features were delicate and most distinctive. Her eyes were very nearly the same quite astonishing shade of blue as Zooey's, but were set farther apart, as a sister's eyes no doubt should be. . . ." Of Zooey, we are assured he has a "somewhat preposterous ability to quote, instantaneously and, usually, verbatim, almost anything he had ever read, or even listened to, with genuine interest." The purpose of such sentences is surely not to particularize imaginary people but to instill in the reader a mood of blind worship, tinged with an understandable envy.

In "Raise High the Roof Beam, Carpenters" (the best of the Glass pieces: a magic and hilarious prose-poem with an enchanting end effect of mysterious clarity), Seymour defines sentimentality as giving "to a thing more tenderness than God gives to it." This seems to me the nub of the trouble: Salinger loves the Glasses more than God loves them. He loves them too exclusively. Their invention has become a hermitage for him. He loves them to the detriment of artistic moderation. "Zooey" is just too long; there are too many cigarettes, too many goddams, too much verbal ado about not quite enough.

The author never rests from circling his creations, patting them fondly, slyly applauding. He robs the reader of the initiative upon which love must be given. Even in "Franny," which is, strictly, pre-Glass, the writer seems less an unimpassioned observer than a spying beau vindictively feasting upon every detail of poor Lane Coutell's gaucherie. Indeed, this impression of a second male being present is so strong that it amounts to a social shock when the author accompanies Franny into the ladies' room of the restaurant.

"Franny," nevertheless, takes place in what is recognizably our world; in "Zooey" we move into a dream world whose zealously animated details only emphasize an essential unreality. When Zooey says to Franny, "Yes, I have an ulcer for Chrissake. This is Kaliyuga, buddy, the Iron Age," disbelief falls on the "buddy" as much as on "Kaliyuga," and the explanatory "the Iron Age" clinches our suspicion that a lecturer has usurped the writing stand. Not the least dismaying development of the Glass stories is the vehement editorializing on the obvious—television scripts are not generally good, not all section men are geniuses. Of course, the Glasses condemn the world only to condescend to it, to forgive it, in the end. Yet the pettishness of the condemnation diminishes the gal'ıntry of the condescension.

Perhaps these are hard words; they are made hard to write by the extravagant self-consciousness of Salinger's later prose, wherein most of the objections one might raise are already raised. On the flap of this book jacket, he confesses, ". . . there is a real-enough danger, I suppose, that sooner or later I'll bog down, perhaps disappear entirely, in my own methods, locutions, and mannerisms. On the whole, though, I'm very hopeful." Let me say, I am glad he is hopeful. I am one·of those—to do some confessing of my own —for whom Salinger's work dawned as something of a revelation. I expect that further revelations are to come.

The Glass saga, as he has sketched it out, potentially contains great fiction. When all reservations have been entered, in the correctly unctuous and apprehensive tone, about the direction he has taken, it remains to acknowledge that it *is* a direction, and that the refusal to rest content, the willingness to risk excess on behalf of one's obsessions, is what distinguishes artists from entertainers, and what makes some artists adventurers on behalf of us all.

UP FROM ADOLESCENCE

by LESLIE FIEDLER

I am not sure why I have liked so much less, this time through, a story which moved me so deeply when I first read it in *The New*

Yorker four or five years ago. I mean, of course, "Zooey," to which "Franny" is finally an appendage, like the long explanatory footnote on pages 52 and 53, the author's apologetic statement on the jacket, the pretentiously modest dedication: all the gimmicks, in short, which conceal neither from him nor from us the fact that he has not yet made of essentially novelistic material the novel it wants to become.

It was, I guess, the novel which "Zooey," along with a handful of earlier stories, seemed to promise to which I responded with initial enthusiasm: the fat chronicle of the Glass family which might have caught once and for all the pathos and silliness of middle-class, middle-brow intellectual aspiration—the sad and foolish dream that certain families, largely Jewish, dreamed for their children listening to the Quiz Kids perform on the radio two long decades ago. For the sake of that novel, Salinger seemed at the point of making a new start, of breaking through certain bad habits picked up along the way from *Good Housekeeping* to *The New Yorker*. Certainly in "Zooey" Salinger had begun untypically to specify the times and circumstances of his characters; to furnish patiently the rooms through which they moved; to eschew slickness and sentimentality and easy jokes in favor of a style almost inept enough to guarantee honesty; to venture beyond an evocation of adolescent self-pity and adolescent concern with sex titillating chiefly to adolescents themselves.

But there is, as yet, no novel—only "Zooey," well-leaded and in hard covers, flanked by apologies and new promises, but still unfulfilled: and it is this, I suppose, which has left me baffled and a little disappointed. In a magazine, Salinger's documentation seemed not quite so irrelevant, his furnishings not quite so disproportionate to the events they frame, the awkwardness of his writing not quite so much a tic of embarrassment or a posture of false modesty.

"Franny" itself, which I had not read before, seems to me an eminently satisfactory piece of reportage, turned in as evidence (at the demonstration trial of the generations, in which it is not clear who is the plaintiff, who the defendant) by a middle-aged eavesdropper on station platforms and at restaurants where the Ivy League young ritually prepare for watching games and getting laid. It is, at least, scarcely ever cute, like much of "Zooey" and all of the mere apparatus with which it ekes out a book; and it ends ambiguously before its author, whose resolutions are often disasters, can manage to be either sentimental or sage. In "Franny" for once Salinger demonstrates that he can write of adolescence without disappearing into it; but "Franny," alas, is completed by "Zooey," which itself completes nothing.

We have been, I begin slowly to understand, living through a revolution in taste, a radical transformation of the widest American literary audience from one in which women predominate to one in which adolescents make up the majority. Controlling the market (it is, for instance, largely to reach them that the more expensive paperbacks were invented and marketed in new ways by new generations of editors scarcely older than themselves), they control also the mode. And the mode demands, in lieu of the teenage novelists who somehow refuse to appear, Teenage Impersonators, among whom one might list, say, Norman Mailer, Jack Kerouac, even William Burroughs—certainly the Salinger who wrote *Catcher in the Rye* and invented Holden Caulfield, a figure emulated by the young themselves, though not by all the young.

Each of the Impersonators I have mentioned speaks only for a portion of our youth: hip or beat or square, straight or queer or undecided. No one writes for all, but inevitably takes his stand: with those who "turn on" or those who do not, with those who write papers on Kierkegaard and Flaubert or those who scrawl on the walls of saloons "Ez for Pres." Salinger, of course, speaks for the cleanest, politest, best-dressed, best-fed and best-read among the disaffected (and who is not disaffected?) young; not junkies or faggots, not even upper-Bohemians, his protagonists travel a road bounded on one end by school and on the other by home. They have families and teachers rather than lovers or friends; and their crises are likely to be defined in terms of whether or not to go back for the second semester to Vassar or Princeton, to Dana Hall or St. Mark's. Their *Angst* is improbably cued by such questions as: "Does my date for the Harvard weekend *really* understand what poetry is?" or "Is it possible that my English instructor hates literature after all?"

I do not mean by reduction to mock the concerns of Salinger's characters; they cannot, in any case, be reduced, and I should

mock myself making fun of them. For better or for worse, a significant number of sensitive young Americans live in a world in which
the classroom and the football game provide customary arenas for
anguish and joy, love and death; and to that world, Salinger has
been more faithful than it perhaps deserves. Which is why in the
end he is a comic novelist or nothing. If the Temple Drake of
Faulkner's *Sanctuary* stands as the classic portrait of a coed in the
twenties, the Franny of Salinger's Glass stories bids to become her
equivalent for the fifties, and the decline in terror and intensity from
one to the other, the descent toward middle-brow bathos is the
fault not of Salinger but of the times. Temple's revolt was against
vestigial Puritanism and obsolescent chivalry and her weapons were
booze and sex; Franny's is against literature and the New Criticism
and her weapon is the "Jesus Prayer."

Certainly, this is fair enough; for, in the thirty years that separate
the two refugees from college, the Culture Religion of Western
Europe has replaced Christianity as the orthodox faith for middle-
class urban Americans; and the pastors to whom our hungry sheep
look up in vain are Ph.D.'s in Literature and the "section men" who
are their acolytes. In a society presided over by this new clergy, to
play with Vedanta or Buddhism or even Catholicism, except as
these are represented in certain recent poetic texts, *i.e.*, to seek a
salvation beyond the reach of art, is considered heresy or madness
or some blasphemous compound of both. Franny, at any rate, who
will not write the proper papers or go out for the next college play,
seems, not only to her elders and her peers, but to herself as well, a
heretic guilty as charged and therefore self-condemned to what her
world calls a "nervous breakdown."

I am less sure this time though than I was the first that Salinger
really understands just how splendid and horrifying a joke this all
is, but begin to suspect that he has only stumbled on the comic
possibilities of his subject in pursuit of a more pathetic theme which
has obsessed him ever since the writing of his popular little tear-
jerker, "For Esmé—with Love and Squalor." It is this theme which
lies at the center of *Catcher in the Rye* and which becomes the main
interest if not of "Franny," certainly of the much longer "Zooey."
I am referring, of course, to Salinger's presentation of madness as
the chief temptation of modern life, especially for the intelligent

young; and his conviction that, consequently, the chief heroism possible to us now is the rejection of madness, the decision to be sane. What suicide was for the young Werther or running away from home for Huck Finn, the "nervous breakdown," Salinger urges us to believe, is for the sensitive adolescent of our time. Having been taught, chiefly by the psychoanalysts (who haunt Salinger's books, ambiguous and omnipresent almost as his teachers), that insanity itself lies within the scope of choice, we have been able to make of it a theme for debate, our own to-be-or-not-to-be.

Before the present volume, Salinger had always presented madness as a special temptation of males; perhaps because, in the myth he was elaborating, it is a female image of innocence that, at the last moment, lures his almost-lost protagonists back from the brink of insanity: a little girl typically, prepubescent and therefore immune to the world's evil, which, in his work, fully nubile women tend to embody. The series which begins with "Esmé" goes on through "A Perfect Day for Bananafish," where the girl-savior appears too late to save Seymour, oldest of the Glass family; and reaches an appropriate climax in *Catcher in the Rye*, where the savior is the little sister and the myth achieves its final form. It is the Orestes-Iphigenia story, we see there, that Salinger all along had been trying to rewrite, the account of a Fury-haunted brother redeemed by his priestess-sister; though Salinger demotes that sister in age, thus downgrading the tone of the legend from tragic to merely pathetic.

In "Zooey," where the brother saves, the sister is redeemed and neither is a child, the myth struggles back toward the tragic dimension; and it is for this, too, perhaps, that I responded so strongly at first to the story, to its implicit declaration of Salinger's resolve to escape what had become for him a trap. Yet though the girl-savior does not operate in "Zooey" to produce the pat Happy Ending of *Catcher in the Rye*, she floats disconcertingly in and out of its action, a not-quite-irrelevant ghost. It is, for instance, the chance meeting with a four-year-old girl at the meat counter of a supermarket that prompts the long letter from his oldest surviving brother, Buddy, which Zooey is reading as his story opens; and in that letter, we are permitted to see at last the haiku found in Seymour's hotel room after his suicide: "The little girl on the plane/Who turned her doll's head around/To look at me."

Buddy, however, released from long silence by his little girl and the memory of Seymour's, has tried to save Zooey, through the mails, by advising him to "act" (Buddy is a teacher of writing, Zooey a TV star); and Zooey, trying in turn to save Franny, can only repeat in Buddy's voice and over Seymour's still-listed telephone the same advice. Behind it all, at any rate, is the inevitable little girl, her message echoed and re-echoed through the linked ventriloquist's dummies of the three brothers, who seem sometimes only three versions of the single author, listening faithfully to Esmé down the years.

But "Zooey" is, at last, a fable of reconciliation as well as of salvation; for the saved Franny, we are left to believe, will return perhaps to school, certainly to "acting," as her brothers recommend, not so much for her own sake as for the sake of what Seymour had been accustomed to call, in their Quiz Kid days, the Fat Lady, *i.e.*, the audience out front. But the Fat Lady, Zooey announces as his story ends, is Christ; the mass audience is Christ. It is an appropriate enough theophany for a popular entertainer, for Salinger as well as Zooey, and the cue for a truce with all the world, with bad teachers, mad television producers, bad psychoanalysts, bad everyone.

Finally, like his characters, Salinger is reconciled with everything but sex. The single voice in his novella which advocates marriage is the voice of Bessie Glass, a stage-Irish comic mother married to an off-stage comic Jew; but she raises it in vain in a fictional world where apparently only women marry and where certainly no father appears on the scene. It is to Zooey she speaks, the one son of hers not already killed by marriage like Seymour, or safe in monastic retirement, secular like Buddy's or ecclesiastical like his Jesuit brother Waker's. Zooey, who fears his own body and his mother's touch on it, turns her aside with a quip; though he might well have repeated what he had cried earlier in deep contempt, "That's just sex talking, buddy. . . . I know that voice." These words, too, he had addressed to her; since for him men and women alike are "buddy," as if unlike the actual Buddy, he needed no little girl to remind him of what Seymour had once tried to teach them all: that "all legitimate religious study *must* lead to unlearning . . . the illusory differences between boys and girls. . . ."

To unlearn the illusory differences: this is what for Salinger it means *to be as a child*. And the Glasses, we remember, are in this sense children, holy innocents still at twenty or thirty or forty, Quiz Kids who never made the mistake of growing up, and whose most glorious hours were spent before the microphones on a nation-wide radio program called "It's a Wise Child." The notion of the Quiz Kids, with their forced precocity, their meaningless answers to pointless questions faked by station employees, as heroes, sages, secret saints of our time is palpably absurd. But Salinger himself ironically qualifies what he seems naïvely to offer by the unfinished quotation he uses to give his only half-mythical program its name. It is with his collaboration, we remind ourselves, that we are able to say of his hidden saints, when they become insufferably cute or clever or smug, "The little bastards!" Surely, this is Salinger's joke, not just one on him and on his world.

IV. Magician, Clubman or Guru

The five writers represented in this section are united in a certain breezy disapproval of Salinger. They refuse to take him quite seriously. Of the quartet, Seymour Krim is the most sympathetic. He evidently admires much of Salinger's work but seems to feel that it is too good to be good—too entertaining, that is. When Krim calls Salinger a penthouse Manhattanite, he has a wildly wrong address for his man. But both in praise and blame, he shows a fine sense of Salinger the performer, the magician. If Updike speaks of him as a fellow writer, Krim speaks of him (figuratively) as a fellow vaudevillian.

The English critic David Leitch brings a note of transatlantic detachment to his comments, an air of amusement about all the fuss that is being made. He offers many of the points also found in the later Kazin and Updike pieces—the withdrawn quality of the Glasses, the questionable aspect of the Parable of the Fat Lady—but he puts them differently. Particularly amusing is the image of the Glass (or Salinger) club.

The short contributions by Joan Didion and Isa Kapp are really rather crude—and cute!—restatements of Kazin, and suggest that it is becoming fashionable to bait Salinger, even though no other critic has yet dismissed him quite so easily as a phony middle-class guru or fictional Norman Vincent Peale. A remark of Leslie Fiedler's applies to both reviews: in mocking the concerns of Salinger's characters, he writes, "I should mock myself." These two pieces are not only mocking, they are brattish. But they are well written.

George Steiner thinks that there has been far too much critical attention paid to Salinger and, incidentally, has expressed the opinion to the editor that this volume itself constitutes a premature "consecration." Be that as it may, Steiner strikes one as judicious in his evaluation of Salinger's work, with the exception of "Seymour" ("a piece of shapeless self-indulgence"). He is rough on his fellow critics, including some of those represented here, but the attack is invigorating.

SURFACE AND SUBSTANCE IN A MAJOR TALENT

by Seymour Krim

J. D. Salinger, author of *Catcher in the Rye*, is probably the freshest new writer that *The New Yorker* has come up with in years. His short stories, which began appearing several years before his novel was published, restored some of the old pep to *New Yorker* fiction; here was a writer (one thought to oneself) who could embody the magic of old-fashioned fiction and also create a new form that did justice to today's life.

Nine of Salinger's stories are now collected in book form, giving us a chance to assess what he has done so far. Read together they are not quite as impressive as they seemed when read individually, but they show us a unique talent, and more, a born writer whom one must read to get the "feel" of. No paraphrase will do him justice, but we can, in the broad sense, trace out his literary ancestry and his themes and perhaps understand his significance a little better for having done so.

J. D. Salinger's closest resemblance is to F. Scott Fitzgerald—that is, close in one sense. Salinger is at home with the details of upper-middle-class life, and, like Fitzgerald, there is much grace, lightness of touch and bittersweet emotion in his stories. But since Salinger is his own man, and hardly an imitator, the analogy with Fitzgerald ends at a certain point; there is a bitterness and intensity in the younger writer's work which is subtly wedded to the charm, and this combination makes Fitzgerald seem romantically old-fashioned by comparison. But both writers have that particular poignance which results from a lyrical identification with subject matter set off by a critical intelligence; they are both lovers, so to speak, who are forced to acknowledge that they have been "had," and this gives their work the emotion of subtle heartbreak.

Salinger's "A Perfect Day for Bananafish" is representative of this. The story is simple: a gifted young man has come back from the war somewhat paranoiac, and goes down to Florida with his conventional, wealthy young wife. We meet him for just a short time, playing on the beach with a four-year-old girl—both are looking for "bananafish" in the water, an invention of the man's which delights his young companion. The climax of their relationship is reached when the little girl says that she has seen a banana-fish with six bananas in its mouth. At this moment there is a sense of complete understanding between the child and the adult which redeems the man's pain and, briefly but poetically, restores happiness to life. But several minutes later, when the young man is returning to his hotel room, he turns on a woman in the elevator and asks her why she is looking at his feet—"If you want to look at my feet, say so. . . . But don't be a God-damned sneak about it." Of course, the woman isn't looking at his feet. When the man gets into his room he casually takes a revolver from his luggage and shoots himself in the head.

And that is the story. It is certainly a "sad" story; but what saves it from being depressing is the author's feeling for textures and situations, and the freshness of his irony. And these cannot be communicated in a summary. The same may be said for "Uncle Wiggily in Connecticut," "Just Before the War with the Eskimos," "Down at the Dinghy," "For Esmé—with Love and Squalor" and "Teddy." They are all imaginative, felt (for the most part) and strikingly fresh. They have that invaluable quality, in Johnson's words, of making the familiar new and the new familiar.

But, gifted as J. D. Salinger is, a reading of his stories, one after the other, reveals certain un-nice qualities which slightly compromise his present achievement. Like many virtuosi, he is sometimes more interested in the way he is saying something than in what he is saying. Owning a keen eye for revealing description and an

D

even keener ear, he sometimes dotes on his superior sensory equipment for its own sake, even though the story he is telling has no
logical room for such arbitrariness. Even worse, he sometimes seems
to think that there is some high purpose in his "asides."

Being gifted, Salinger is at the mercy of his own gift; and going
deeper, one guesses that his sleight-of-hand is often the cover-up
for an unsure grasp of the meaning of his material. Like Faulkner
in his more inferior moments, this unsureness results in an intensification of surface brilliance, as if to distract the reader from a certain hollowness underneath by a dazzlement above. In the technical
sense, this means that Salinger, apart from overusing his ear and
eye (he will repeat certain conversational bits somewhat affectedly
when the reader doesn't deserve such disingenuousness), will
"mark time" in the middle of a story by irrelevant observations,
often fascinating in themselves, but not contributing to a well-knit
whole.

To reduce it to fundamentals, I believe that Salinger is not quite
clear about the meaning of his material; he is extremely deft, sometimes oversophisticated in his surface technique, and for the most
part it is a pure pleasure to follow his artistic strokes. But
underneath, where it is a question of values and finally of the iron
moral grasp of meaning, one suspects a dodging of issues.

However, one point should be stressed: when you come down to
it, the chivvying of a genuine writer is a form of complimenting
him. In the majority of cases the "magic" simply isn't there, and
one makes criticism a form of duty; in Salinger's instance, where the
gem of his talent shines, there is real concern that the author make
the very best use of it. Such freshness isn't given freely, and its
ownership implies a responsibility which transcends self.

[This review appeared in 1953. Late in 1961, Krim continued his
examination of Salinger.]

J. D. Salinger is a beautiful workman who sometimes—not unlike
Faulkner—gets a kick out of making the reader eat from his hand.

Gifted men often find it hard not to revel in talent for its own
sake and Salinger is no exception. In his first offering in eight
years (and not truly brand-new in that it's compromised of two

almost freakishly long stories which appeared in *The New Yorker*),
we see how his technical dexterity has increased to the point where
he is on the verge of inventing a really unique storytelling method.
This method, as in the ultimate accomplishment of Proust and
Faulkner, comes out of tremendous greased fluency of expression,
which allows Salinger to spin around in mid-air, so to speak, and
observe his own tail. It's a marvelous feat, like wing-walking. But
Salinger at this point can easily become the victim of his own
brilliance. Ultimately, we may get only a breath-taking performance
ten thousand feet higher than it need be.

This is theater, finally, as critic Alfred Kazin recently pointed
out when pitting himself against J. D. in the sober pages of the
Atlantic Monthly. And it is therefore no accident that the parents
of the Glass family, Salinger's mythic Irish-Jewish clan, are ex-
vaudevillians. This is a perfect touch to anyone who knows the
mystique of New York life, its love of show business and consequently its own showiness.

Salinger in this sense is a genuine New Yorker, a real way-up-in-
a-penthouse Manhattanite as distinguished from a Bronx or Brooklyn rube, because he loves the glitter of bright lights as only a city
hipster can. His stories read like slow-motion close-up movies
instead of conventional fiction because the flair of theater is in his
bones. And since Salinger is identified with *The New Yorker*, this
deep-down admiration of flashiness has been restrained by taste,
fine toothcombed by that magazine's positive horror of vulgarity.

It may surprise the reader to find the tender Salinger accused
of showiness (let alone the insinuation that he is the product of
a literary manufacturing house). But stop and think. If it weren't
for his shimmering night-club performance in prose, would you
read him with such fascination? Hardly.

Salinger can take the simplest, most prosaic facts in these
chronicles about Franny and Zooey Glass and recall them with such
precision that you are hynotized, as by a Dunninger. The most
familiar objects—a razor, a lipstick, a hairbrush, are raised from the
commonplace by this prestidigitator and made to seem more rare
than they are.

Salinger brings back to us the things we have taken for granted
and that is why he evokes something close to love in his readers.

He is a sentimental purveyor of nostalgia, held under the strictest leash of taste and clarity so that there isn't even a whisper of sloppiness.

But the significance of his themes evaporates in the ardors of the technique until we are left, as in these two monumental miniatures, with a puzzle: "Why so much shuck for so little nubbin?" (as Sherwood Anderson is reputed to have said when he saw the smallish William Faulkner wrapped in a huge overcoat).

In other words, are Salinger's sentimental jazz ballads worth such symphonic orchestration?

Still, there is no getting around the loveliness of the writing, nor should there be; one reads books for pleasure, among other reasons, and few Americans writing today—if any—can give as much bitter-sweet, civilized pleasure. He is a romantic with a flawless eye, a bright documentarian of the slightly lower upper-crust.

Few if any writers in history have so lovingly tried to reproduce the accents of a Bennington girl or a Yale boy, have winced so exquisitely at the cut of a suit, examined a martini or a smoldering cigarette with such superprofound airs. Salinger, as befits a born performer, imbues the most insignificant objects with the mumbo-jumbo of mystery; and because he *feels* it he makes us feel it.

Magic is thus very much a part of Salinger's appeal. But how "magical" do we want our suicides, nervous breakdowns, quests for truth and religion to be? This thought intrudes on our enjoyment of the present book, which is so concerned in both stories with Franny Glass's slow mental collapse.

Franny, as *New Yorker* readers already know, has become all worn out in the search for truth, and falls apart in her comfortable New York home after a disastrous weekend with a Yale man who says "Goddam" as regularly as a robot (and is just as convincing).

But along the route of Franny's collapse, as fastidiously and conscientiously as a street cleaner looking for gems, J. D. gives us every external detail of this seemingly serious business. We therefore suffer, as readers, from a peculiar gap in our emotional response: we can't be deeply moved because the author appears to be more interested in the Christmas wrapping of experience than in uncovering what's in the box.

Thus, when Professor Salinger (he has changed costume for the last act and become an Eastern mystic) gives us an incredibly long discourse on an obscure religious book which fascinates his young heroine, it all seems oddly pretentious in view of what has preceded it.

There is snob appeal in this performance, witting or unwitting, and a healthy, democratic soul will reject it no matter how nicely, even exquisitely, our artificer is embroidering his own fantasies.

THE SALINGER MYTH

by DAVID LEITCH

One night, in Rome about a year ago, an American friend, well known for his sobriety and serious-mindedness, phoned in a state of great excitement to say that he had met Seymour Glass's brother-in-law in a bar and would I go and meet him. Feeling that the Salinger myth was getting out of hand I said no. Since then I have occasionally wondered about the *soi-disant* Glass and on the whole feel more disposed to believe in him now than I did then. In fact, it wouldn't surprise me if Holden Caulfield had been in the bar as well. Wearing his red hunting cap.

For Jerome David Salinger and the families about whom he writes—Glasses, Gladwallers and Caulfields—exist in a mysterious world that is half literary and half real. Salinger is more than a successful writer; a whole cult of the whimsical and eccentric has arisen round him. I felt it was appropriate that forty-five minutes after ordering *The Catcher in the Rye* and "For Esmé—with Love and Squalor" at the British Museum, an assistant arrived and solemnly presented me with a copy of *Our Friend Mrs. Goose.* Again I wasn't altogether surprised when copies of the *Saturday Evening Post, Collier's, Harper's* and *The New Yorker,* listed in the periodicals index as containing Salinger short stories, had a habit of turning up with the relevant pages torn out.

One section of the community in the United States follows the doings of the Glasses with the same breathless wonder that rather a different one here reserves for the Royal Family. When *The New Yorker* printed "Franny," a typically vague but by no means impenetrable story about Frances Glass on a football weekend with Lane Coutell, her rather inadequate boy friend, it found itself with a heavy post from worried readers. They had grasped that Franny had something on her mind without being quite sure what, and so wrote demanding to know whether she were pregnant. It is all slightly reminiscent of those agonized people who gathered on a New York quay to meet the ship which was carrying the last installment of *The Old Curiosity Shop*. "Is Little Nell dead?" they called to the crew.

Readers who send questions to Salinger himself probably don't receive any answers, or even signed photographs. His desire for anonymity is almost an affectation. In one of his few published comments, Salinger has said of *The Catcher*: "I'm aware that many of my friends will be saddened and shocked, or shocked-saddened, over some of the chapters in *The Catcher in the Rye*. Some of my best friends are children. In fact, all my best friends are children. It's almost unbearable for me to realize that my book will be kept on a shelf out of their reach." The mixture of whimsy and sentimentality is typical; the emphasis on children recurs. A laconical note that he delivered to *Harper's* with the manuscript of "Down at the Dinghy" in 1949 stated, "I almost always write about very young children." This is less true now as his most recent stories have all been concerned with members of the Glass family who have grown up; Franny (Frances), the youngest, is in her mid-twenties, Zooey (Zachary Martin) is thirty, and Seymour, whose suicide was described in the story "A Perfect Day for Bananafish," in 1948, was then thirty-one. But though he is dead his ghost still stalks the Glasses' East Seventies apartment, and meetings with children, or memories of childhood, play an important part in all the stories.

What is true of the Glasses is also true of the Salinger devotees: "We are, all of us, blood relatives, and we speak a kind of esoteric family language." Salinger is obsessed with the family and the relationships within it. But in a way the Glasses have been made to seem like members of a peculiarly intimate club, a club which Salinger readers are overtly invited to associate themselves with if not actually join. Anyone can join who is young, or obsessed with

youth, sensitive, vague and eccentric, mystically inclined and profoundly conscious of being set apart from the run-of-the-mill human
beings he sees around him—in short, anyone who can speak the
language. Members, or associates, of the family/club, are sensitive,
they know the truth when they see it and they enjoy discussing the
important things in life with similarly inclined fellows. Communication with outsiders is not only useless and impossible, it is apt, if
attempted, to cause unpleasant situations. When a member wants
to know what happens to the ducks on the lagoon near Central
Park South in the wintertime and asks, say a cabdriver, for this
information, he only too soon discovers "Most people aren't interested in that kind of stuff."

"To get straight to the worst, what I'm about to offer isn't really
a short story at all but a sort of prose home movie . . . the fact is,
I've been producing prose home movies, off and on, since I was
fifteen." This is how Buddy Glass, "writer in residence at a girls'
junior college in upstate New York," describes his literary method
at the beginning of "Zooey," and Salinger's own is very similar. To
read a lot of his work at once is like traveling between London
and Aberdeen in the same compartment with one of those middle-
aged women who delight in treating strangers to endlessly detailed
family chronicles, including their husband's opinions about politics
and league football and the minor illnesses suffered by their children
over the preceding twenty years. Characters keep appearing out of
the blue, but the devoted and sharp-eyed reader, or the man who
has listened carefully to the earlier part of the conversation, will
quickly catch on to their genealogy. He will realize that Lionel
Tannenbaum (in "Down at the Dinghy") is Seymour's nephew, that
the soldier who was killed in Japan in 1945 and who the drunken
Eloise remembers with such affection in "Uncle Wiggily in Connecticut" is, in fact, Walt Glass—the first of the family's casualties.
Holden Caulfield himself is much given to family allusion. We are
told about D. B. being a prostitute in Hollywood and about Allie,
the younger brother: "He's dead now. He got leukemia and died
when we were up in Maine, on July 18, 1946. You'd have liked him."
The tone is very intimate and friendly. Salinger's readers are per-
petually being invited to draw their chairs up to the fire for a chat
in the family apartment, or in Buddy's isolated cottage on the other

side of a mountain in upstate New York. It's a friendly, reassuring world of affection and security that is offered, everyone is as good and innocent as a child, communication is immediate and complete (if slightly esoteric) and you can bet your life there won't be a flit or a phony in sight.

Understandably many people accept Salinger's invitation. A return to childhood innocence has always had a wide appeal, and particularly in American novels. Writing of the American novel in general, Leslie Fiedler refers to the number of books which seem "not primitive, perhaps, but innocent, unfallen in a disturbing way, almost juvenile," and again to the recurring "level of sentimentality that seems precisely that of a preadolescent." These descriptions can fairly be applied to Salinger. His characters fear, dislike and despise the adult world; their response to it is a rapid withdrawal into fantasies of childhood. Seymour's suicide is the most complete withdrawal. His marriage to Muriel Fedder, a middle-class American girl who appears at the beginning of "A Perfect Day for Bananafish" lacquering her nails and reading a magazine article on sex, is an attempt to bridge the gap between himself and ordinary, everyday people. His first reaction to her and her mother—who insists on his being analyzed—is to drive the family car into a tree; his second is to shoot himself. Salinger's characters find almost any contact with outsiders virtually impossible. Holden's reaction to the news that Stradlater is "dating" a member of the club who qualified, among other reasons, because she refused to move her kings out of the back row when playing checkers, is typical.

> "Jane Gallagher. Jesus." I couldn't get her off my mind. I really couldn't. "I oughta go down and say hello to her, at least."
> "Why the hell *don't*cha, instead of keep saying it?" Stradlater said. . . .
> "I'm not in the mood right now," I said. I wasn't, either. You have to be in the mood for those things.

So Holden doesn't actually meet her. Instead he reminisces about playing checkers the summer before and worries about her date. "If you knew Stradlater you'd have been worried too." Later, in New York, he makes a plan to speak to her over the telephone by pretending he is her uncle. Again he doesn't do it. "You have to be in the mood for those things."

Unlike the uninhibited Stradlaters, Holden and his literary family sheer away from sex. They are at their happiest with family affection, the love of brother and sister. Although this family love often carries a strong erotic charge (to me it always seems that Holden comes nearer to having a sexual relationship with Phoebe than he does with anyone else), on the face of it, at least, it is pure, innocent and childlike.

The Catcher in the Rye is Salinger's only novel to date. His technique is no different from that in the short stories—in fact two long sections of *The Catcher* were originally published in short-story form. There is no plot to speak of and the reader's interest is held entirely by the narrator's internal monologue. It is Holden's language, above all, that provides the excitement, the surprises and the clues to character. The reader learns about Holden not from what he does, nor even what he thinks, but from the way that he expresses his thoughts.

The idiom of a metropolitan, American teenager—banal, stylized and repetitive—does not seem a very likely medium for subtle expression. But Salinger uses it with such virtuosity that by the end of the book even Holden's adjectives "pretty," "crumby," "terrific," "lousy," "stupid," "old," "quite" have taken on a vivid and exact significance. His constant use of an additional phrase at the end of a sentence, for emphasis—"I really did, I honestly did, I mean it, for Godsake, for Chrissake"—in a way suggests that he is not always sure he's telling the truth, or, for that matter, what the truth is. His occasional excursions into jargon, "It has a very good academic rating, Pencey. It really does," act as reminders that he is poised between the schoolboy and adult worlds. The language conveys an impression of someone trying desperately to express the truth; sometimes he fails through a lack of the right words to express his thoughts, and sometimes because the world around him is so corrupt that he can't be quite sure whether his own integrity has been affected. And, in fact, the phonies win in the end. Those at Pencey, those in the night club and the theater, Sunny, the young prostitute, and Maurice, the pimp, the treacherous Mr. Antolini and the people all over the world who go round writing dirty words on walls, they are all too much for him. His response is to search for comfort with his sister Phoebe and the other children in the park. He imagines himself to be "the catcher," and then prepares to pursue his last, bleak dream—of "hitching out west" to take a job at a filling station and pretend he is a deaf mute. Unfortunately he is prevented, presumably by the intervention of his parents, from going through with this escape. He goes home and the epilogue implies he has had some kind of breakdown, though we are not told about it in any detail—"that stuff doesn't interest me too much right now."

The last sentences of the book hint that Holden is somewhere near coming to terms with it all. "About all I know is, I sort of *miss* everybody I told about. Even old Stradlater and Ackley, for instance. I think I even miss that goddam Maurice. It's funny. Don't ever tell anybody anything. If you do, you start missing everybody."

This hint is made more explicit in the later short stories, although the message is slightly cryptic because of the Glass family's preoccupation with mysticism and their continual references to the Bhagavad-Gita, Sri Ramakrishna, Chuang-tzu and other mystical sources. In these stories Salinger is trying to express his personal version of the doctrine of salvation through love. When Buddy Glass (the writer, who is narrator of the family chronicles) has an impulse to say something "mildly caustic" about his junior-college students he refrains, turning to brother Seymour as his ethical authority.

> There isn't one girl in there [the classroom], including the terrible Miss Zabel, who is not as much my sister as Boo Boo or Franny. They may shine with the misinformation of the ages but they shine. This thought manages to stun me: there's no place I'd rather go right now than into Room 307. Seymour once said that all we do our whole lives is go from one little piece of Holy Ground to the next. Is he *never* wrong?

The clearest exposition of the idea comes at the end of "Zooey." Franny Glass, like Holden, is on the verge of a breakdown. Like him, she is obsessed by phonies. She visualizes one of them, Professor Tupper, a visiting philosophy teacher from Oxford, going into the men's room before his classes "to muss up his hair" and so make his appearance conform to his idea of himself. Zooey fastens on this anecdote as an example of her wrong approach to people. He explains to her how once when he was a child and didn't want to brush his shoes, Seymour (with typical obliqueness) said that he must do them "for the Fat Lady."

"*There isn't anybody out there who isn't Seymour's Fat Lady.* That includes your Professor Tupper, buddy. And all his goddam cousins by the dozens. There isn't anyone *any*where that isn't Seymour's Fat Lady. Don't you know that? Don't you know that goddam secret yet? And don't you know—*listen* to me, now—*don't you know who that Fat Lady really is?* . . . Ah, buddy. Ah, buddy. It's Christ Himself. Christ Himself, buddy."

Franny's response to this is joy and understanding. She feels "as if what little or much wisdom there is in the world were suddenly hers." Her problems have been solved.

Although some readers may feel less content than Franny with Zooey's answer, many, among them those who regard Salinger as a spokesman, have greeted it with delight. Although it is offered as a great step forward, this "blanket" love shows no progression beyond the conclusion of *The Catcher;* it is simply another variation on Salinger's perpetual theme of withdrawal and escape. To love everybody indiscriminately, simply because they are human, is as efficient a way of avoiding any commitment to them as hitchhiking out west to masquerade as a deaf mute. As Holden says: "A horse is human, for Godsake."

Zooey's answer is a comfortable and accommodating one. It leaves the lovers undisturbed in their world of childhood and innocence, secure in the knowledge that they will never be forced to actually have any relationship with the fat ladies. They can love from a convenient distance and remain unspotted.

The idea of the unfallen preadolescent has exercised an extraordinary strong appeal in the last few years, stronger it seems than at any time since Dickens showed the Victorians an endless source of titillation in the beloved sisters, child wives and girlish, though often corrupted, innocents about whom he loved to write. The young Jean Simmons, appropriately as Estella in *Great Expectations,* did a lot toward starting a fashion in film stars that was carried on by Leslie Caron and Audrey Hepburn. James Dean, who was worshiped by his fans with a religious love that has been accorded to no one else except Valentino, also based his film appeal on a kind of child-ishness. In his relationships with both Judy (Natalie Wood) in *Rebel Without a Cause* and, though to a lesser degree, Abra (Julie Harris) in *East of Eden,* the sexual aspect was strongly under-played. He was seen not as a lover but a close, childhood friend. In *Rebel* the three teenagers, Jim, Judy and Plato, make up a family that, during their brief idyll in the deserted house, provides them with a security and happiness lacking in their real home lives. "Play-ing at families," they find the game infinitely preferable to the real thing. Jim, like "the catcher," is a big brother and protector. In his mannerisms—the disconnected, hesitating speech, his slouching walk and unexpected, whimsy gestures—he expresses a childish un-certainty and confusion similar to that suggested by Holden through language. Above all Jim is good.

And so is Colin MacInnes's teenage hero of *Absolute Beginners,* the nearest thing to *The Catcher* that has appeared here. Some-times, indeed, he is so good that the effect is like reading a school story by Talbot Baines Reed.

Like Holden he reaches a point at which he is so shocked by the corruption of society that he has an impulse to escape from it. Although in every way more down to earth than his American counterpart, his attitude to sex is respectable enough to reassure the most prudish parent, reading the book in the hope of gaining some information about teenage morality. For him sex should be reserved for "the person you really dig, with all of yourself, your other half you'd give your life to." Otherwise it is only "a head, bodies and legs thing."

Associate members of Salinger's club, clasping memories of child-hood to them as they reluctantly join the adult world, are unlikely to parade their dissatisfaction. Their world is one of dreams and they will take refuge in it, secretly. While the beats express their revolt dramatically, so that all the squares in the world can see, the whimsical rebels for whom Salinger writes will be content to live theirs in a mental world of escape and disaffiliation. The people who find in Holden Caulfield, and to a lesser extent in James Dean, an expression of their own most fundamental attitudes are more complicated and less pliable than advertising copywriters and mem-bers of government committees on youth like to think. They even seem to want different things. Recruits to the ranks of the dis-affiliated, they regard society from a safe distance, convinced of one thing at least. For them it has nothing to offer.

FINALLY (FASHIONABLY) SPURIOUS

by JOAN DIDION

When I first came to New York during the fall of 1956, I went to a party on Bank Street which I remember with particular clarity for a number of reasons, not the least of them my surprise that no one present wished William Knowland were running for President. (I had only been in New York a few days, and the notion that Democrats might be people one met at parties had not yet violated what must have been, in retrospect, my almost impenetrable Western innocence.) There were a couple of girls who "did something interesting" for *Mademoiselle* and there were several rather tweedy graduate students from Princeton, one of whom intimated that he had a direct wire to the PMLA, baby; there was, as well, a stunningly predictable Sarah Lawrence girl who tried to engage me in a discussion of J. D. Salinger's relationship to Zen. When I seemed unresponsive, she lapsed into language she thought I might comprehend: Salinger was, she declared, the single person in the world capable of *understanding her*.

Five years work certain subtle changes. I have become downright blasé about Democrats at parties; that particular Sarah Lawrence girl found that she could, after all, be understood well enough for everyday purposes by someone else, an electronics engineer; and nobody, not even on Bank Street, thinks much any more about Adlai Stevenson for President.

The idea that J. D. Salinger is a kind of middle-class American guru, however, has somehow resisted those gently abrasive sands. Among the reasonably literate young and young in heart, he is surely the most read and reread writer in America today, exerting a power over his readers which is in some ways extraliterary. Those readers expect him to teach them something, something that has nothing at all to do with fiction. Not only have his vague meta-physical hints been committed to rote by *New Yorker* readers from here to Dubuque, but his imaginary playmates, the Glass family, have achieved a kind of independent existence; I rather imagine that Salinger readers wish secretly that they could write letters to Franny and Zooey and their brother Buddy, and maybe even to Waker (who is a Jesuit and apparently less disturbed than his kin), much as people of less invincible urbanity write letters to the char-acters in "As the World Turns" and "The Brighter Day."

What actually happens in *Franny and Zooey* is really nothing much. In "Franny," Franny Glass arrives at Princeton for a football weekend and is met by her date, strictly another of those boys with a direct wire to the PMLA, baby. He has frogs' legs for lunch and talks about Flaubert, all of which gets on Franny's nerves, especially because all she wants to do at the moment is say something called the "Jesus Prayer." ("The thing is," she explains, "the marvellous thing is, when you first start doing it, you don't even have to have *faith* in what you're doing . . . then eventually what happens, the prayer becomes self-active. Something *happens* after a while.")

When her date somehow fails to get the point about the Jesus Prayer, Franny faints. In "Zooey," which picks up the action the next morning, we find Franny laid up at home with what her brother, a television actor named Zooey, calls "a tenth-rate nervous break-down." She is tired of everybody's ego, not excepting her own. ("Just because I'm choosy about what I want—in this case, en*light*enment, or *peace*, instead of money or pres*tige* or *fame* or any of those things —doesn't mean I'm not as egotistical and self-seeking as everybody else.") Zooey eventually effects a cure of sorts by convincing Franny that everybody out there—no matter how given to ego, to eating frogs' legs and "*name*-dropping in a terribly quiet, *casual* voice" and wanting "to *get* somewhere"—is "Christ Himself. Christ Himself, buddy." ("Don't you know that? Don't you know that goddam secret yet?")

To anyone who has ever felt overexposed to the world, to anyone who has ever harborèd hatred in his or her heart toward droppers of names, writers of papers on Flaubert, toward eaters of frogs' legs, all of this has a certain seductive lure; there is a kind of lulling charm in being assured in that dazzling Salinger prose that one's raw nerves, one's urban hangover, one's very horridness, is really not horridness at all but instead a kind of dark night of the soul; there is something very attractive about being told that one finds en*light*enment or *peace* by something as eminently within the realm of the possible as tolerance toward television writers and section men, that one can find the peace which passeth understanding simply by looking for Christ in one's date for the Yale game.

However brilliantly rendered (and it is), however hauntingly right in the rhythm of its dialogue (and it is), *Franny and Zooey* is finally spurious, and what makes it spurious is Salinger's tendency to flatter the essential triviality within each of his readers, his predilection for giving instructions for living. What gives the book its extremely potent appeal is precisely that it is self-help copy: it emerges finally as *Positive Thinking* for the upper middle classes, as *Double Your Energy and Live Without Fatigue* for Sarah Lawrence girls.

EASY VICTORY

by Isa Kapp

In spite of the intellectual sponginess of our time, it is still strange to see the optimistic American reader gobbing up J. D. Salinger's stories of defeatism, self-deprecation and nervous breakdown. Like the hero of *Catcher in the Rye*, Franny spots pedants and name droppers everywhere, and has become, for moral reasons, a quitter. She gives up a good role in a play (she cannot stand "all those egos running around feeling terribly *charitable* and *warm*"), considers dropping her English courses and faints away just before the football game. She complains that the faculty poets aren't leaving behind "a single solitary thing beautiful," that wisdom is no longer the goal of knowledge.

All in all, it looks as though Franny might turn into an Underground Girl. But as a reader you are only briefly disturbed. Because you can be sure, if it's Salinger, that there's only a short tunnel to the Revelation.

A spiritual crisis in these pages is mainly a question of sweating it out and taking slugs of the truth like a boxer. In the long story, "Zooey," Franny's older brother explains that her crusade against academics has been too personal, and that she cannot find salvation by mumbling the Jesus Prayer because she does not really understand or admire the character of Christ. After this first round, Zooey's shirt is sopping wet, Franny is down, sobbing but still alert, and both are tinglingly conscious of their form and courage.

There follows a good deal of circling and springing about and bruising of vanity before Franny drags herself wearily to her feet for the last round. From the knockout blow she learns that it is her duty to do the best she can with her talents for the sake of the "Fat Lady" (the Glass household term for the ordinary human ignoramus, a figure even more abject than the liberals' vanishing "little man"). But there is more to come; in the moment before sleep and transfiguration she hears Zooey's voice affirm: *"Don't you know who that Fat Lady really is?* Ah, buddy. Ah, buddy. It's Christ Himself. . . ."

I don't know what an orthodox Christian would make of this democratization of the Spirit, but I resent the liberties Salinger takes with the word. The unappetizing image of the Fat Lady is only one rude plank in his program for educating us by adopting a recklessly chummy attitude toward ideas and moral concepts ("who besides Jesus really knew which end was up?"). Salinger gives a fast great-books course, but in name only. He seems to be deathly embarrassed by any token of erudition, and must bolster a mention of Epictetus or Zen Buddhism by a frank, virile burst of swear words, or an apologetic phrase like "as Kafka, no less, has told us."

No matter how inspirational his reading list, Salinger himself persists in a low opinion of mankind. If one of his characters happens to find a friend, the chosen person is usually between ten and fourteen years old, or dear because departed. Holden Caulfield's one decent roommate commits suicide. When Franny, in emotional turmoil, is asked if she would like to speak to her brother, Buddy, on the telephone, she answers plainly and with small regard for material considerations: "I want to speak to Seymour." Seymour has been dead (also by suicide) since an earlier story, "A Perfect Day for Bananafish," and his idealism is therefore beyond question. This uncompromising writer wastes no unction on the human condition unless it is extreme.

Is Salinger sincere? Alfred Kazin has made the sensible point that he cares less about the failure of feeling than about the failure of art in these stories. Certainly, there is a lot of unlucky language in *Franny and Zooey*: "If you do anything at all beautiful on a stage, anything nameless or joy-making . . ." Almost every page contains some coy, self-conscious formulation; and, unfortunately, a person who is very conscious of himself and overly concerned with appearances is not able to concentrate on the content of what he is saying. Ardent as Salinger is in his pursuit of truth and beauty—an incredible number of actions are designated as beautiful or not in the course of this short book—ambitious as he is to take some critical stand on the H-bomb or "the joys of television and *Life* Magazine every Wednesday," his confrontations grow shallower and briefer as the problems get larger.

The silly collegiate mannerisms despised by Franny, and the "phonies" who crowd the road from Pencey Prep to Penn Station (in *Catcher in the Rye*) seem, theoretically, to make good material for fiction. But a novelist or story writer has to want more than the kick of discovering someone in a fraudulent position. Proust and Camus, who also dealt with hypocrisy and self-deception, were interested in exactly how they operated in the big world as well as in the small ego. You cannot find out much about society from Salinger, who only worries about what this crude body has done to violate his own or his hero's integrity.

When Céline tells us it's a rotten universe, he is an honest witness. He gives you the details and admittedly partakes of the general corruption. Salinger lets you infer that he has somehow managed to remain untainted by the humbug, ignorance and academicism that surround him. It is an easy victory, often quietly insinuated by situations in which the hero is involved with only one or two other people, remarkable as himself, fine in spirit and able to grasp his metaphors.

This cliquish note of self-congratulation is the most antagonizing aspect of Salinger's writing. Maybe it comes of trying so hard to handle ethics when questions of taste are really his specialty. Like Franny, he is better at telling what personal affectations he doesn't like than locating the moral enemy. He is reliable for homelier tasks, like itemizing the furniture of a middle-class apartment or the contents of the medicine chest.

The best section of *Franny and Zooey* describes Mrs. Glass, with her old kimono and an abstracted expression, barging into the bathroom to talk to Zooey, who makes scathing comments from behind the shower curtain. There is also a well-handled scene in which, over snails and olives, the heroine and her boy friend dramatize the victories and humiliations in the classroom. On the level of such psychologizing, small in scope and safely outside the responsibilities of philosophy, a reader may be impressed by the Salinger touch.

THE SALINGER INDUSTRY

by GEORGE STEINER

In themselves, all the critical exaggerations and pomposities about J. D. Salinger are of no great importance. But they do point to some of the things that are seriously wrong with contemporary American criticism.

First of all, they get Salinger's work badly out of focus and could do him a great deal of harm if he were so misguided as to read them (most probably he does not). Mr. Jerome David Salinger is neither Molière nor Chekhov. He is not yet Mark Twain (and by a long shot). Why should he be? He is a gifted and entertaining writer with one excellent short novel and a number of memorable stories to his credit. He has a marvelous ear for the semiliterate meanderings of the adolescent mind. He has caught and made articulate the nervous, quizzical, rough-edged spirit of the moment. He very obviously touches on major or traditional motifs: the failure of the bridges that are meant to link young and old, the mending power of a general, nonsexual love between human beings (something between friendship and compassion). "For Esmé—with Love and

Squalor" is a wonderfully moving story, perhaps the best study to come out of the war of the way in which the greater facts of hatred play havoc in the private soul. "The Laughing Man" and "Down at the Dinghy" are fine sketches of the bruised, complicated world of children. But neither holds a candle to Joyce's *Araby* or to the studies of childhood in Dostoevsky. Of late, Salinger has begun parodying Salinger. His most recent chronicle of the Glass family is a piece of shapeless self-indulgence. (*The New Yorker* is notoriously vulnerable to the delights of sheer length.) The writer himself, moreover, is interesting. He has adopted a T. E. Lawrence technique of partial concealment. He does not sign books at Brentano's nor teach creative writing at Black Mountain. "I was with the Fourth Division during the war. I almost always write about very young people." That's about all he wants us to know.

Salinger's virtues account for part of his vast appeal. But only for part. The rest is less exalted. The young like to read about the young. Salinger writes *briefly* (no need to lug home a big book or something, Lord help us, not available in paperback). He demands of his readers nothing in the way of literacy or political interest (in my time, college bull sessions raged over *Doctor Faustus;* but that meant having heard of Hitler or Nietzsche or being dimly aware of a past writer called Goethe). Salinger flatters the very ignorance and moral shallowness of his young readers. He suggests to them that formal ignorance, political apathy and a vague *tristesse* are positive virtues. They open the heart to mystic intimations of love. This is where his cunning and somewhat shoddy use of Zen comes in. Zen is in fashion. People who lack even the rudiments of knowledge needed to read Dante, or the nerve required by Schopenhauer, snatch up the latest paperback on Zen. "Salinger's constant allusions to the Bhagavad-Gita, Sri Ramakrishna, Chuang-tzu, and the rest are only efforts to find alternate ways of expressing what his stories are about," says Mizener. I wonder. They are more likely a shrewd insight into the kind of half-culture which the present college generation revels in. Twelfth-century madrigals are bound to come soon into the lives of Franny or Zooey or the late lamented Seymour.

These are the main facts. Why is literary criticism so determined to get them out of proportion?

First, there is a matter of language. Having added to the legacy of Germanic scholarship the jargon of the New Criticism, many American academic critics are no longer able to write with plainness or understatement. They have a vested interest in the complex and the sublime. (Hence Messrs. Heiserman and Miller's capitalized Quest and their pious statement, "We use the medieval term." . . .) A new, probably rather minor achievement comes along, and at once critical language soars to sublimity. The result is a serious devaluation of critical coin. If one writes about Salinger as do Gwynn and Blotner, just how is one to write about Cervantes or Turgenev? The entire sense of discrimination between values which should be implicit in a critic's language gets lost.

Secondly, there is a matter of economics. The young assistant or associate professor must publish in order to get advancement or to obtain one of those Fulbrights, Guggenheims or Fords which mark the ascent to Parnassus. Now suppose he is still faintly alive and does not care to write yet another paper on imagery in Pope or cancel-sheets in Melville. He wants to test his critical sense against a contemporary work. He does not know enough French or German to write about European masters. What is he to do? He turns to the American scene. The giants are no longer about. Faulkner is making tape recordings and Hemingway is adding further gore to *Death in the Afternoon* (surely one of the dullest books in our time). Along comes a small though clearly interesting fish like Salinger and out go the whaling fleets. The academic critic can do his piece with few footnotes, it will be accepted by critical reviews or little magazines, and it is another tally on the sheet of his career.

American literary criticism has become a vast machine in constant need of new raw material. There are too many critical journals, too many seminars, too many summer schools and fellowships for critics. One is reminded of the ambitions of Marcia, a character in the New York *Herald Tribune* comic strip "Miss Peach." Asked what she wished to become in life, the little brute answered, "A critic." And whom would she criticize? "Every man, woman, and child in the United States." There has never been, and cannot be, enough good literature produced at any given moment to supply a critical industry so massive and serious. The immediate past, moreover, has been a classic period for critics. With Eliot, Pound, Leavis, Edmund

Wilson, Trilling, Blackmur, Tate and Yvor Winters in the field, just how much use is there in writing yet another essay on Dante or Shakespeare or Yeats? The quarry of greatness having been exhaustively mined, younger critics turn their big guns onto the smaller targets.

All this has serious consequences. There is, at the moment, a gross devaluation of standards (the Cozzens ecstasy of a few seasons back is a case in point). If criticism does not serve to distinguish what is great from what is competent, it is not carrying out its proper task. If it conspires to suggest that transcendent values are made articulate in anything quite as loose and glossy as the maunderings of Zooey, it is betraying its responsibilities. Of course, Salinger is a most skillful and original writer. Of course, he is worth discussing and praising. But not in terms appropriate to the master poets of the world, not with all the pomp and circumstance of final estimation. By all means, let us have Esmé, Daumier-Smith and all the Glasses. But let us not regard them as the house of Atreus reborn.

v. A Slight Case of Incest

The critics represented in this section share a high regard for "well-made" fiction and a heavy reliance on depth psychology. Maxwell Geismar, who calls Holden a half-creation, suggests that Salinger is simply not a very good craftsman. Cogently and skillfully, Geismar expresses what nags so many other critics: a sense of limitation, of narrowness, about Salinger's fictional world. He mixes his criticism, however, with an astonishing amount of social and class consciousness; does it really matter so much that Holden is an "upper-class orphan" (in point of fact, he is neither) or well-to-do? Is it pertinent to suggest that Salinger disguises Jews behind Anglo-Saxon names (and what of Tannenbaum and Glass)? It takes a rather special point of view to discover hints of murder in "Bananafish," to find Franny as unpleasant as Lane, or to see contempt in Holden's compassion. In literary terms, Frederick Gwynn and Joseph Blotner take Salinger far more seriously, but they too show their disapproval of his craftsmanship by praising his earlier, well-made stories and dismissing his later ones as ambitious failures; in fact, they go so far as to tell Salinger where "Zooey" should have started (much later). The critics particularly seem to overrate "Esmé," with their carefully numbered, philosophical correlations.

As for these writers' psychoanalytic interpretations, they verge on parody. Geismar wonders whether Esmé's charm and affection "can replace the need for mental therapy," and he is downright angry at "revisionist" dissenters from Freudian orthodoxy. Gwynn and Blotner, in discussing "De Daumier-Smith's Blue Period," discover that the hero is, psychologically, a suffering castrate and that the story's theme is really incest. All this is an extreme instance of that flourishing literary specialty, psychocriticism.

The Gwynn and Blotner contribution is taken from a pamphlet on Salinger's fiction which, for Salinger students, is a useful catalogue and contains much painstaking work. One is quite dazzled by some of their scholarly leaps, as when they compare the foot-kissing episode in "A Perfect Day for Bananafish" with Raskolnikov kissing Sonia's foot. They regard the name Seymour Glass as symbolyzing perceptiveness and sensitivity ("he sees more than others and shatters like glass"), a point on which they differ from Geismar, who considers "Glass" to be standing for mirror, hence narcissism. The authors also note, and no one else can make this claim, that some of the most important scenes in the Glass legend take place in bathrooms, but the explanation they offer— "family shyness"—is somewhat disappointing. Surely psychocriticism could have done better than that.

THE WISE CHILD AND THE
NEW YORKER SCHOOL OF FICTION

by Maxwell Geismar

He worked on *The Catcher in the Rye* for about ten years, J. D. Salinger told us, and when it appeared in 1951, it evoked both critical and popular acclaim. Here was a fresh voice, said Clifton Fadiman in the Book-of-the-Month Club *News*. "One can actually hear it speaking, and what it has to say is uncannily true, perceptive and compassionate." The novel was brilliant, funny, meaningful, said S. N. Behrman. It was probably the most distinguished first novel of the year, said Charles Poore in *Harper's Magazine*. The real catch in the *Catcher*, said *Time*, was novelist Salinger himself, who could understand the adolescent mind without displaying one.

Salinger's short stories in *The New Yorker* had already created a stir. In undergraduate circles, and particularly in the women's colleges, this fresh voice, which plainly showed its debt to Ring Lardner, but had its own idiom and message, began to sound prophetic. Salinger was the spokesman of the Ivy League Rebellion during the early fifties. He had come to express, apparently, the values and aspirations of college youth in a way that nobody since Scott Fitzgerald (the other major influence in his work) had done as well. He is interesting to read for this reason, and because he is a leading light in the *New Yorker* school of writing. (He is probably their *ultimate* artist.) And besides, Salinger's talent is interesting for its own sake.

But just what is the time spirit that he expresses? The *Catcher's* hero has been expelled from Pencey Prep as the climax of a long adolescent protest. The history teacher who tries to get at the causes of Holden Caulfield's discontent emerges as a moralistic pedagogue, who picks his nose. ("He was really getting the old thumb right in there.") During his farewell lecture, Holden is restless, bored—"I moved my ass a little bit on the bed"—and then suddenly uneasy. "I felt sorry as hell for him all of a sudden. But I just couldn't hang around there any longer." This refrain echoes through the narrative; and the rebellious young hero ends up by being "sorry" for all the jerks, morons and queers who seem to populate the fashionable and rich preparatory-school world.

He is also scornful of all the established conventions as "very big deal." (Another standard refrain in the story.) He seems to be the only truly creative personage in this world, and, though he has failed all his courses except English, he has his own high, almost absolute, standards of literature, at least.

"They gave me *Out of Africa* by Isak Dinesen. I thought it was going to stink, but it didn't. It was a very good book. I'm quite illiterate, but I read a lot." By comparison, *A Farewell to Arms* is really a phony book, so we are told. As in Saul Bellow's work, the very human hero of *The Catcher*, who is a physical weakling, who knows that he is at least half "yellow," is also a symbol of protest against the compulsive virility of the Hemingway school of fiction.

The action of the novel is in fact centered around the athlete Stradlater, who is "a very sexy bastard," and who has borrowed Holden Caulfield's jacket and his girl. Stradlater is "unscrupulous" with girls; he has a very *sincere* voice which he uses to snow them with, while he gives them the time, usually in the back seat of the car. Thinking about all this, Holden gets nervous ("I damn near puked"). In his room, he puts on his pajamas, and the old hunting hat which is his talisman of true rebellion and creativity, and starts out to write the English theme (which Stradlater will use as his own) about his dead brother Allie's baseball mitt. Yet when the athlete returns from his date, full of complacency about Holden's girl and of contempt for Holden's essay, this weakling-hero provokes him into a fight. "Get your dirty stinking moron knees off my chest," says Caulfield to Stradlater. "If I letcha up," says Strad, "willya keep your mouth shut?" "You're a dirty stupid sonuvabitch of a moron," says Holden Caulfield.

Later, nursing a bloody nose as the price of his defiant tongue, he wanders into old Ackley's room for companionship. "You could also hear old Ackley snoring. Right through the goddam shower curtains you could hear him. He had sinus trouble and he couldn't breathe too hot when he was asleep. That guy had just about everything. Sinus trouble, pimples, lousy teeth, halitosis, crumby fingernails. You had to feel a little sorry for the crazy sonuvabitch." But he can find no comfort or solace in the room, which stinks of dirty socks. Ackley is even more stupid than Stradlater. "Stradlater was a goddam genius next to Ackley." A familiar mood of loneliness and despair descends upon him. "I felt so lonesome, all of sudden, I almost wished I was dead. . . . Boy, did I feel rotten. I felt so damn lonesome." He counts his dough ("I was pretty loaded. My grandmother'd just sent me a wad about a week before") and says goodbye:

> When I was all set to go, when I had my bags and all, I stood for a while next to the stairs and took a last look down the goddam corridor. I was sort of crying. I don't know why. I put my red hunting hat on, and turned the peak around to the back, the way I liked it, and then I yelled at the top of my goddam voice, "Sleep tight, ya morons!" I'll bet I woke up every bastard on the whole floor. Then I got the hell out. Some stupid guy had thrown peanut shells all over the stairs, and I damn near broke my crazy neck.

These are handsome prose passages, and The Catcher in the Rye is eminently readable and quotable in its tragicomic narrative of preadolescent revolt. Compact, taut and colorful, the first half of the novel presents in brief compass all the petty horrors, the banalities, the final mediocrity of the typical American prep school. Very fine—and not sustained or fulfilled, as fiction. For the later sections of the narrative are simply an episodic account of Holden Caulfield's "lost weekend" in New York City which manages to sustain our interest but hardly deepens our understanding.

There are very ambiguous elements, moreover, in the portrait of this sad little screwed-up hero. His urban background is curiously shadowy, like the parents who never quite appear in the story, like the one pure adolescent love affair which is now "ruined" in his memory. The locale of the New York sections is obviously that of a comfortable middle-class urban Jewish society where, however, all the leading figures have become beautifully Anglicized. Holden and Phoebe Caulfield: what perfect American social register names which are presented to us in both a social and a psychological void! Just as the hero's interest in the ancient Egyptians extends only to the fact that they created mummies, so Salinger's own view of his hero's environment omits any reference to its real nature and dynamics.

Though the book is dedicated to Salinger's mother, the fictional mother in the narrative appears only as a voice through the wall. The touching note of affection between the brother and sister is partly a substitute for the missing child-parent relationships (which might indeed clarify the nature of the neurotic hero), and perhaps even a sentimental evasion of the true emotions in a sibling love. The only real creation (or half-creation) in this world is Holden Caulfield himself. And that "compassion," so much praised in the story, and always expressed in the key phrase, "You had to feel sorry"—for him, for her, for them—also implies the same sense of superiority. If this hero really represents the nonconformist rebellion of the fifties, he is a rebel without a past, apparently, and without a cause.

The Catcher in the Rye protests, to be sure, against both the academic and social conformity of its period. But what does it argue *for?* When Holden mopes about the New York museum which is almost the true home of his discredited childhood, he remembers the Indian war canoes "about as long as three goddam Cadillacs in a row." He refuses any longer to participate in the wealthy private boys' schools where "you have to keep making believe you give a damn if the football team loses, and all you do is talk about girls and liquor and sex all day, and everybody sticks together in these dirty little goddam cliques." Fair enough; while he also rejects the notion of a conventional future in which he would work in an office, make a lot of dough, ride in cabs, play bridge or go to the movies. But in his own private vision of a better life, this little catcher in the rye sees only those "thousands of little children" all playing near the dangerous cliff, "and nobody's around—nobody big, I mean—except me" to rescue them from their morbid fate.

This is surely the differential revolt of the lonesome rich child, the conspicuous display of leisure-class emotions, the wounded affections, never quite faced, of the upper-class orphan. This is the *New Yorker* school of ambiguous finality at its best. But Holden Caulfield's real trouble, as he is told by the equally precocious Phoebe, is that he doesn't like *any*thing that is happening. "You don't like any schools. You don't like a million things. You *don't.*" This is also the peak of well-to-do and neurotic anarchism—the one world of cultivated negation in which all those thousands of innocent, pure little children are surely as doomed as their would-be and somewhat paranoid savior. "I have a feeling that you're riding for some kind of a terrible, terrible fall," says the last and best teacher in Holden's tormented academic career. But even this prophetic insight is vitiated by the fact that Mr. Antolini, too, is one of those flits and perverty guys from whom the adolescent hero escapes in shame and fear.

He is still, and forever, the innocent child in the evil and hostile universe, the child who can never grow up. And no wonder that he hears, in the final pages of the narrative, only a chorus of obscene sexual epithets which seem to surround the little moment of lyric happiness with his childlike sister. The real achievement of *The Catcher in the Rye* is that it manages so gracefully to evade just those central questions which it raises, and to preserve both its verbal brilliance and the charm of its emotions within the scope of its own dubious literary form. It is still Salinger's best work, if a highly artificial one, and the caesuras, the absences, the ambiguities at the base of this writer's work became more obvious in his subsequent books.

I am conscious of treating severely, or at least analytically, a book which is most entertaining, but which is also so typical and so illuminating as an example of its class. *Nine Stories*, in 1953, had already established Salinger's reputation with an elite group of magazine readers. Among these tales, "A Perfect Day for Bananafish" was notable for the unpleasant suicide of a disturbed war veteran.

Seymour Glass has shot himself, seated on the bed next to his sleeping wife. Shortly before this, while carrying on a whimsical conversation with one of Salinger's innocent little girls, he has pushed the child ever deeper into the Florida ocean. There are intimations of a murder before the suicide; and similarly in another well-known story in the collection called "Teddy," a jealous sister pushes a child prodigy into an empty swimming pool. Here the little genius has anticipated and even welcomed his own death, however, while here indeed the morbid, the more than neurotic emotions which are implicit in Salinger's first novel take a more prominent place in his writing. The obsessive affection for little children has usually been accompanied, in the major writers, by other untoward elements of the psyche (child seduction, child rape), as witness Dostoevsky, Dreiser, or Nabokov. But like the post-Freudian and revisionist psychologists of the fifties, Salinger has also attempted to deny or reject the darker urges that are present in the idyl of pure childhood.

One of the best tales in the volume describes the drunken binge of an unhappy exurbanite wife, whose lonely little daughter kills her imaginary playmate, Jimmy Jimmereeno. Two other stories deal with the comfortable bourgeois New York Jewish society in which, again, the leading figures are called Ginnie, Selena, Franklin, Eric, etc. That is to say, Jewish and not Jewish: this "assimilated" German-Jewish urban group, not wishing any longer to be identified with their religious and cultural minority group, whose bright children now attend the fashionable American Christian schools like "Miss Basehoar's." If Salinger has primarily been concerned with the pure, the isolated, the *causeless* child, one sees that he can describe the milieu of their origin very well indeed when he chooses to, even under its pseudonymic and self-protective coloring.

Or at least, up to a point. In "Down at the Dinghy," Boo Boo Tannenbaum, who, we are told, is "a stunning and final girl," discovers that her son believes a "kike" to be something that flies in the sky: a tricky little bit of anti-anti-Semitism. (Boo Boo and Seymour Glass are to be heard from again.) "For Esmé—with Love and Squalor" concerns a beautiful, dignified, precocious upper-class English maiden of thirteen who saves an American soldier from a nervous breakdown. There is no doubt of Esmé's grace and charm (or of her social standing), but only whether, in this case, an adolescent's romantic affection can replace the need for mental therapy. The young hero of "De Daumier-Smith's Blue Period" has a similar background: disturbed and Continental. The mother, divorced, remarried, has died in Europe. Back in New York, the second husband and the lonesome son have gradually discovered "that we were both in love with the same deceased woman."

What was curious about Holden Caulfield's chronicle, besides the shadowy mother, was the absence of any father relationship at all. Perhaps here, through the device of the second husband or the "false father," the writer can express humorously and even gaily what was more difficult to describe seriously. At nineteen, at any rate, the present hero invents a "deceased wife," a false name, a small estate in the south of France, a kinship with Daumier and "poor Picasso," and goes off to teach art at an obscure correspondence school in Canada. The school and its inscrutable Japanese owners, and the types of students who use it, are all brilliantly described in the story; the young hero is engagingly and wildly adolescent, and falls in love, by mail, with a certain Sister Irma of St. Joseph's whose portraits of Christ have caught his fancy.

On a walk through the provincial town he is also fascinated by the window display of the local orthopedic appliances shop:

> Then something altogether hideous happened. The thought was forced on me that no matter how coolly or sensibly or gracefully I might one day learn to live my life, I would always at best be a visitor in a garden of enamel urinals and bedpans, with a sightless wooden dummy-deity standing by in a marked-down rupture truss.

This is engaging and illuminating imagery; and perhaps the rupture-truss deity, before whom the hero has his moment of mystic insight, leads directly to the Eastern gurus who are invoked in Salinger's later and more famous short story "Franny," which took up considerable space in *The New Yorker* of January 29, 1955, and caused another minor sensation in the undergraduate (feminine) academic world. The central question was whether the story's heroine was pregnant, or insane, or both—or neither.

As in any good Scott Fitzgerald tale, it is the weekend of the Yale game. The young men are waiting on the station platform for their dates. In his Burberry raincoat, Lane Coutell is reading Franny's passionate love letter and thinking that station-platform kisses are "rather inhibited in the follow-through." (The collegiate atmosphere is done very well.) Yet their dinner at Sickler's—a symbolic name—turns into a catastrophe. Lane is talking about his paper on Flaubert's concern for the *mot juste*. Franny, listening to him "with a special semblance of absorption," is overcome by her distaste for his vanity, his complacency. He is indeed a dreadful portrait of a college intellectual, who will become a typical graduate student in English, a "section man," and then perhaps a minor contributor to the *Partisan Review*.

That is what Franny tells him in effect, as she feels her "destructive" impulses coming to the fore, with the disloyalty and guilt "which seemed to be the order of the day." (She has had to strain to write him her last [false] love letter.) Lane's self-absorbed egoism can't stand criticism; the conversation becomes a controversy. Up to this point the story is sharp and sensitive. Then comes the mysterious scene in Sickler's ladies' room, where Franny collapses:

> Without any apparent regard to the suchness of her environment, she sat down. She brought her knees together very firmly, as if to make herself a smaller, more compact unit. Then she placed her hands, vertically, over her eyes and pressed the heels hard, as though to paralyze the optic nerve and drown all images in a voidlike black. . . . She held that tense, almost fetal position for a suspensory moment—then broke down. She cried for fully five minutes. She cried without trying to suppress any of the noisier manifestations of grief and confusion, with all the convulsive throat sounds that a hysterical child makes when the breath is trying to get up through a partly closed epiglottis. And yet, when finally she stopped, she merely stopped, without the painful, knife-like intakes of breath that usually follow a violent outburst-inburst. When she stopped, it was as though some momentous change of

polarity had taken place inside her mind, one that had an immediate, pacifying effect on her body. Her face tear-streaked but quite expressionless, almost vacuous, she picked up her handbag from the floor, opened it, and took out the small pea-green clothbound book.

And, armed with this mysterious weapon of spiritual guidance, but periodically overcome by other symptoms of nervous collapse, she proceeds to tell her lover off.

It is not only him, it is his whole life of habits, values, standards that she cannot bear. She ends up not only with an indictment of upper-class American society, but almost of Western culture itself. "It's *everybody*, I mean. Everything everybody does is so—I don't know—not *wrong*. . . . But just so tiny and meaningless and—sadmaking." She thinks she is going crazy, she says; she is sick of "ego, ego, ego." While her teeth chatter, she explains that her little green book, *The Way of a Pilgrim*, is the story of a Russian peasant's attempt to find salvation through prayer. "Lord Jesus Christ, have mercy on me" is the prayer that Franny herself keeps repeating incessantly, while Lane, not impressed by her religious conversion, reeking of garlic from his frogs' legs, discusses his psychoanalytic paper on Flaubert, *i.e.*, his own literary ego.

Here is the central conflict, in collegiate terms, of the life of renunciation *versus*—just what? For Lane is certainly not an artist (which also implies a form of self-renunciation) but closer to a boor. There are references in Franny's hysterical outbursts (she is more learned than one might suspect) to the Nembutsu sects of Buddhism and the Indian meditation on the "Om." "You get to see God. Something happens in some absolutely nonphysical part of the heart— where the Hindus say that Atman resides, if you ever took any Religion—and you see God, that's all." But Lane says it is really a matter of the most elementary *psychology*, and adds that she should take a rest in the room he has reserved for them. "When was that Friday night? Way the hell early last month, wasn't it?" And that maybe Franny's real trouble comes from another source. "Too long between drinks, to put it coarsely." Left alone, while he goes off to make the necessary arrangements, Franny begins to pray. "Her lips began to move, forming soundless words, and they continued to move." It is the Jesus prayer she is saying, to keep herself from fainting again; but then why does the story also leave such an unpleasant or disagreeable impression?

It is mainly, of course, the trickiness. After Lane's parting words we are still left wondering whether the painful description of Franny's "fetal" position was the opening of pregnancy or of mystical incantation. The descriptions both of Western materialism and Eastern spiritualism in Franny's adolescent terminology are hardly convincing, and her insistent tone finally loses her the original sympathy she had gained in the story. Both the central characters become almost equally unpleasant toward the close; and there are still more personal elements of Salinger's own philosophic conflicts involved here. For the remaining obscurities in "Franny" were developed, if not entirely clarified, in its sequel, "Zooey," to which *The New Yorker* devoted even more space—almost the entire issue— about two years later, on May 4, 1957.*

"Zooey" is an interminable, an appallingly bad story. Like the latter part of "Franny," it lends itself so easily to burlesque that one wonders what *The New Yorker* wits were thinking of when they published it with such fanfare—or what they might not have done with it, were it published elsewhere. Yet in terms of Salinger's career, and of the fashionable school of writing which he represents, it is also a very illuminating story. One notices, first of all, the uneasy tone of the prose. The writer's artistic conscience is at war with the apparent urgency of his message. What is here offered, we are told, isn't really a short story at all, "but a sort of prose home movie, and those who have seen the footage have strongly advised me against nurturing any elaborate distribution plans for it."

True enough, and the tale is full of these uneasy insights, or with a kind of Woukian ambiguity, where the artist both is and is not responsible for what he is saying. For the narrator of the "prose home movie" turns out to be Buddy Glass (at least Salinger won't

---

* "Raise High the Roof Beam, Carpenters," in *The New Yorker* of November 19, 1955, tells the story of Seymour Glass's disastrous marriage to the girl, whose name is difficult to locate, on the other bed in "Bananafish"—his wife, I mean, when he commits suicide. This is in fictional terms the best story in the series, because Salinger's philosophical and mystic preoccupations had not yet got the better of his craftsmanship. But it is simply an entertaining tale, with rather morbid undertones, comment on which is omitted here since most of the material in it is repeated with far more emphasis in "Zooey."

say he isn't), a brother of the late Seymour Glass and of Boo Boo Tannenbaum, both of whom we have met.

Risking the "aesthetic evil" of a footnote, Salinger indeed gives us a detailed chronology of the entire Glass family, including the dead twin Walt, and Waker, a Roman Catholic priest. One begins to realize that this is a sort of Yoknapatawpha County on Park Avenue. All of the Glass children have starred on the famous radio program "It's a Wise Child." They are all, apparently, prodigies (like the deceased and also famous Teddy, who should be related). And just as we remember that Boo Boo was "a stunning and final girl," so the present "hero" of the new story, Zooey, is "surpassingly handsome, even spectacularly so." Boo Boo has in fact described Zooey as "the blue-eyed Jewish-Irish Mohican scout"—an odd bit of childhood romance.

The Glass children all seem to admire each other no end. Zooey is indeed in the bathtub, reading Buddy's four-year-old letter, when the story finally begins to move (in its static way), and when Mrs. Glass herself slips into the bathroom to have a family conference with her handsome, talented and naked son. (There is a shower curtain drawn between them, which apparently obviates both the Oedipal and the pornographic factors here.) Franny Glass is still pursuing her nervous breakdown in the living room, and Zooey now repeats, in greater detail, the nature of her spiritual conflict, and the meaning of her quest for what is now a clear case of Zen Buddhism.

While Bessie Glass would appear to have all the anxious, doting traits of a Jewish matriarch, she turns out in fact to be a sort of mystic Irish druidess. She is indeed the Ideal Mother, understanding, perceptive, wise in her eccentric way, hiding her grief for her two dead sons, and crossing and uncrossing her remarkable legs throughout this whole scene. But there are really only two people talking—or one—in any given area of "Zooey," and now the camera moves on to the prone and ailing Franny. Zooey has already dissuaded his mother from calling in a psychoanalyst ("Just think of what analysis did for Seymour").* Now he instructs his sick sister

---

* Salinger's description of a "good" analyst is couched, alas, in about the same terms that Graham Greene uses for the Catholic analyst (another servant of God) in *The Potting Shed*. But isn't this revisionist concept of psycho-

E

that what is totally wrong in her personal revolt against the Western ego is her inadequate view of Buddha, the Indian Japam and the Bible itself. (During this scene Franny continues to fondle the altered tomcat Bloomberg, who is apparently the only honest Jewish character in the tale.)

Zooey proceeds to explain that she has never understood Jesus Himself from the time she was a child. "Your age has nothing to do with what I'm talking about. There are no big *changes* between ten and twenty—or ten and eighty, for that matter"—an interesting rationalization for the perennial world of childhood. "You keep talking about *ego*," he adds. "My God, it would take Christ himself to decide what's ego and what isn't. This is *God's* universe, buddy, not yours, and he has the final say about what's ego and what isn't." Moreover, Jesus was far superior to earlier prophets. Moses "was a nice man, and he kept in beautiful touch with his God and all that—but that's exactly the point. He had to keep in touch. Jesus realized there *is* no separation from God."

This is again an odd synthesis of Eastern and Western thought which might not have the approval of Christian or Jewish scholars; and yet Zooey's own final picture of Christ is closer to the religious fantasies of a John Steinbeck or a Bruce Barton. "Jesus was a supreme *adept*, by God, on a terribly important mission," he says:

> "This was no St. Francis, with enough time to knock out a few canticles, or to preach to the *birds,* or to do any of the other endearing things so close to Franny Glass's heart. I'm being serious now, God damn it. How can you miss seeing that? If God had wanted somebody with St. Francis's consistently winning personality for the job in the New Testament, he'd've picked him, you can be sure. As it was, he picked the best, the smartest, the most loving, the least sentimental, the most un*i*mitative master he could possibly have picked. And when you miss seeing that, I swear to you, you're missing the whole point of the Jesus Prayer."

---

analysis contrary to Freud's whole scientific and antireligious orientation—as is the modern fusion of depth psychology and Eastern mysticism in the disciples of Jung, or even the recent Zen Buddhism itself of the Erich Fromm school? But perhaps the primary historical function of psychoanalysis (to cut through all these forms of supernatural myths, fantasies, illusions and prejudices) was too ruthless, too cruel, for the civilizations which live on such illusions.

Isn't it odd, too, in Salinger's synthesis of Eastern and Western religions, that only the Jewish faith, like the Jewish father of the family, should be barely mentioned, and in effect is omitted? Nevertheless, Franny, under the spell of this therapeutic magic, or that of Buddy's continuous, insistent, repetitious, sermonizing lecture, somehow achieves her peace of mind, and falls asleep.

There is no doubt also that Salinger is deadly serious about all this, and that his continual use of collegiate phrases is no longer for the purposes of satire, but of persuasion of his mainly collegiate audience. Yet to read "Zooey" seriously is indeed like being in a lunatic asylum, as the heroine says about the Glass family, where it is difficult to distinguish between the doctors and the patients, as these self-appointed spiritual saviors play out their dubious roles. What is obvious of course is that these roles are all identical; and the literary "personages" in the narrative are merely the splintered parts of the same literary ego, persuading, opposing, convincing and arguing with itself. Thus there is the almost deliberately static effect of the story: the lack of all inner or outer action, the monotonous and repetitious use of the same trite and paralyzed gestures—as though, finally, we were hearing one voice speaking endlessly in an empty room. This is close to a catatonic tale.

And perhaps those buried monsters and horrors, always hinted at in Salinger's work, are having their say here. *"Yes. Yes. Yes. All right. Let me tell you something now, buddy . . . Are you listening . . . I'll tell you a terrible secret. Are you listening to me?"* And yet "Zooey" is also the logical climax of Salinger's career to this point. We have noticed the narrow range of his literary orbit, its uneasy base, its superstructure of sham. This predominantly Jewish middle-class urban circle, which ends up with its exotic Irish and druidic thespians! This inner psychological world of highly confused parental images, of effusive, sentimental and false sibling affection, which arrives at a Super Mother and a whole clan of brilliant child prodigies! The family name of Glass could hardly be better as a symbol of the pervading narcissism of all these identical "characters"—their ego-bound armor of self-vanity which is so illusory and so fragile.

Nowhere in this whole literary scene is there a genuine parent, or perhaps a genuine child. The true existence of the "glass" family is indeed on the perennial radio program of the Wise Child. And perhaps the almost compulsive naturalism of "things" in "Zooey" is the writer's unconscious attempt to substitute a material solidity of furnishings for the missing social, economic and psychological bases of his craft. Very likely these stories represent the writer's search, too, for his lost origins. Yet this family is still so evasive in its origins, so histrionic in its nature, so unnaturally handsome, talented, beautiful, wise and sensitive in all its component parts (parents, children, furnishings, atmosphere), and so brilliantly artificial in the end! It also represents the failure of the writer really to understand his own, true, life experience and to fulfill himself.

Is this indeed the "terrible secret" that is contained and never revealed in the tormented latest story of Salinger's? For a serious writer it could be. The buried depths of the past, which are the core, the source, the dark and ever-fresh quarry of his work, have failed. Thus, too, the satiric study of formal American education, with which Salinger opened his career, has its own limited focus. It is not really concerned with all those jerks, morons and queers that Holden Caulfield feels sorry for. It is directed at the failure of this educational system to understand the solitary "creative" rebel who protests against it. And Salinger's scathing references to the "normalcy" of those people who read the *Times*, care about the H-bomb, join the Westport or Oyster Bay Parent-Teachers' Association (not. Bronx, Brooklyn or Manhattan) proceed from the same source. This is an Exurbanite Radical Party of One.

We might say much the same thing about Salinger's disdain for the mass entertainment of Broadway and Hollywood from the superior vantage point of the *New Yorker* school of entertainment. Gifted, sensitive, perceptive, such high verbal talents as, say, John Cheever, Irwin Shaw or Edward Newhouse, among the *New Yorker* Impressionists, exist in a cultivated and most knowledgeable void. Maybe Salinger's real wish is simply to be the brightest of all these bright children. "Always, always, referring every goddam thing that happens right back to our lousy little egos," says Zooey, in sober truth. But what a perfect solution Salinger's mode of Zen Buddhism offers for this uneasy and unresolved conflict. In favor of a higher ego renunciation, it "transcends" all the solid material facts of environment and personality which this writer has ignored or evaded in his own literary career. In behalf of a kind of oceanic moral grandeur, it dispenses with any attempt at self-knowledge.

In a desperate spiritual revulsion against a devouring infantile egoism, is the answer really to repudiate our whole notion of Western individuality? Is there really no such thing (as Zooey tells Franny) as time or change or growth in our concept of human personality? In the Zen quest for "No-Knowledge" (as Buddy Glass tells his split-half Zooey), is it true that all legitimate religious study must lead to unlearning "the illusory differences between boys and girls, animals and stones, day and night, heat and cold?" Then indeed, Lord Jesus Christ, have mercy on us—and perhaps we should also invoke the practical, hard-headed, wrathful Jehovah whom Salinger has always repudiated. For the universe surely has a final transcendent unit. But meanwhile, here on earth, it is the legitimate business of the writer, in his mortal and un-Zenish career, to make clear just what those "illusory" differences are between boys and girls, day and night, animals and stones.

"Cleverness was his permanent affliction," the latter part of Salinger's literary personality (whom we might call Zen Buddy) has also announced, in another of those brilliant half-insights which never make an artistic whole. And we may remember that little Teddy himself, the first of these precocious Eastern mystics, was attracted to Oriental philosophy just because it negated the "mind" which had distinguished him in favor of the pure and primary world of childhood sensation. That lost world of childhood indeed to which, somehow or other, Salinger, like the rest of the *New Yorker* school, always returns! The pre-Edenite community of yearned-for bliss, where knowledge is again the serpent of all evil: but a false and precocious show of knowledge, to be sure, which elevated without emancipating its innocent and often touching little victims. . . . The root of the matter is surely here, and perhaps all these wise children may yet emerge from the nursery of life and art.

ONE HAND CLAPPING

by FREDERICK L. GWYNN and JOSEPH L. BLOTNER

At the outset, it might be well to consider Salinger's major fictional victory—the victories being the only reason for considering any of the failures that punctuate his unique career. The high point of his art, the moment at which particular narrative and general truth are identified most successfully with one another, comes in his most famous story, "For Esmé—with Love and Squalor," when Sergeant X, stationed in Bavaria after V-E Day, reads a German inscription in a German book and caps it with a Russian quotation written in English. The four agents in this process are perfectly chosen, and three of them are presented simply and at top speed. The reader is told that the book is *Die Zeit Ohne Beispiel* by Joseph Goebbels, that one inscription is by a thirty-eight-year-old unmarried woman, "a low official in the Nazi Party," and that the other inscription is from Dostoevsky. The fourth agent, Sergeant X, whose gesture of quotation sounds the depths of the human condition, thereby prepares himself and the reader for the salvation he receives from someone else's gesture later in the story.

What Goebbels represents should be obvious to anyone over thirty, but surely the range of this evil cannot be fully registered on the generation that adores Salinger, and it may even have dimmed in the more timeworn mind. To make any kind of contact with Joseph Goebbels is to be overwhelmed by the very type of psychotic hatred for everything weaker or more human than itself. His diaries show him to be "the unflagging motive force behind the vicious anti-Semitism of the Nazi regime," as Hugh Gibson says, whose "aim was the extermination of all Jews"; an ex-Catholic, he planned to "deal with the churches after the war and reduce them to impotence." It was this man, the holder of a *bona fide* doctorate, who in 1933 personally selected and had burned thousands of printed pages in which man had communicated with man. Less known than the genocide and the book-burning is Goebbels' hatred for humanity itself. In 1925 he wrote in his diary: "I have learned to despise the human being from the bottom of my soul. He makes me sick in my stomach." A year later he concluded that "The human being is a *canaille*."

But as Louis Lochner says, "Nobody who has not lived under Nazism can grasp how absolute was Goebbels' control of the German mind." It was this irresistible influence that (we may guess) had stimulated the second agent in the Salinger situation first to her Nazi party activities and later to the revulsion that she expressed by penning in the Goebbels book that X finds:

"Dear God, life is hell." To X, "the words appeared to have the stature of an uncontestable, even classic indictment," and he impulsively writes a comment underneath, one of Father Zossima's exhortations in *The Brothers Karamazov:* "Fathers and teachers, I ponder 'What is hell?' I maintain that it is the suffering of being unable to love.'"

The woman's substitution of the Christian God for Hitler and Goebbels is paralleled by the sergeant's reference to Russian Christianity, and her implicit recognition of *Die Zeit Ohne Beispiel*— The Unprecedented Era—as unprecedented hell is paralleled by Zossima's and X's awareness of the nonlove that brings about disintegration and war; together these form not only a "classic indictment" but a profound objective correlative for the love and "squalor" experienced by Sergeant X—and the reader—in the rest of the story. (It is the young Esmé who asks Sergeant X to write her an "extremely squalid and moving" story, adding the question, "'Are you at all acquainted with squalor?'" The sergeant's answer is typically ironic but correct: "I said not exactly but that I was getting better acquainted with it, in one form or another, all the time. . . .") We may now see exactly what is correlated.

The conflict of "Esmé" places the protagonist, Sergeant X, against four "squalid" forces in the four chronological sections of the story. (1) In 1950, the present, he is set off against his wife, "a breathtakingly levelheaded girl," and his mother-in-law. (2) Back in April, 1944, he is set off against the dullness of pre-Invasion training and the incommunicativeness of his sixty male mates, as well as against his wife and his mother-in-law, the women who write selfish civilian letters to this soldier about to be landed in France. (3) In the long year from D Day in 1944 to V-E Day in 1945 (referred to only briefly in the story), the protagonist is set off against war itself (which has resulted in his nervous breakdown) as well as against his jeep-mate, Corporal Clay. (4) In May, 1945, Sergeant X's combat fatigue is set off against the insensitivity of the loutish Clay, as well as against the selfish civilian triviality of his brother (who writes asking for souvenirs) and Clay's girl Loretta (who sits at home callously and amateurishly derogating X's psyche).

To balance these "squalid" antagonists there are four demonstrations of "love." (1) In 1950, exactly six years after X met Esmé, and apparently without any communication between them during this period, he receives an invitation to her wedding that makes him want to fly to it, "expenses be hanged." (2) In 1944, he has met Esmé, a brave English orphan of thirteen, who, nervous like X ("her nails were bitten down to the quick," "her hand, as I'd suspected, was a nervous hand, damp at the palm"), is also precociously sensitive to artistic, intellectual and emotional values. (3) Set opposite X's shattering experience in the war against Germany is the simple inscription in the book that communicates to him the shattering experience of a German in the war against the Allies. In answering the *cri de coeur* of an enemy whom he has actually just arrested as a criminal, Sergeant X equates himself with her simply as human beings against the total war they have suffered in—"a method of existence that is ridiculous to say the least," as Esmé naïvely but perceptively describes World War II. (4) Finally, in 1945, X receives the wrist watch which Esmé mailed to him the day after D Day, almost a year before. It is a stunning gesture for a titled gentlewoman who is "usually not terribly gregarious" thus to give her father's watch to a G.I., a foreigner casually and briefly met, a man who had countered almost every one of her statements with an ironic answer. The gift, which belonged to a British nobleman, "s-l-a-i-n in war (in her younger brother's hearing she spells out crucial words), helps restore the possibility of life ("f-a-c-u-l-t-i-e-s") for the American Staff Sergeant X.

[The authors then catalogue Salinger's early stories, in an extremely useful account that will be found in Appendix A (page 259). They move on to the work of his "classic period," 1948-1951, taking up "A Perfect Day for Bananafish," "Uncle Wiggily in Connecticut," "Just Before the War with the Eskimos," "The Laughing Man," "Down at the Dinghy" and *The Catcher in the Rye*. Pointing out the rarity of Salinger's approach—"the utilization of transcendental mysticism in satiric fiction"—they turn to "De Daumier-Smith's Blue Period."]

Salinger is in fine control in this fantastic and subtle tale, a humorous treatment of the classic Oedipal situation, wherein re-direction of love to a conventional object is surprisingly achieved by means of religious impulse. The narrator's attitude toward his stepfather throughout childhood and adolescence is one of ill-concealed hostility. The strength of his feeling for his mother is made clear in his glib fantasy of a job-application letter ("I said I had just left my small estate in the South of France, following the death of my wife") and in a retrospective comment in another letter ("The happiest day of my life was many years ago when I was seventeen. I was on my way for lunch to meet my mother, who was going out on the street for the first time after a long illness.") Shortly after he finally articulates the nature of the situation with his stepfather ("we gradually discovered that we were both in love with the same deceased woman"), he leaves his rival's shelter and support.

Not only is there the representation of love for the mother with its repressed sexual component, but there are also repeated symptoms of father-hatred, even to the point of some unobtrusive castration imagery. The narrator thinks he has found escape and fulfillment when, under the name of Jean de Daumier-Smith, he secures a job as an instructor in a Montreal correspondence art school, Les Amis Des Vieux Maitres, but it develops that he has only tossed himself into another family situation. The sole instructor-proprietors of the art school are Monsieur Yoshoto, a small man who barely speaks to the narrator, and Madame Yoshoto, taller and more attractive, who in-spires his affection and shows some concern about his wishes, asking him on two occasions if he would prefer an egg to the fish she serves. Furthermore, he occupies the room of the Yoshotos' absent son.

Before the appearance of the third father-figure, the narrator encounters by correspondence the force and the experience which will liberate him and resolve the problem of his psychological development. One of the pupils who falls to his lot is a Sister Irma of the Order of St. Joseph (still another father reference). Her painting technique is amateurish, but she has a remarkable talent.

De Daumier-Smith immediately falls in love with her; and it is this love for a sweet and good woman (she teaches art and cooking to classes of "kittys") that permits him to make the transition from the Oedipal phase of the story's beginning to the normal and nearly adult heterosexual plane of the story's end. He lies awake thinking of her: "I tried to visualize the day I would visit her at her convent. I saw her coming to meet me—near a high wire fence—a shy, beautiful girl of eighteen who had not yet taken her final vows and was still free to go out into the world with the Peter Abelard-type man of her choice." Since she is, despite the age he specifies, essentially a mother-image, he must minimize the sexual side of his feeling: "I saw us walking slowly, silently, toward a far, verdant part of the convent grounds, where suddenly, and without sin, I would put my arm around her waist."

De Daumier-Smith's wildly emotional letter to Sister Irma, a desperate attempt to communicate with another sensitive spirit, as well as a covert but transparent declaration of love, results in the withdrawal of Sister Irma from the art course. But it is not Sister Irma who severs the relationship; it is Father Zimmermann, who has already registered forcibly in de Daumier-Smith's mind in a connection that suggests castration, his name being that of the dentist who had pulled out eight of his teeth. This recollection is very close to the sketch de Daumier-Smith had done earlier, on an easel set between his and his stepfather's twin beds, which showed "a cavernous view of the mouth of a man being attended by his dentist. The man's tongue is a simple, U.S. Treasury hundred dollar bill, and the dentist is saying, sadly, in French, 'I think we can save the molar, but I'm afraid that tongue will have to come out.' It was an enormous favorite of mine." One may also note here another castration image set forth in a letter from the protagonist to Sister Irma: ". . . as I was coming into the Avenue Victor Hugo, which is a street in Paris, I bumped into a chap without any nose. I ask you to please consider that factor, in fact I beg you. It is quite pregnant with meaning." (The student of Salinger may also be reminded of the Laughing Man, the noseless monster originally created by Hugo in *L'Homme Qui Rit.*)

It is at this point that the reader may appreciate fully the richness of an earlier reference of de Daumier-Smith's. By calling himself a

"Peter Abelard-type man," the youth identifies himself both as what he would like to be—a popular academic teacher, a philosopher and a successful lover—and what his fantasies reveal him actually to be psychologically—a suffering castrate. Like Abelard with Eloise, further, he is a monk ("I live like an evil-minded monk," he writes Sister Irma) who falls in love with a pupil (Eloise entered a convent *after* the event) and who is punished for it by her protector, Irma's Father Zimmermann and Eloise's Canon Fulbert both being instruments of emasculation.

The resolution of all this chaos comes about when de Daumier-Smith, reacting against the loss of Sister Irma as a pupil, successively experiences the mystic's dark night of the soul and then an illumination. His concerns with religion, possibly quite as strong and demanding as those with sexual and psychological maturation, have already been indicated by his identification of himself as an agnostic acquainted with Buddhism, Roman Catholicism and Protestantism. His art school is directly above an orthopedic appliances shop (he is psychologically crippled as we first see him), and it is while gazing into the windows of the shop that he experiences both phases in his religious progress. In the first phase, his fantasy represents him as a nonbeliever witnessing the Crucifixion of Christ: "The thought was forced on me that no matter how coolly or sensibly or gracefully I might one day learn to live my life, I would always at best be a visitor in a garden of enamel urinals and bedpans, with a sightless, wooden dummy-deity standing by in a marked-down rupture truss." In the second phase ("my Experience"), a girl removing the truss from the dummy does a comic pratfall, but "Suddenly (and I say this, I believe, with all due self-consciousness), the sun came up and sped toward the bridge of my nose at the rate of ninety-three million miles a second. Blinded and very frightened—I had to put my hand on the glass to keep my balance. The thing lasted for no more than a few seconds. When I got my sight back, the girl had gone from the window, leaving behind her a shimmering field of exquisite, twice blessed enamel flowers." It is then that de Daumier-Smith, released by his love and his Experience, writes in his diary, "I am giving Sister Irma her freedom to follow her own destiny. Everybody is a nun." More than a statement of release, it is also a declaration of his own independence from the pure image he has subconsciously tried to preserve of his mother. The last sentence is, moreover, a profound if cryptic attempt to summarize the whole human condition: every human being, the boy seems to be saying, is cut off from others in one respect, yet has in him or her the possibility of spiritual achievement, and it is sin for another human being to jeopardize those possibilities by making purely personal demands on him or her.

Both the ending and the beginning of "De Daumier-Smith's Blue Period" affirm the fact of the narrator's belated maturation. For a nineteen-year-old, the normalcy of the pursuit that occupies him after his resignation from the staff of Les Amis Des Vieux Maitres is patent: "I packed up and joined Bobby, my stepfather, in Rhode Island, where I spent the next six or eight weeks, till art school reopened, investigating that most interesting of all summer-active animals, the American Girl in Shorts." Nor is this all. The very telling of the story (we are forcefully informed in its very first paragraph) is in itself a mature act demonstrating his release from jealousy of his stepfather. Bobby, says de Daumier-Smith, "was an adventurous, extremely magnetic, and generous man. (After having spent so many years laboriously begrudging him those picaresque [sic] adjectives, I feel it's a matter of life and death to get them in here.)"

The explication above does not by any means exhaust the subtleties and nuances of this ingenious story. The imagery that reinforces the basic theme is much more pervasive than indicated. For example, in contrast to Sister Irma and her work, de Daumier-Smith's other students and their efforts are completely secular and highly sexual. A young housewife with the pseudonym of Bambi Kramer has enclosed a photograph of herself in a strapless bathing suit and has submitted a picture of "three small boys fishing in an odd-looking body of water, one of their jackets draped over a 'No Fishing!' sign." Another student's submissions include one that "satirized the familiar, everyday tragedy of a chaste young girl, with below-shoulder-length blond hair and udder-sized breasts, being criminally assaulted in church, in the very shadow of the altar, by her minister. Both subjects' clothes were graphically in disarray." A completely nameless man sends a landscape dominated by "a forest of phallic symbols."

Another facet of this story is the subtlety with which it dramatizes the isolation suffered by de Daumier-Smith. The *cul de sacs* are Kafkaesque. We never learn the narrator's real name and he never learns the real names of three of his four students, one of whom is a woman with the name of a male deer. He has gone to Canada with a bogus identity and a false background to teach in a correspondence school bearing a French name and run by two Japanese, whose name is not even a legitimate Japanese cognomen. M. Yoshoto never responds to the protagonist's compulsive conversational attempts, and other efforts to bridge the gap are just as futile: after ingratiatingly revealing that he is a student of Buddhism, de Daumier-Smith learns that the Yoshotos are Presbyterians. Every night he hears "a high, thin, broken moan" from behind their wall. "I never did find out which of the Yoshotos it came from," he says, "let alone why." Laboring in the instructors' room of the Les Amis slum tenement, he is isolated from his students (all but Sister Irma) quite as much by their failure of sensitivity as by the physical distance that separates them. And when he releases Sister Irma with the words *"Tout le monde est une nonne,"* he means partly that everyone, in his aloneness, is like a nun cloistered from the normal contact of humanity.

Even the title bears on the progress from conflict to resolution in the tale. De Daumier-Smith, like the Picasso he claims to know as a family friend, proceeds through the Blue Period of melancholy concern with unfortunate *isolatoes*. But it is merely a period, and de Daumier-Smith, through Sister Irma, comes out of it to chase the American Girl in Shorts. As the story stands, it can hardly escape the label *tour de force*, but if only the protagonist were less precocious and the Yoshoto sequence less fantastic, the tale might take its place with "For Esmé," with love again resolving "squalor."

[From "Teddy" ("memorable and even inspirational") the authors turn to *Zen Buddhism and The Glass Menagerie*.]

With this concluding achievement in mind, the reader can go back and work on the epigraph to *Nine Stories:*

> We know the sound of two hands clapping.
> But what is the sound of one hand clapping?

To the merely literary, this might appear comic, possibly some echo of the Krishna ceremony in Forster's *A Passage to India*, where the Hindu Godbole lays down one cymbal so that he can adjust his pince-nez, while with the other cymbal he clashes the air. To the merely critical, the saying might stimulate symbolic application to the stories, with something made of the isolation, the "one hand clapping," of Seymour, Eloise and so many others. But students of comparative religion would recognize this as the most famous of the seventeen-hundred-odd koans of Zen Buddhism, those surrealistic unanswerable conundrums designed to stir up and readjust one's view of things. "Zen has always specialized in nonsense," Aldous Huxley puts it, "as a means of stimulating the mind to go forward to that which is beyond sense. . . ." A koan thus makes a perfect epigraph for a writer who wishes to entitle his book of nine stories *Nine Stories:* the reader has not to apply the quotation *to* the tales but simply to be thereby aware that the tales present problems which he may or may not solve for himself by supersensory perception.

Yet the background of the koans may be explored here a little more, since it provides a clue to what the characters in Salinger's most recent stories are in conflict with and what they are seeking. Zen Buddhism, even according to its adepts, is as impossible to define and describe as any transcendentalism. It is not a religion, not a philosophy, not an ethic and not even a psychology (though to a Westerner it certainly sounds like all these), but a Way, an attitude with intuitive spiritual enlightenment as its goal. ". . . Zen is above all an experience, nonverbal in character," says Alan Watts, "which is simply inaccessible to the purely literary and scholarly approach. To know what Zen is, and especially what it is not, there is no alternative but to practice it. . . ."

For readers of the Glass family saga, possibly the most helpful comments on Zen are two by its most famous explicator in the West, Professor Daisetz Suzuki of Columbia, whose work is said to have stimulated Salinger. (1) "The basic idea of Zen is to come in touch with the inner workings of our being, and to do this in the most direct way possible, without resorting to anything external or superadded." (2) "As I conceive it, Zen is the ultimate fact of all philosophy and religion. . . . Therefore Zen is not necessarily the fountain of Buddhist thought and life alone; it is very much alive also in Christianity, Mohammedanism, in Taoism, and even in positivistic Confucianism. . . . Zen is what makes the religious feeling run through its legitimate channel and what gives life to the intellect."

What Seymour, Zooey and Franny Glass seem to want to do is "to come in touch with the inner workings" of their beings, to achieve nonintellectual enlightenment—what Zen Buddhists call satori, "to be in a state of pure consciousness" (this is Buddy Glass quoting Dr. Suzuki) that "is to be with God before he said, Let there be light." With all religions at their fingertips, the Glass siblings utilize anything Zen-like, and it is their comparative success or failure in this enterprise that forms the basic conflicts of their stories. Furthermore, the farther away from this conflict a story gets, the more unsuccessful it is as a work of art.

[After explaining some of the Glass family relationships, Messrs. Gwynn and Blotner discuss "Raise High the Roof Beam, Carpenters," whose point they feel is obscured by a mass of detail and which resembles "an eye's investigation of itself in a mirror." On the other hand, "Franny" "works out quite well" and is, because of its relative brevity, "the best chapter in the Glass history." And so, on to "Zooey," which the authors consider the "longest and dullest" story ever to appear in *The New Yorker*.]

Any reader who gets through it and happens to turn back a hundred pages to the opening will agree heartily with the narrator (Buddy again) that the piece "isn't really a short story at all but a sort of prose home movie," and with "those who have seen the footage" who "have strongly advised me against nurturing any elaborate distribution plans for it." If Salinger is currently putting together a novel about the Glasses, one hopes that "Zooey" will undergo the same shaping consideration that the author gave to his first Caulfield family stories when he came to write *The Catcher in the Rye*.

For "Zooey" has eight undesignated parts to it—two or three of which might have served by themselves to advance the case history of Franny and/or the Glasses; as they stand, none is in happy proportion to one another or to the whole. Part 1 is a totally unnecessary first-person introduction by Buddy Glass, whose stylistic master is S. J. Perelman. Buddy then disappears as narrator, but Part 2, which describes Zooey and the Glass family in un-Perelmanian terms (including a long footnote) is merely a prelude to Part 3, which consists of "an almost endless-looking letter" from Buddy to Zooey on the third anniversary of Seymour's suicide. Zooey is sitting in the Glass bathtub reading the letter (which exhorts him to *Act with all your might*) years after it was written. (Could there be any significance in the fact that one of the links among these last three Salinger stories is the fact that in "Roof Beam" Buddy reads Seymour's diary in the bathroom, in "Zooey" Zooey reads Buddy's letter in the bathroom, and in "Franny" Franny reads *The Way of a Pilgrim* in a ladies' room? An answer might be that it signifies the family shyness carried to an extreme in Seymour's agoraphobia.) Part 4, also laid in the bathroom, is a prolix causerie between Zooey and his mother that serves only to characterize Zooey and his mother —something the classic Salinger could have done in a phrase (*e.g.*, "my wife, a breathtakingly level-headed girl," or "Poor Uncle Wiggily"). Part 5 at least gets Zooey out of the bathroom and into the living room, where he and Franny converse, also at length. This is where the story should have begun, for herein Franny and her arrogant brother touch on not only Franny's crisis but Zooey's, both of which, in terms of their education by Seymour and Buddy, could be described as the dark night of the soul. In Part 6, which also could have been condensed and utilized in a good story, Zooey cruelly lectures his sister on her having a wrong attitude to the Jesus Prayer: she is having "a tenth-rate nervous breakdown" because she is not really saying the prayer to Jesus but to herself, and "This is *God's* universe, buddy, not yours. . . ." But the basic conflict is once again interrupted by Part 7 while Zooey enters and examines the room formerly occupied by Seymour and Buddy; untenanted for seven years, it still contains Seymour's listed telephone. In Part 8 Zooey calls up Franny on this phone and pretends to be Buddy, but when exposed, reverts to his lecture on Franny's self-interest.

Here, however, he begins to make some sense, and in the conclusion—which the magazine reader may have suspected was coming only in a later issue—he neatly resolves the conflict of what could have been a good episode in Franny's spiritual progress. He reminds Franny of how Seymour used to make them shine their shoes before the radio quiz program. Why? For the Fat Lady out there, in the audience whose sordid life he left them to envision. All right; Franny is forgetting that the people whom she finds spiritually frustrating are all Seymour's Fat Lady. "There isn't anyone *any-where* that isn't Seymour's Fat Lady. Don't you know that? Don't you know that goddam secret yet? And don't you know—*listen* to me, now—*don't you know who that Fat Lady really is?* . . . Ah, buddy, Ah, buddy. It's Christ Himself. Christ Himself, buddy." The effect of Zooey's dramatic sincerity is to give Franny "joy" (*i.e.*, satori) and to allow her to fall into a deep sleep.

Salinger has said something morally profound here, but hardly aesthetically original. Zooey's first secret, that everyone is Seymour's Fat Lady, is merely a Broadway version of Christ's second commandment, already exemplarily embodied in Holden Caulfield: Thou shalt love thy neighbor as thyself. Something very much like his second secret has already served as the revelation ending the Blue Period of Jean de Daumier-Smith: "Everybody is a nun." Furthermore, the end of this saga is one Salinger had already brilliantly utilized for his best story: Esmé's gesture of love, like Zooey's, enabled Sergeant X, like Franny, to go to sleep, and "You take a really sleepy man, Esmé, and he *always* stands a chance of again becoming a man with all his fac—with all his f-a-c-u-l-t-i-e-s intact." For Salinger, it would seem, the dark night of the soul is not quite Scott Fitzgerald's three o'clock in the morning, but the symptom of its end is sleep.

Buddy quotes Fitzgerald's Nick Carraway at the beginning of "Zooey," going on to say that his own cardinal virtue is to "know the difference between a mystical story and a love story. I say that my current offering isn't a mystical story, or a religiously mystifying story, at all. *I* say that it's a compound, or multiple, love story, pure and complicated." And it is a multiple love story in the sense that several kinds of love—spiritual, universal, and familial (sexual love is notably absent in the Glass house) are discussed and occasionally displayed. But once again Salinger's fine eye for the insignificant detail has dissolved a promising multiple love story into the very "prose home movie" that Buddy also labels it. As a dramatic director, Buddy-Salinger is most often "a regular Belasco" (in Scott Fitzgerald's phrase), loading the stage with real snow for Setting, or bringing out Character according to the Contents-of-Small-Boy's-Pockets school—as with the lists of what Mother Glass's kimono pockets contain (ten items), what the Glass medicine cabinet contains (fifty-five items, plus "quite a good deal more"), what the Glass living room contains (more than four dozen items, not to mention eight titles of books in the bookcases), plus twelve quotations, given in full, out of the twenty-dozen odd inscribed on the door of Seymour's room. Indeed, the home movie is just what the masked Buddy describes his own letter to Zooey as being: "virtually endless in length, overwritten, teaching, repetitious, opinionated, remonstrative, condescending, embarrassing," even if it is also "filled, to a surfeit, with affection." As with "For Esmé," "there is love and squalor, but it is the verbiage rather than the human condition that is squalid here. . . ."

Admirers of this writer are, of course, entitled to worry a little. J. D. Salinger learned too long ago that everyone in the world is Seymour's Fat Lady, just as he learned and then forgot that an artist can make use of depth psychology without retailing every item of a case history. Whatever is going on right now with the Glass family evidences a curious aesthetic amnesia in the realm of these basic discoveries, and the sympathetic reader can only hope that all is not lost. Or he may find himself involuntarily crying out, in Zooey's accents: "Ah, buddy. Ah, buddy. Can't you get *off* this turntable? Fiction's a lot more than just *talk—you* know *that*. It's *action* and *conflict*, buddy. And you can turn 'em out *again*, buddy, with one of those hands tied behind your *back*. The *other* hand is the one that makes the *clapping* sound."

VI. The Cures for Banana Fever

These two related pieces by William Wiegand mark a sharp turn from the criticism presented in the preceding sections. He believes that the absence of a very clear social context in Salinger's work is not a fault but necessary for what the author is trying to do. Wiegand disagrees with the view of Holden and other Salinger characters as rebels against society, and sees that their troubles are within, not without. His diagnosis of "banana fever" for those inner troubles is perhaps a little forced, but he seems to come closer to the truth with it than a lot of other literary specialists. As he describes it, the disease has two symptoms: a kind of incapacity to purge one's emotions, and a chronic hypersensitivity or sense of loss. His clinical examination of where these symptoms come from, and the various cures Salinger tries on them, has the merit of flexibility. More than other critics, he sees that Salinger changes, experiments ("remedies come and go"), and that the change represents progress rather than regression. He is one of the few critics to say a kind word for the technique used in "Seymour," and also one of the few to note that Salinger's "cherishing" of the Glasses is by no means unchanging throughout. Ultimately, however, Wiegand may try to apply his banana fever diagnosis to more patients than seems quite reasonable. Werther's case is clearly recognizable; but with Tristan and Thomas Mann's characters, the disease surely deserves another name and requires, perhaps, a very different treatment.

THE KNIGHTHOOD
OF J. D. SALINGER

by WILLIAM WIEGAND

In his latest work of fiction, J. D. Salinger, speaking through a favorite narrator, makes the following observation about P. B. Shelley, a writer some one-hundred-odd years his senior: "I surely think," he says, "that if I were to ask the sixty-odd girls in my two Writing for Publication courses to quote a line, any line, from 'Ozymandias' or even just to tell what the poem is about, it is doubtful whether ten of them could do either, but I'd bet my unrisen tulips that some fifty of them could tell me that Shelley was all for free love and had one wife who wrote *Frankenstein*, and another who drowned herself."

Probably, it would be another safe bet, and one must assume Salinger knows it, that for every ten of Salinger's fans who know anything about the intellectual basis of Zen, a pet subject of his, or the contents of the Bhagavad-Gita, there are at least fifty who know that Holden Caulfield had to go to a psychiatrist ("it killed him, really it did"), and that Franny Glass wasn't pregnant after all. Salinger's Zen is to the faithful like Shelley's Platonism—vague and a little dry. But Holden and Franny—that's different. They are the author's kin, as much kin as Shelley's wives were to Shelley. Information about them is more than mere information; it is intimate lore. And discovering it has led naturally and indiscriminately to the quest for information about the paterfamilias, Salinger himself.

Nobody can fail to recognize that this rampant curiosity about the author—"lurid and partly lurid," Salinger calls it—is one of the most interesting aspects of his reputation. Just how intense the interest is may be hard to gauge, but if his experiences are anything like those of Buddy Glass, the writer through whom Salinger has written much in the last few years, the fifty are already beating a path to his door, planting tire tracks in his rose beds and asking him silly questions about "the endemic American *Zeitgeist*," just as they have done with Buddy.

This is remarkable devotion in a generation as cagey as the present one is supposed to be, and yet it might all be conceded to

Salinger gracefully enough (fads being what they are) if the body of Salinger's admirers was confined purely to that undergraduate group which sees that it can follow Holden Caulfield's nice line between colloquial earthiness and colloquial mysticism without feeling either too far In or too far Out. But the group is much larger than that, and some people, outside it, have wondered why. About the only explanation Salinger has offered, as he no doubt recalls all the bad imitations of Holden Caulfield, is Buddy Glass's crack, "I have been knighted for my heart-shaped prose."

Going beyond that answer, certain critics, like Maxwell Geismar and John Aldridge, have tried to explain Salinger's appeal by examining some of his favorite themes. Geismar calls Salinger "the spokesman of the Ivy League Rebellion of the early fifties." "Ivy League" means to Geismar that it is a rebellion founded mostly on a dislike for the fancy prep-school phony who abounds in *Catcher in the Rye* and Salinger's other fiction. For Geismar, and for Aldridge too, the rebellion never quite transcends this adolescent pique at wrong guys and boring teachers. The sympathy of the undergraduate with Salinger can, by this line of reasoning, be reduced to the fact that he doesn't like his roommate any better than Holden does and that he may also share Holden's wish for deafness, or Teddy's wish for death and reincarnation in a quieter world where nobody, for God's sake, is lecturing at him on Western civilization three of four mornings a week. For Geismar and Aldridge, the "rebellion," thus interpreted, seems irresponsible and "adolescent."

It is hard to argue with their opinion, except to observe that the derogation of "adolescent" has also been applied at different times to Goethe, Schiller, Sterne, Byron, Shelley, Keats, Fitzgerald, Wolfe, Hemingway and others. The trouble with such a reduction is that it tends to cancel out Geismar's equally interesting opinion that Salinger is "the ultimate artist of the *New Yorker* school of writing," a compliment which ought to have some bearing on our question. Beyond that, their assessment does not do much about telling why the "lurid or partly lurid" curiosity that has always distinguished the interest in Shelley turns today to somebody like Salinger rather than to other writers who are concerned with adolescent and preadolescent characters.

Salinger's subject matter is not unique, nor are his positions quite as intelligible as the talk about rebellion would indicate. He has undercut almost every position he has taken, so much so lately that to call him the spokesman for anything seems bold. Probably, if we could find the True Blue Salingerite, that ideal reader who would remain stanchly superior to any *ad hoc* image of Salinger, he would be no more addicted to rebellion than he would be to Zen. He would, I think, be likely to say that he is interested in Salinger for no better reason than that Salinger's characters are so uncomfortably alive that one has a kind of irrational desire to keep after them and see if something can't be worked out. If pressed, he might guess further that Salinger made them uncomfortable quite deliberately, and that there is an apparently conscious development toward isolating and then enlarging upon the discomforts of the people he is writing about.

This may be put in terms of two propositions; first, that Salinger is offering something different, something presumably more provocative than other writers of his "school"—certainly a good reason for popularity. And, second, that he becomes increasingly interesting to follow because he has changed (and is changing) his own methods after a conscious pattern.

The first proposition is fairly easy to demonstrate. Compare any of Salinger's stories—they all deal more or less with the indigestible past—and the work of most of the other writers of Reminiscence fiction in *The New Yorker* and the little quarterlies. The difference is in the half-embarrassed attitude of Salinger's characters ("I did something very stupid and embarrassing." "Why do I go on like this?" "I'm a madman, really I am.") This is a bit more than a trademark; the writers of conventional Reminiscence avoid any tinge of self-consciousness like the plague. While they may be just as jealous of their hunting caps and crocus-yellow neckties as Holden Caulfield and Buddy Glass are, they make it all sound blithely natural and healthy. Where Salinger lurks off in the shadow of his banana tree, they plant themselves under a spreading chestnut, anyway something more solid and less sickly green. They may experience the same reaction against Today, the same cherishing of Yesterday, but seldom see any implications in so much nostalgia.

The second proposition may be a little subtler. All writers develop in some fashion or other, but Salinger's development has been especially interesting. As with a singer who evolves a style slowly, much of the pleasure of the audience comes from knowing the stages in his growth.

Salinger's method has depended all along on a close personal touch with the reader, the shy advance and retreat, and candor about making mistakes, and the tacit assurance that his defenses will be seen through; but in its most recent manifestation it feels for the reader's very heartbeat, tries to catch every flicker of interest or disaffection. By reaching for this kind of communion, it must promise, above all, candor in the difficult writer-reader relationship. Many readers find this concern for staying honest with them particularly appealing; they truly believe (and why not?) that Salinger is trying to get at a more intimate and accurate vision of things than if he took one of the short cuts of form where truths become so facile that they seem more like lies.

Why can this be regarded as a "development"? Because in Salinger's early work, even the best, there was the tendency to take these short cuts, to slide through by means of an easy symbol or two, to settle for one of the standard explanations, or appearances of explanation. There, Salinger was criticizing a formulated and formulable society, and his writing derived from some wing of the proletarian tradition in which the gulf between the "lover" and the corrupted bourgeoisie causes most of the suffering of the protagonist.

But after *Catcher in the Rye*, an impulse which was latent in the early work began to assert itself. It was an impulse to deal cautiously, but exclusively, with the emotional graph of a single personality: no moments of sudden truth to give the nice terminal epiphany, but rather a series of tentative illuminations, which confess, explicitly and implicitly, the speaker's lack of any all-encompassing revelation. In "Teddy" and "Franny," the strain of having to contrive a well-made story had started to show, and afterward Salinger began his experiment with the longer novella. His distrust of what he calls "beginning-middle-end" fiction stemmed then most probably from his awareness of the easy facility not only of the work of others, but of his own. ("Pretty

Mouth and Green My Eyes" may have seemed terse and calculable; "A Perfect Day for Bananafish" almost too tidily abtruse.) When Salinger returns to Seymour Glass in the middle fifties in order to do him right, Buddy Glass, Seymour's brother, is moved in to afford a kind of analysis that completely rejects conventional structural formula. Also, in the course of the three most recent stories, the social context in which Seymour moved has been largely forsaken.

At the same time, Salinger has found new ways to keep the reader oriented. While he violates most of the rules of the well-made story as well as the usually sacrosanct convention of self-effacement of the author, he still retains certain organizing principles. In "Seymour: An Introduction," the device is one familiar in lyric poetry. As the poets have catalogued the charms of their ladies, in "Seymour" Buddy takes up one at a time the pertinent characteristics and activities of his brother. A rather droll solution, it nevertheless provides a goal for the story; namely, to make the reader feel Seymour less as a saint and more as a human being. If I pull myself together, Buddy says, Seymour who has killed himself may yet be reconstructed—his eyes, his nose, his ears may rematerialize, even his words may be heard without the echo of the tomb. He is not a dead saint, Buddy tells us, and we don't want to think of him as ectoplasm; hence, a tormenting effort to describe his features, his clothes, his poems—anything to make him imperishable.

One by one, the items are ticked off. The poems may be the most embarrassing part of it; they are the hope held in reserve, the means of making Seymour immortal. They are the magic elixir which Buddy keeps half-concealed in the pocket of his coat. He does not really trust the elixir's effectiveness, so he rationalizes his failure to have had the poems published. The reader may not like them, so he advertises their merits in advance. The English departments may not like them so he prepares to deny their denials of Seymour's immortality.

The consequences of this method are considerable, for in the course of the story, Buddy becomes almost indistinguishable from Seymour. Buddy himself notices this. The object-observed has become the observer. All the air has been pumped out of the bell jar, time and space continuums are sacrificed, and Buddy and Seymour react so intuitively to each other that there is no reverberation. Consequently, the description of the relationship is so great an effort that Buddy breaks into a cold sweat or sinks to the floor, or falls ill for weeks in the torture of trying to present a report without any of the ordinary points of reference or means of control.

The objective of the story then in a manner fails. If Seymour in fever was in danger of becoming a saint, Buddy, who identifies too much, has no better luck avoiding the same impression of Seymour in health. No longer the bananafish, Seymour is here metamorphosed into a "curlew sandpiper." He is faster than the Fastest Runner in the World; he makes his profoundest observations in the twilight. He is ephemeral, and no matter how many homely anecdotes are told about him, he has grown too diffuse to look at in the daytime; his talents have become supernatural. Only reincarnation ("and here the first blushes will be the reader's, not mine") could bring him down to earth again, and Buddy knows it, knowing the agonizing failure of his heart-shaped prose to do the job.

To use the word "failure" about the story itself is, however, probably almost meaningless to the true Salingerite, for there is a great difference between a failure of purpose ("Does the writer accomplish what he set out to do?") and a failure of effect. In the tradition in which Salinger is now writing, effect is attained not through achieving any goal, any resolution, but rather by getting the effort toward the goal down on the page. However vague that may seem as a criterion, the technical equipment required to meet it with intelligence, integrity and variety is great. Salinger has submitted to the challenge with particular rigor in the last three stories where the dramatic action in the present has grown increasingly less, and in "Seymour" becomes almost totally expressed in the drama of the individual consciousness, anchored by incidental reports of Buddy's getting up, going to class, getting sick. The past is funneled through by means of letters and personal journals, but remains a part of the struggle of the present.

Corollary to this, it has been important for his enduring appeal that Salinger's narrative procedure has not been associative or "stream of consciousness," a conventional modern reaction against overrigid form. His syntax is sophisticated and lucid, and in spite of the destruction of the time continuum, he proposes his objectives and makes his digressions (if we want a fictional forebear) with an aplomb like Sterne's, whose techniques those of "Seymour" perhaps most resemble.

Compare, for example, this from *Tristram Shandy*:

> . . . It is one comfort at least to me that I lost some four-score ounces of blood this week in a most uncritical fever which attacked me at the beginning of this chapter; so that I still have some hope remaining, it may be in the serious or globular parts of the blood and in the subtle aura of the brain. . . .

with Salinger's:

> . . . I'm really not up to anything that *intime* just here. (I'm keeping especially close tabs on myself, in fact. It seems to me that this composition has never been in more danger than right now of taking on precisely the informality of underwear.) I've announced a major delay between paragraphs by way of informing the reader that I'm just freshly risen from nine weeks in bed with acute hepatitis. . . .

There are dangers in this kind of writing. Sometimes it verges on whimsy, and certainly it can lead to cultishness, as it did with Sterne or with Byron and Shelley, all of whom on occasions got *intime* with their readers. Also, and particularly with temperaments like Salinger's, it may depend too much on wit to relieve and to steady it. When the humor shows signs of exhaustion and despair, as Byron's and Sterne's did at times, as Salinger's does in "Seymour," the writer may be in trouble.

The body of Salinger's work has been an exploration chiefly of the problem of loss and mutability, free from theories about how a solution may be found. Inasmuch as poets have largely lost interest in such quests since about the time of Tennyson's *In Memoriam* and that it has made few real inroads into English or American fiction (unlike French and German) since Tennyson, the Salinger vogue is not surprising. It answers a need for a different kind of treatment of experience.

When Buddy Glass asks, "How can I record what I've just recorded and still be happy?" he doesn't answer the question. But there are hints that he is happy with his persistence, and that many of his readers who are up to anything *intime* are happy with it too.

SEVENTY-EIGHT BANANAS

In simple terms, Salinger's heroes are a family of nonconformists, and Salinger documents their brotherhood by presenting several of them as brothers and sisters in "Franny," "Raise High the Roof Beam, Carpenters," and "Zooey." However, this is not traditional nonconformity. Logically, the enemy of the nonconformist is society or some oppressive segment of society; and in the recent tradition from Sinclair Lewis' Arrowsmith and Hemingway's Frederick Henry right down to Ayn Rand's Howard Roark, the nonconformist hero is constantly threatened by external forces which seek to inhibit and to destroy him. With the Salinger hero, however, the conflict is never so cleanly drawn. Holden does not leave the fencing team's foils on the subway because of any direct external pressure, nor does he flunk out of Pencey and the other schools because of unreasonable demands made on him. Holden knows this as well as anybody. He is a victim not so much of society as of his own spiritual illness.

Salinger has spent much of his career seeking a cure for this illness; however, before we examine that search, we need a somewhat more precise definition of the illness. Perhaps it is best described in "Raise High the Roof Beam, Carpenters," a work which amplifies and explains the first of the Nine Stories, "A Perfect Day for Bananafish." The earlier story describes the last few hours in the life of Seymour Glass and is a brief, impersonally told and slightly obscure work. The later story, seven or eight times as long, tells of Seymour's wedding day some years before his death. Its main scene is a long interlude in a taxicab in which Seymour is discussed by several interested parties, including his brother Buddy. It concludes with sections from Seymour's personal journal, material designed to explain why he leaves his bride at the altar, and to suggest why he kills himself after several years of marriage. Without "Carpenters" the suicide which closes "Bananafish" appears motivated chiefly by Seymour's inability to put up with his bourgeois wife. With "Carpenters," however, we see Seymour as a man not deprived of, but rather surfeited with, the joy of life. Salinger's sole excuse for Seymour's desperate social irresponsibility is this same curious surfeit of sensation.

We learn, for example, in the course of "Carpenters," that Seymour does not show up for his wedding because he is too "happy," or as he puts it in his journal, he is "too keyed up . . . to be with people." The nature of this happiness is further illuminated through the use of a boyhood experience of Seymour's: at the age of twelve he threw a stone at a young girl, scarring her for life. Seymour's brother, the narrator, explains the incident this way:

> We were up at the Lake. Seymour had written to Charlotte, inviting her to come and visit us, and her mother finally let her. What happened was, she sat down in the middle of our drive-way one morning to pet Boo Boo's cat, and Seymour threw a stone at her. He was twelve. That's all there was to it. He threw it at her because she looked so beautiful sitting there in the middle of the driveway with Boo Boo's cat. Everybody knew that, for God's sake—me, Charlotte, Boo Boo, Waker, Walt, the whole family.

Seymour's own understanding of his malady is a more poetic one. He writes in his journal:

> If or when I do start going to an analyst, I hope to God he has the foresight to let a dermatologist sit in on the consultation. A hand specialist. I have scars on my hands from touching certain people. Once, in the park, when Franny was still in the carriage, I put my hand on the downy pate of her head and left it there too long. Another time, at Loew's Seventy-second Street, with Zooey during a spooky movie. He was about six or seven, and he went under the seat to avoid watching a scary scene. I put my hand on his head. Certain heads, certain colors and textures of human hair leave permanent marks on me. Other things too. Charlotte once ran away from me, outside the studio, and I grabbed her dress to stop her, to keep her near me. A yellow cotton dress I loved because it was too long for her. I still have a lemon-yellow mark on the palm of my right hand. Oh, God, if I'm anything by a clinical name, I'm a kind of paranoiac in reverse. I suspect people of plotting to make me happy.

The "skin disease" which Seymour sees himself afflicted with in 1942 apparently becomes worse. By 1948, the date of his suicide, the "lemon-yellow marks" have attained weight and shape; he has become mortally ill.

During the course of his interlude with the little girl on the beach in "A Perfect Day for Bananafish," he says to her:

> "You just keep your eyes open for any bananafish. This is a perfect day for bananafish."
> "I don't see any," Sibyl said.
> "That's understandable. Their habits are very peculiar. . . . They lead a very tragic life. . . . You know what they do, Sibyl?"
> She shook her head.
> "Well, they swim into a hole where there's a lot of bananas. They're very ordinary-looking fish when they swim *in*. But once they get in, they behave like pigs. Why I've known some banana-fish to swim into a banana hole and eat as many as seventy-eight bananas. . . . Naturally after that they're so fat they can't get out of the hole again. Can't fit through the door."
> . . . "What happens to them?"
> . . . "Well, I hate to tell you, Sibyl. They die."
> "Why?" asked Sibyl.
> "Well, they get banana fever. It's a terrible disease."

In other words, Seymour, a bananafish himself, has become so glutted with sensation that he cannot swim out into society again. It is his own banana fever, not his wife who is at fault, or his mother-in-law. If they are stupid and insensitive, "Carpenters" shows them also to be without malice, and hence basically as in-culpable for the bananafish's condition as is the Matron of Honor, who represents the whole level-headed society in criticizing Seymour for his peccadilloes.

In general, the bananafish diagnosis applies to all the Salinger invalids. Holden Caulfield's trouble, for example, is not that he hates, or that he fears, or, as Aldridge suggests, that he has no goals —but rather that he has no capacity to purge his sensations. He is blown up like a balloon, or like a bananafish, with his memories. He says at the very end of the novel: "About all I know is, I sort of *miss* everybody I told about. Even old Stradlater and Ackley, for instance. I think I even miss that goddam Maurice. It's funny. . . ." Thus, with the good things he remembers like Allie, his dead brother, and like Jane, the girl who kept her kings in the back row, he retains the bad things as well—until nothing is either good or bad after a point, but simply retained and cherished as a part of himself, submerging him with the sheer weight of the accumulated burden.

The important word in the passage quoted above is "miss." What is unbearable is not that some people are bad, but that experience is fleeting. Everything must be retained. The image Holden has for himself of being "the catcher in the rye" is the perfect metaphor for this objective. He wants to guard the children from falling off the edge of the rye field; likewise he tries to guard each experience from falling into oblivion. With this perspective he fails to discriminate between "important" and "unimportant" experiences to determine which to retain and which to reject—and the bananafish becomes the more bloated and uncomfortable. The "perfect day" is the day when the bananafish is able to end all his suffering by killing himself.

In going back, we find the bananafish in embryo even in Salinger's very early stories. Most of those which appeared in the *Saturday Evening Post* and *Collier's* during the war years are rather standard pieces about GI's which the magazines were full of then. But what is distinctive about them perhaps is a particular undertone of very imminent tragedy: the moment imperiled by what is to come. Even the glimpses of life we get away from the front are fraught with a fragile sense of impermanence. Everything is in a state of flux. There is no arrested moment.

The hero of three of these stories is John (Babe) Gladwaller. For the most part, Babe is a Hemingway soldier who suffers in silence. Occasionally, however, there are clues of self-torment in the character, traits which are to become the hallmark of the Salinger heroes in the late stories. In "The Last Day of the Last Furlough," Babe speaks of a girl he loves. "The more unrequited my love for her becomes" (he says) "the longer I love her, the oftener I whip out my dumb heart like crazy X-Ray pictures, the greater the urge to trace the bruises."

"The Stranger" closes with Babe's little sister jumping off the curb into the street as Babe walks beside her. "Why was it such a beautiful thing to see?" he asks, as if with an urge to fight the feeling for its very largeness. In *Catcher*, the same situation is echoed in Phoebe's carousel ride. Holden says of it, "I felt so damn happy all of a sudden, the way old Phoebe kept going around and around. I was damn near bawling, I felt so damn happy, if you want to know the truth. I don't know why. It was just that she looked so damn *nice*, the way she kept going around and around, in her blue coat and all. God, I wish you could've been there."

The Babe Gladwaller stories therefore foreshadow what is to become the chief concern in Salinger's fiction, but they remain unfocused. The war is still an irrelevant part of them—irrelevant because it was too easy to blame the war for the hero's state of mind, when probably Babe Gladwaller had an incipient case of banana fever. It took Salinger some years to define Babe's feelings as a disease, to recognize, in other words, that so-called normal people were not affected with these strange symptoms of chronic hypersensitivity and sense of loss.

With the publication of his stories in *The New Yorker*, beginning with "A Perfect Day for Bananafish," he makes his first inroads into understanding. In "Bananafish," his awareness that his hero is "diseased" is still intuitive, I think. Although the "bananafish" metaphor is brilliant in itself, the insight is somewhat neutralized by Salinger's apparent blame of the wife and the mother-in-law for Seymour's suicide. The two women are, at any rate, mercilessly satirized in the telephone conversation through the mother-in-law's constant interruption of the impassioned discussion of Seymour's perilous mental health with questions like "How's your blue coat?" and "How's your ballerina?" As a result, Seymour seems as clear a victim of an external force, namely, the bourgeois matriarchy, as Babe Gladwaller was of "the war." When the important bananafish symbol arrives later in the story, it is impossible to do much with it. There is no demonstrated connection between society's insensitivity and Seymour's zaniness.

The problem recurs in the next story, "Uncle Wiggily in Connecticut," but not without growing evidence that Salinger is ready to resist the easy answer that the bourgeoisie and/or the war is responsible for the bananafish's condition. Here, for example, it is quite clear that it is Eloise Wengler's tormenting memories of her lost lover, Walter, that make her unable to swim out of the cave into her proper place in Exurbia. Although "the war" is a factor in her despair, since her lover is killed in it, he dies not in battle but in an "absurd" camp accident; likewise, her militantly bourgeois husband may contribute to her unhappiness, but she is allowed to repay him in kind. No mere victim of society, Eloise is a bitch, not only with her husband, but with her daughter and her maid as well. She takes the revenges of an invalid.

This story contains the first clear explanation of banana fever: it is the sense of what is missing that causes the suffering. Here, the lover's death brings the loss. Death, of course, is the most primitive way of making loss concrete; it is the villain of the war stories and it is still the villain here. In "Uncle Wiggily," however, we have Salinger's first sign of awareness that this sense of loss ought to be overcome; the first sign, in other words, that remembering too much is a bad thing. Eloise, for example, resents her daughter's habit of inventing invisible playmates, Mickey Mickeranno and Jimmy Jimmereeno, to take to bed with her at night. Unconsciously, Eloise knows that Walter, her lost lover, is as invisible as Ramona's boyfriends. She forces Ramona to move into the middle of the bed to prevent her daughter from lying with an invisible lover as she has had to lie with one in the years since Walter's death. She knows the consequences: her bitchiness.

These "consequences" show that Salinger was not yet willing to settle completely for a story about somebody with banana fever. In the war, he learned that actions not only had social causes but also social consequences, so he must indicate that Eloise's unhappiness affects others. In this way he absolved himself from having written an isolated, clinical report about one of the hypersensitive.

After "Uncle Wiggily," the desire to blame somebody or something generally vanishes. No longer was the evil out there somewhere; rather it was a microbe within us. We were not oppressed; we were sick.

The stories of Salinger's middle period, from "Uncle Wiggily" to "Franny," are stories of the search for relief. Having evidently rejected impulsive suicide as a cure ("A Perfect Day for Bananafish") and having seen the futility of trying to forget ("Uncle Wiggily in Connecticut"), Salinger alternately considered the following remedies: sublimation in art ("The Laughing Man"), the bare-faced denial of pain ("Pretty Mouth and Green My Eyes"), the love and understanding of parents ("Down at the Dinghy"), the love and understanding of children ("For Esmé" and *The Catcher in the Rye*), psychiatry (*The Catcher in the Rye*), a mystic vision ("De Daumier-Smith's Blue Period"), a mystic faith ("Teddy") and a mystic slogan ("Franny"). It is interesting to note that each of the remedies seems to furnish at least a temporary restoration of balance for the protagonist.

In "For Esmé—with Love and Squalor" we have an interesting development in the record of the bananafish: Salinger allows himself his first *explicit* statement of what is wrong with his heroes. Actually, he allows Dostoevsky to make the statement for him: "Dear God, life is hell. . . . Fathers and Teachers, I ponder 'What is hell?' I maintain that it is the suffering of being unable to love." Although Dostoevsky's lament probably does not accurately describe Sergeant X's condition, nor that of Salinger's other heroes for that matter, most of whom love too much, still the God that the sergeant requires is clearly a God of redemption, not of justice. What the bananafish needed was to be saved; where justice lay was no longer certain.

This can be seen even more sharply in *The Catcher in the Rye,* which appeared shortly after "Esmé" but which had taken ten years to complete. It is possible to trace how Holden's need for redemption grew in these years. The bright Holden-Phoebe relationship, for example, was undoubtedly conceived early. Not only does it follow closely the Babe-Mattie relationship of the Gladwaller stories, but the framework of the first bedroom scene between Holden and Phoebe appears in an early *Collier's* story called "I'm Crazy," in which Holden Caulfield is first introduced as a character. Later, part of the skating rink episode with Sally appeared in *The New Yorker*. In these early versions, it is hard to see Holden as much more than brash and irrepressible. *The Catcher* makes him both a kinder and a sicker person, no longer just a boy but with half his hair gray. The final chapter in the rest home, as well as the long and important scene with Mr. Antolini, must have been written late in the ten years.

In Antolini, the bananafish faces the demand for an agonizing judgment. Antolini has represented for Holden the last bastion of

F

moral conscience; that is, Holden has called on Antolini in this crucial moment in his progress because Antolini "finally picked up that boy that jumped out of the window. . . . He didn't even give a damn if his coat got all bloody." This is a moral value to Holden. Also, Antolini shares Holden's sentiments about D. B.'s sellout to Hollywood. When Holden arrives at Antolini's, however, he finds his teacher half high and obviously married to a woman he does not love. Holden is bored with him and disappointed in him. His disappointment increases to revulsion when he awakens during the night to find Antolini "petting me or patting me on the goddam head." Terrified, he leaves at once. But the next morning, in thinking it over, he says, ". . . I wondered if just maybe I was wrong about thinking he was making a flitty pass at me. I wondered if maybe he just liked to pat guys on the head when they're asleep. I mean how can you tell about that stuff for sure? You can't."

What Holden refuses to do, in effect, is to make an ultimate judgment on Mr. Antolini. The result is that the bananafish, having abandoned the emotional outlet of condemnation, grows more and more frustrated, a consequence of the acceptance of a purely aesthetic frame of reference (*i.e.*, "This seems ugly to me" or "This seems beautiful to me"). Note Holden's plaintive comment on Phoebe's last carousel ride: "It was just that she looked so damn *nice* going around and around in her blue coat and all." No absolute value can be assigned.

The stories published since *The Catcher in the Rye* ("De Daumier-Smith's Blue Period," "Teddy," "Franny," "Raise High the Roof Beam, Carpenters" and "Zooey") explore a solution for the bananafish, first in terms of union with God, and finally in terms of reunion with society.

The stories demonstrate that although the bananafish is incapacitated by the weight of his experience, he is also afflicted with a psychological conflict between the desire to participate in and the need to withdraw from society. He is a nonconformist, but a paralyzed one, unlike Arrowsmith, for example, who was moving full-tilt toward a private goal, or Huckleberry Finn, who was making his precipitate escape away from society, unwilling to be captured. The Salinger hero, on the other hand, is carried along in the currents of his own psyche, neither toward nor away from anything. He drifts in a course more or less parallel to that of society, alternately tempted and repelled, half inclined to participate, and half inclined to withdraw.

In "De Daumier-Smith's Blue Period," the miracle regeneration of "For Esmé" recurs, this time in terms of a frankly mystical Experience. Salinger himself, only half ironically, uses the capital "E" to describe it, perhaps to indicate that it takes a momentary union with God in order to achieve a real insight into a man's relationship with his fellows.

The reconciliation to the idea of participation without illusion is pushed to fantastic new extremes in "Teddy," in some ways Salinger's most unexpected story. In "Teddy," reconciliation becomes Oriental resignation. The transition from the personal mysticism to the formal Eastern self-immolation which Teddy practices does not occur, however, without certain schizophrenic symptoms in both the form of the story and in its main character. It is the only one of Salinger's stories that is utterly incredible, and yet he goes to his usual pains to document its reality.

What Teddy, this ten-year-old Buddha, has achieved in Salinger's bargain with the East is, of course, invulnerability, the persistent wish of all bananafish. The knowledge that de Daumier-Smith comes to by hard Experience, Teddy is granted early through mystic revelation. He then withdraws, as all great religious figures have, to be better able to participate. In Teddy's case, he removes himself from the boorish concerns of a society represented by his father and sister in order that he may be invulnerable to the malice of his father and sister, and be able to do good in return. He writes in his diary, for example: "See if you can find daddy's army dog tags and wear them whenever possible. It won't kill you and he will like it."

The publication of "Franny" revived the dilemma of participation or withdrawal. Here, the Zen Buddhist material is not as well integrated on a story level as in "Teddy," since Franny merely wishes to believe in a way of living the validity of which Teddy has had satisfactory mystic revelation. But because the tension is more psychological in "Franny," and because God is sought this side of oblivion, it is a more touching story.

In the main scene in the restaurant with her boyfriend, Franny is graphically split between the desire to withdraw and the need to participate. She has arrived to spend the weekend with Lane, already apprehensive that she will find the kind of insensitivity she has found in him many times before. She would like to be the good-time girl that Lane wants, but this time she cannot bear his egocentricity, his counterfeit participation in the world. She retreats to the stall in the ladies' room to weep for him and for all the others, one presumes, who, like Lane, are devoted to the Flaubertian view of society, that mean focus on personal vanity, which so offends Franny. Franny, a bananafish, sees all the beautiful possibilities instead, and she suffers for it. She tries to communicate with him again, finally withdraws once more and falls insensible to the ground. Her courage, however, has touched something in the boy at last. After her final collapse, he is kind to her, half understanding, but she ends making her final whispered appeal to God.

Pity for the bananafish ends with "Franny." The functions of Salinger's two more recent stories, both long, didactic and largely unsymmetrical, is to restore the stature of the bananafish. In "Raise High the Roof Beam, Carpenters," he removes the shame from the disease by showing Seymour Glass as a superior man. In "Zooey," he shows that reconciliation with society is possible if the bananafish, with courage, practices the act of Christian love.

"Raise High the Roof Beam, Carpenters" affirms the bananafish in spite of the fact that the reader knows that Seymour Glass is to end as Teddy did, embracing death. Its very title, first of all, is a paean for the bridegroom, a singularly appropriate symbol for all the Salinger heroes, who are young people, people uninitiated, unconsummated, unassimilated. The story thus is a celebration of experiences, rather than a dirge for them. Moreover, it celebrates for the first time the sensitivity of the hero, marking perhaps a final surrender of the author's identification with the hero and a beginning of appreciation for him. If Seymour is a sick man, he is also a big man, and that becomes an important thing here.

While the story explains the suicide of Seymour in "Bananafish," it also makes that suicide seem a little irrelevant. It is Seymour's life, his unique way of looking at things that concerns Salinger here, and although he is obliged to mention the subsequent death of Seymour early in the story, he refers to it simply as "death," rather than suicide. For a change, the remark seems incidental, rather than a calculated understatement, the device Salinger consistently uses when he talks about what touches him particularly.

Concerned with Seymour's life rather than his death, Salinger is at last able to expose the bananafish here. Banana fever no longer seems the shame that it did in "Pretty Mouth," "The Laughing Man," "For Esmé" and in "A Perfect Day for Bananafish" itself, where Seymour can express himself only to a little girl, and ambiguously at that. The secretly prying eyes of others he is unable to bear. Witness the curious scene on the elevator when he accuses a woman in the car of staring at his feet. This happens less than a minute before he puts a bullet through his head.

In "Raise High the Roof Beam, Carpenters," the frank advocacy of Seymour enables Salinger to transcend the limits of the tight pseudo-poetic structure which hamstrings so much of modern short fiction. Because the story is partisan, it must be analytic as well as metaphoric. No longer deceived into thinking his characters are prey to simple grief or to bourgeois insensitivity, rather than to beauty, he is able to expose them at last. The loosening of form, which begins with "Esmé," culminates with Seymour's throwing the stone at Charlotte, the affirmation of the effort for expression and communication even at the expense of exposure and pain.

Finally, it takes Zooey, in the story which bears his name, to communicate the new awareness and to act upon it. The redeeming union with the divine is the same as union with society, Zooey believes. If Buddy remains unreconstructable, Zooey, the youngest Glass son, comes to recognize that to be a deaf-mute in a high silk hat or a catcher in the rye is not the privilege of many.

Essentially, Zooey is a man of action. Appropriately enough, his profession is acting. Although he does not care much for a great deal of the world, he participates in it. He performs in television scripts which he detests; he meets people for lunch he does not like; he argues with his mother; he challenges his sister; he even dares to deface the shrine of the long-dead Seymour. In none of these things is he remotely self-immolating or contemplative, in the manner of Teddy; in none of them does he seek an "affinity." It is suggested that it is because Zooey alone among the Glasses has "forgiven"

Seymour for his suicide that he is enabled to take a more involving and distinctly Western view of society. Zooey's final advice to his sister Franny, who has had aspirations to the stage, is: "The only thing you can do now, the only *religi*ous thing you can do, is *act*. Act for God, if you want to—be *God's* actress, if you want to. What could be prettier? You can at least try to, if you want to—there's nothing wrong in *trying*."

Action then is the remedy here, and although remedies come and go in Salinger, it is perhaps most important because when action becomes an end in itself, it becomes possible to distinguish again between the deed and the doer. Zooey remonstrates with Franny about it: ". . . what I don't like—and what I don't think either Seymour or Buddy would like *eith*er, as a matter of fact— is the way you talk about all these people. I mean you just don't despise what they represent—you despise them. It's too damn personal, Franny. I mean it." Zooey's aim is to recognize that principles exist by which men live; and that without action, things are neither good nor bad. Principles vanish. The bananafish's mind is full of still photographs; action thaws these photographs; action again makes judgments possible. It forestalls the rapt contemplation of moments that have no meaning to others and which tend to isolate each individual in his own picture gallery. To transcend the particular for the sake of the general is to overcome the paralyzed moment for the sake of the principle which animates it.

Although this is a new step for Salinger, one must observe that throughout the story, he keeps Buddy's opinion in abeyance. In the speech quoted above, Zooey suggests that Buddy and Seymour agree with him about the distinction between the deed and the doer. But the shadow of Buddy and Seymour would suggest otherwise. Zooey's consent to participate is as much rebellion from as it is practice of the way of life of his older brothers. As a matter of cold fact, principles have always gotten in the way for the bananafish because principles, ideas, systems are too far away from life as the bananafish lives it. That is why every participation in the social system has turned out to be counterfeit in the end.

Where Salinger fits in the mainstream of American fiction remains uncertain. As I have noted earlier, his is not what is ordinarily termed social fiction, except insofar as all novels and short stories must concern themselves with the fabric of human relations. The "disease" which I have discussed at length is innate, not social, and society's reaction to it hardly affects its virulence. If anything, society is a palliative force. Occasionally, a hero like de Daumier-Smith becomes infected with the health of society. For those who remain in the sanitarium, the remedies are many, but the truly sick seldom recover. Like Camille, they cough their way through their eternal confinement—not brave, but sometimes witty invalids, hating the disease that Salinger has diagnosed, even as Fitzgerald had diagnosed Gatsby's.

Call the disease Illusion or Delusion, Salinger stands, in regard to the nature of his insight, as close to Fitzgerald as he does to any American author. Both are concerned with the effect of the immaculate moment on men. These moments are so complete in themselves that better balanced heroes could assimilate them as the minor aesthetic experiences which the "well adjusted" know them to be. Fitzgerald has always emphasized the ideational attraction. That the response of Gatsby to Daisy, of Avery to Rosalind, of Dick Diver to Nicole, and of Anthony West to Gloria is hardly sexual at all has been generally recognized. Attraction arises out of a conceptual ideal that some men have, the kind that Goethe's Werther had over a century earlier, and that Salinger's heroes were to have a generation later.

Salinger, in resisting the dominant trend of determinism in American fiction during the last fifty years, has simply succeeded a little better than Fitzgerald in isolating the hero's response by keeping the "passion" as remote from sexual connotation as possible. Where the object of delight is found in women, these women are often little girls or nuns, and what is admired is sexless in essence, some capacity for charity or candor, sensitivity or simplicity. Fitzgerald's heroes, on the other hand, usually confused glamour with beauty. To this extent, they were far more conditioned by a particular social climate than Salinger's are. If, however, they mistook Duessa for Una more often than not, it was not because they were especially at fault, but because the ideal had been corrupted by the *Zeitgeist*. One is compelled to feel that Fitzgerald would have been as sympathetic to Gatsby as Goethe was to Werner and as Salinger is to Seymour Glass if only Daisy Buchanan had been less obviously phony.

Fitzgerald moralizes because Daisy is a social by-product. Salinger, in his best work, does not, because he sees that the terrible fascination with other human beings is apart from any good-ness or bad-ness in society as a whole or in particular individuals. This attitude places him at a little distance from Fitzgerald, and, of course, at a great distance from other American writers who have handled "fatal fascination" with traditional Puritanism, assuming that what was fascinating was necessarily either voluptuous or evil or both. Authors from Hawthorne and Poe all the way down to Faulkner are victims of this fallacy, but Salinger is not.

For this reason, Goethe's Werther (whom Salinger himself mentions in "A Girl I Knew") seems to be a more likely forebear of the bananafish than anybody in our own literature. Werther was distracted by what was fair. Plain enough. So was Tristan. And in modern German fiction, so is Thomas Mann's Aschenbach in *Death in Venice*. In each case, there is an effort to aestheticize the passion, that is, to idealize its object, to see it perhaps for the purposes of the story as the hero sees it. This is Romantic, of course, and with the concomitant additions of irony, peculiarly German-Romantic— a habit of mind which many regard as archaically self-indulgent.

A part of Thomas Mann's subject matter—disease and the non-conformist, as treated in *Death in Venice, Tonio Kröger, Little Herr Friedemann*, and in much of *The Magic Mountain* and *Buddenbrooks*—is the whole of Salinger's. Both explore the non-conformist's ambivalent attitudes toward bourgeois society. Stylistically both write with wit, with a gift for the well-turned phrase and lack of timorousness about didacticism. Allowing that Salinger has neither the intellect nor the creative energy of Mann, it seems reasonable to suppose he could benefit from the security of a form and a tradition more sympathetic to his genius than our own: for all his fidelity to the native idiom and the native scene, Salinger, like his characters, is himself hardly more than a "visitor in this garden of enamel urinals."

VII. Sensitive Outsider *vs.* Vulgarian

The essay that fills this section is, on the whole, densely and forbiddingly written, and makes a formidable, almost painful effort to follow Salinger's flights with the heavy tools of scholarly analysis. But it will repay careful reading, because it also contains many observations made with unusual grace and clarity. Hassan's description of the typical Salinger conflict as taking place between the "sensitive outsider" and the "vulgarian" sounds sociological, but it is not; Hassan knows that Salinger is "too loving and particular" for sociology. The fact that he detects "self-hate" in the Glasses is interesting in view of the fact that so many other critics see only self-love. And in pointing to the strain that exists between loathing phonies and trying to love them, between denouncing sham and calling no man Fool, Hassan manages to avoid using the word "dichotomy," surely a notable achievement.

Finally, any Salinger fan will want to put certain quotations from this essay on his door, among them:

"The retreat to childhood is not simply an escape,"

and

"The right kind of emotional excess nowadays can be as effective as the sharpest irony."

THE RARE QUIXOTIC GESTURE

by IHAB HASSAN

> Through our own recovered innocence we discern the innocence of our neighbors.
>
> —THOREAU

> We know the sound of two hands clapping. But what is the sound of one hand clapping?
>
> —A ZEN KOAN

Salinger has written some of the best fiction of our time. His voice is genuine, new and startlingly uneven. In his work we find no showy or covert gesture in the direction of Symbolism or Naturalism, Gothic design or Freudian chiaroscuro; and indeed there was a time when we were unsure whether his intentions came closer to those of Fielding or Firbank, Twain or Chekhov. If close to anything, Salinger's intentions are probably more in keeping with Fitzgerald's idea of self-created innocence and Lardner's biting renderings of corruption, with the spiritual assumptions of Martin Buber, and, more recently, with those of primitive Christianity and Zen. Yet to speak of his uniqueness in these terms is simply to indulge in the small talk of criticism. We are more anxious, nowadays, to discover the opportunities of literary significance, the conditions of heresy and protocols of formal excellence. We question *Kitsch* and middle-brow art to the extent that we consume it in prodigious quantities, and are adversely disposed to any serious work that carries the aura of either. It is in response to this line of criticism that the work of Salinger proves itself to be seriously engaged by a current and a traditional aspect of reality in America.

The traditional aspect wears no elaborate disguise. It is the new look of the American Dream, specifically dramatized by the encounter between a vision of innocence and the reality of guilt, between the forms love and power have tended to assume in America. The natural focus of that conflict in the work of Salinger is childhood and adolescence. In them the counterplay of hope and despair, truth and mendacity, participation and withdrawal, commands a full range of comic, that is ambivalent, reference: it is the old story of the self against the world in outlines blurred by a mass society. To say as Fiedler does that the "images of childhood and adolescence haunt our greatest works as an unintended symbolic confession of the inadequacy we sense but cannot remedy" is to view a profound truth in a partial perspective. Nostalgia is the result of our compulsion to re-enact the story of the American fall. We do not always resist it well. But nostalgia, when it is known to itself, has its ironic and artistic uses. The retreat to childhood is not simply an escape; it is also a criticism, an affirmation of values which, for better or worse, we still cherish; and the need for adolescent disaffiliation, the refusal of initiation, expresses the need to reconceive American reality.

Yet it is hard for some critics to recognize that no act of denial in Salinger's work is without some dramatic and social correlative, which is more than we can generally say of equally serious novelists writing today. The urban, suburban and exurban society which circumscribes Salinger's child and adolescent characters—the white dinner, not black leather, jacket circle—is usually well specified. About that society we have recently learned a good deal. We know that it exhibits a sad decay of genuine sensibility and even of simple truth. There are, no doubt, many opportunities of significant action still left in it, and we are justified in requesting our best writers to discover them. But the nature of action is such that its results are seldom commensurate with its motives. And the reverse is no less true. The anger of a child confronted for the first time with the force of anti-Semitism, the spirit of an adolescent who dons a red hunting cap in New York City, the tender cruelty of a woman, who is bereaved of her lover, toward her child, even the suicide of a misfit genius, can suggest possibilities of action which we hastily reject in favor of a mechanical gesture at the polling booth. Social realities are no doubt repressed in the work of Salinger—note how gingerly he handles his Jews—and this puts a limit on the total significance we can accord to it. Yet it is by what an author manages to *dramatize* that we must finally judge him.

The dramatic conflict which so many of Salinger's stories present obviously does not lend itself to sociological classification. It is more loving and particular, and it partakes of situations that have been traditionally available to literature. The conflict, however, suggests a certain polarity between what might be called, with all

due exaggeration, the Assertive Vulgarian and the Responsive Outsider. Both types recur with sufficient frequency to warrant the distinction, and their interplay defines much that is most central to
Salinger's fiction. The Vulgarian, who carries the burden of squalor,
stands for all that is crude, venal, self-absorbed and sequacious in
our culture. He has no access to knowledge or feeling or beauty,
which makes him all the more invulnerable, and his relationship
to the world is largely predicated by Buber's I-It dyad. He or she
can be rich or poor: Evelyn Cooney in "Elaine," Mrs. Ford and
the Croftses in "The Inverted Forest," Sandra and Mrs. Snell in
"Down at the Dinghy," Joanie in "Pretty Mouth and Green My Eyes,"
the Matron of Honor in "Raise High the Roof Beam, Carpenters,"
Maurice, Stradlater, or any number of others in *The Catcher in the
Rye*. These, in a sense, are Spiritual Tramps, as Seymour called
his wife in "A Perfect Day for Bananafish," though he might have
better said it of her mother. The Outsider, on the other hand, carries
the burden of love. The burden makes of him sometimes a victim,
and sometimes a scapegoat saint. His life is like "a great inverted
forest/with all foliage underground." It is a quick, generous and
responsive life, somehow preserved against hardness and corruption,
and always attempting to reach out from its isolation in accordance
with Buber's I-Thou dyad. Often there is something in the situation
of the Outsider to isolate him, to set him off, however slightly, from
the rest of mankind. He might be a child or an adolescent, might
wear glasses or appear disfigured, might be Jewish, though seldom
is he as crippled or exotic as the characters of Capote and McCullers often are. His ultimate defense, as Rilke, to whom Salinger
refers, put it, is defenselessness. Raymond Ford, Boo Boo Tannenbaum (Glass) and her son, Lionel, Seymour and other members
of the Glass family, Holden and Phoebe, in the previous stories, are
examples of that type.

The response of these outsiders and victims to the dull or angry
world about them is not simply one of withdrawal: it often takes
the form of a strange, quixotic gesture. The gesture, one feels sure,
is the bright metaphor of Salinger's sensibility, the center from
which meaning drives, and ultimately the reach of his commitment
to past innocence and current guilt. It is a gesture at once of pure
expression and of expectation, of protest and prayer, of aesthetic

form and spiritual content—as Blackmur would say, it is behavior that sings. There is often something prodigal and spontaneous about it, something humorous or whimsical, something that disrupts our habits of gray acquiescence and revives our faith in the willingness of the human spirit. But above all, it gives of itself as only a *religious* gesture can. In another age, Cervantes endowed Don Quixote with the capacity to perform it, and so did Twain and Fitzgerald endow their best creations. For the gesture, after all, has an unmistakably American flourish. The quest of American adolescents has always been for an idea of truth. It is this very idea of truth that the quixotic gesture is constantly seeking to embody. The embodiment is style in action: the twist and tang, the stammering and improvisations, the glint and humor of Salinger's language. Hence the examples of the deserted husband who memorizes his wife's farewell note backward, the woman who, out of pity, starts smacking her husband at the sight of any dead animal, the man about to commit suicide who makes up a story about bananafish for a little girl, the lover who calls the sprained ankle of his sweetheart Uncle Wiggily, the young man who insists on giving half a chicken sandwich to a stranger, the college girl who trains herself to pray incessantly and does so in the toilet of a restaurant, and the bridegroom who is too happy to appear at his wedding. Out of context these may well sound trite or crazy; in their proper place they are nodes of dramatic significance.

But gesture is language too. The quixotic gesture, the central dramatic metaphor, to which Salinger has committed himself defines the limits of his language and the forms his fiction takes. When the gesture aspires to pure religious expression—this is one pole—language reaches into silence. To a writer of fiction, this is a holy dead end, much as the experiments of Mallarmé, say, impose a profane—that is, aesthetic—limit on the language of poetry. (One of the "Four Statements" of Zen, we recall, is: "No dependence upon words and letters.") When, on the other hand, the gesture reveals its purely satiric content—this is the other pole—language begins to lapse into sentimentality. This is the most persistent charge leveled against Salinger. Salinger's "sentimentality," however, is not obedient to the *New Yorker* doctrine of sardonic tenderness, which is really a way of grudging life emotions that the writer feigns to indulge. But if sentimentality means a response more generous than the situation seems objectively to warrant, then Salinger may choose to plead guilty. And he would be right to do so, for the spiritual facts of our situation invite us to reconceive our notions of dramatic objectivity, and the right kind of emotional excess, nowadays, can be as effective as the sharpest irony.

Between the poles of silence and sentiment, language reels and totters. Salinger's cumbersome experiments with character, tense and point of view in his most recent stories betray his efforts to discover a language which can reconcile the wordless impulse of love to the discursive irony of squalor. In the past, while the quixotic gesture could still convey the force of his vision, reconciliation took the shape of the short story, that genre so richly exploited by the single lyric impulse seeking embodiment in dramatic form. But the quixotic motif seems no longer commensurate with the complex spiritual states by which Salinger has lately been possessed. Language must be refracted into its components—speech, letters, diaries, etc.—and the form of the short story itself must be broken and expanded into something that is neither a short story proper nor yet a novelette. In this development, the risks Salinger has taken with his art are contained in the risks he must take with his religious view of things.

In the two decades which constitute Salinger's professional career, he has published one novel, three novelettes and some thirty short stories. This fair-sized body of work—fair-sized by contemporary standards but slim in comparison with the output of many earlier writers—may be classified into four "periods": the early tentative efforts, up to "The Inverted Forest," 1947; the fine stories which appeared in *The New Yorker* and were later included in the collection *Nine Stories*, 1953; *The Catcher in the Rye*, 1951; and finally the more recent narratives, beginning with "De Daumier-Smith's Blue Period," 1953, which express a new religious bent. Since the focus of our inquiry is the American novel, it is natural that the longer works of Salinger must receive our greatest attention. Salinger, however, is the kind of writer who returns to favored themes and characters with some consistency. *The Catcher in the Rye* was in fact developed from six earlier stories in which the two

Caulfield brothers, Vincent and Holden, appear; and the central sibling relation between Holden and Phoebe is prefigured by the relation of Babe Gladwaller to his sister, Mattie. There is also the hope some critics entertain that the Glass family stories—all seven of them and perhaps more to come—will be someday transmuted by a miracle of chance or art into a novel. Finally, one must defer to the opinion Salinger expressed of himself, even though it was expressed in 1945: "I've been writing short stories since I was fifteen. I have trouble writing simply and naturally. . . . I am a dash man and not a miler, and it is probable that I will never write a novel." It seems therefore an act of necessity rather than piety to consider Salinger's longer works in the light of his shorter pieces.

The earliest stories of Salinger appeared, for the most part, in magazines to which we refer as slicks, though four of these were also published in the now defunct *Story*. The majority of these pieces make an uneasy lot, and some are downright embarrassing —it is gratifying to find that Salinger has excluded them all from his collection. One recalls Matthiessen's comment: "In the years just before, and now after, the war, there has been a special importance in the little magazine for the experimental writer who found that what he had to say did not fit in the mode of the slick magazines. . . . It was often an acute conflict between the outer and the inner, which came to expression not in a sustained form but in a short story." Narratives like "Elaine" and "The Long Debut of Lois Taggett," which center on female protagonists and possess a certain quickness of perception which other stories of Salinger's early period lack, reflect the conflict of which Matthiessen speaks. More often the conflict is translated into the situation of wartime America—"The Last Day of the Last Furlough," "A Boy in France," "The Stranger," "The Hang of It," etc. But the war is treated blandly —there is nothing here comparable, say, to the urgency of John Horne Burns—and the form which the stories assume is only remotely experimental. What we do sense, however, is Salinger's awareness of *craft*, of a structure that owes much less to Kipling than to Lardner, who may have directed Salinger's interest in the first-person point of view, the diary and letter devices, the uses of irony and slang. And we sense, too, the gradual assertion of a dramatic theme—the quixotic gesture, in "Soft-Boiled Sergeant," the predicament of the sensitive outsider in "The Varioni Brothers."

It is, of course, the outsider theme which figures largely in "The Inverted Forest," tagged by *Cosmopolitan* as a short novel. The piece is at best terrifying, at worst awkward, and its style vacillates between glamour and doom. The story unfolds ponderously; the introduction, midway, of a narrator who sees the action both in the first and third person seems like the intrusion of a Nick Carraway gone slightly schizophrenic. Yet the piece strikes with the impact of an old theme given a new Freudian wrench. Raymond Ford, the poet genius, once under the domination of his unspeakably coarse mother, grows up only to throw over marital love and self-respect for a woman every bit as offensive as his parent. The Oedipal surrender is complete, the regression almost savage. But what Thomas Mann presented, in *Tonio Kröger,* as the metaphysical attraction of health and normality for the artist is here rendered as the pathological submission of the outsider to the vulgarian. The symbols of submission are Ford's renunciation of his glasses, the result of long, devoted study, and his practice of eye exercises to suit the taste of his mistress. Without love or irony, Ford bows to squalor.

The second phase of Salinger's career includes at least three stories which are among the very best he has written: "Uncle Wiggily in Connecticut," "Down at the Dinghy," and "For Esmé—with Love and Squalor." This phase also marks the level of his most sustained achievement. The cellophane transparency and geometric outlines of the earlier pieces give way to a constant energy of perception and irritation of the moral sense. Here, in a world which has forfeited its access to the simple truth, we are put on to the primary fact of mendacity. Here, where the sources of love are frozen and responsiveness can only survive in clownish attire, we are jolted by the Zen epigraph: "We know the sound of two hands clapping. But what is the sound of one hand clapping?" (Buber, who did much to introduce Zen to the West, suggests another parable of love: "There is no *I* taken in itself, but only the *I* of the primary word *I-Thou* and the *I* of the primary word *I-It.*") Here, too, are three of the Glass stories.

In "A Perfect Day for Bananafish," the taste of life's corruption is so strong in the mouth of Seymour Glass, and the burden of self-alienation, even from his wife, Muriel, is so heavy, that suicide seems to him the only cleansing act possible. While Muriel is engaged in a drab and vindictive long-distance conversation with her mother, for whom the mere name of a fashionable analyst is insurance against all the ills and mysteries of the universe, Seymour entertains a little girl at their hotel beach, whose foot he has just kissed:

Sybil released her foot. "Did you read 'Little Black Sambo'?" she said.

"It's very funny you ask me that," he said. "It so happens I just finished reading it last night." He reached down and took back Sybil's hand. "What did you think of it?" he asked her.

"Did the tigers run all around that tree?"

"I thought they'd never stop. I never saw so many tigers."

"There were only six," Sybil said.

"*Only* six!" said the young man. "Do you call that *only*?"

"Do you like wax?" Sybil asked.

"Do I like what?" asked the young man.

"Wax."

"Very much. Don't you?"

Sybil nodded. "Do you like olives?" she asked.

The contrast between the monstrous and psychotic Seymour, as seen by his mother-in-law—she is genuinely worried about her daughter—in the first half of the story, and Seymour with Sybil at the beach makes the silent ironic statement of the piece. Yet even Sybil cannot prevent the world, ruthless as it is with the power of spiritual vulgarity, from collecting its toll. One feels, however, that the story needs the background of the later Glass family narratives to give Seymour's suicide its full reference.

If Seymour Glass, like Raymond Ford, concedes the victory to the world much too easily, Walt Glass and Eloise, in "Uncle Wiggily," do not. The plight of Eloise, who survived the tender and imaginative Walt to lead a conventional married life in Connecticut, is clear. The hysteria of Eloise focuses on her lonely and sensitive daughter, Ramona, who *could* be the illegitimate child of Walt, and is certainly the living reminder of the vision Eloise has compromised and the innocence she has lost. Again the contrasts between the embittered and knowing Eloise and her inane visitor, Mary Jane, between Walt, the dead lover, and Lew, the oafish husband, serve to heighten the inability of the self to reveal itself to another. All that is left to Eloise by way of recognition is the spontaneous and quixotic gesture of kissing the glasses of Ramona, whom she has bullied into conformity and disillusionment. In another story, "The Laughing Man," the end of Innocence is more obviously compounded with the end to Romance, and the pressure of adult on boyhood disenchantment is rendered particularly effective by the use of a narrator who, like Lardner's narrators, serves to elicit from the situation more irony than he intends. The narrator recollects a crucial experience of his childhood in which the primary figures are John Gedsudski, nicknamed the Chief by the admiring boys who are his charges in the Comanche Club, and Mary Hudson, a girl from a more sophisticated background. The Chief tells the boys of the Comanche Club a serial and fantastic story about the Laughing Man, who is really an idealized projection of himself. When the love affair between John and Mary fails, the Laughing Man dies. Here the story of the fabulous Laughing Man is itself the quixotic gesture which has the power to influence the youthful audience of boys, including the narrator of Salinger's story, but is powerless to save Gedsudski himself.

Wistful as these stories may appear, Salinger's ideas of innocence and romance, of the urgency of truth and readiness of imagination, take on a broad social meaning. The stories present in poignant, ironic and roundabout ways the radical absence of communion; they define the scope of our guilt. (It is this helpless sense of *shame* that pieces like "Just Before the War with the Eskimos" and "Pretty Mouth and Green My Eyes" dramatize so fastidiously.)

The easy, efficient gestures of social amenities, which usually conceal an abyss of human failure, are not even present in "Down at the Dinghy." Quite simply, the story is that of sensitive, four-year-old Lionel Tannenbaum, who hears the housemaid, Sandra, denounce his father as a "big sloppy kike." Lionel does not fully understand the opprobrium of the term, but the tones and inflections of hate are unmistakable. He runs away to hide the shame and fear in a dinghy, from which his wise mother, nee Boo Boo Glass, attempts to rescue him back to a troubled world:

"Well, that isn't *too* terrible," Boo Boo said, holding him between the two vises of her arms and legs. "That isn't the *worst* that could happen." She gently bit the rim of the boy's ear. "Do you know what a kike is, baby?"

Lionel was either unwilling or unable to speak up at once. At any rate, he waited till the hiccupping aftermath of his tears had subsided a little. Then his answer was delivered, muffled but intelligible, into the warmth of Boo Boo's neck. "It's one of those things that go up in the *air*," he said. "With *string* you hold."

The ignorance of Lionel is as consonant with the immediate requirements of the story as it is with Salinger's larger intentions. Here as elsewhere, what Salinger has undertaken to discover is that old, ironic discrepancy between illusion and reality. But in an age of mass reactions and semantic instability, the distance between illusion and reality must increase to the extent that the opportunities of self-deception are multiplied. In these circumstances, the child becomes both the dramatic analogue and corrective to our modes of awareness, both the victim and savior of our squalor. His lack of experience is at once parallel and antithetical to our blind immersion in experience and his natural sagacity is the corrective to our practiced insensibility. It is much as if Salinger meant innocence to be, in our particular situation, the redemption of our ignorance. And it is perhaps only by the grace of something like the tender playfulness which Boo Boo exhibits toward her outraged son that we can recapture the sense of reality, beyond ignorance, beyond innocence. We concede this ungrudgingly, and in conceding still ask: is this all that so gifted an author can do with the deep-down complexity of a Jew's fate in our culture?

The mode of irony, shield of Perseus against the Medusa face of our time, qualifies the elegiac motive of Salinger's stories. But even irony must exhaust its resources, and a time must come for love to show its face in the noonday light. To the unabashed lyricism of "For Esmé—with Love and Squalor," one can only respond joyously. The story is a modern epithalamium, written on the occasion of

Esmé's wedding. The narrator, who carries his autobiographical burden sprightly and high, recollects the time he was a sergeant stationed with the invasion forces in England. On a rainy afternoon he wanders into a church, and is struck by the angelic voice of Esmé, a girl singing in a choir. Later, he meets her, escorted by a governess and a younger brother, in a tearoom. She rescues him from boredom and loneliness by her wonderful gifts of pertness and sensibility—precocity, which is the concession adults make to the understanding of children, is not the point of the story. The young lady—for she has a title—promises to write him, and in return asks him to write for her a story of squalor. Sometime afterward, we see him at the front, in the third person, suffering from an acute case of battle fatigue. The intolerable Clay, an eternal vulgarian, is his only companion. Squalor, real and tangible like the dust of death, has settled all about him—until he finds a battered package from Esmé, in which she has quixotically enclosed her dead father's watch. The narrator can finally fall asleep, for he knows that hell, which Dostoevsky defined as the suffering of being unable to love, has been kept in abeyance for another day. The inscription a German Nazi woman had scrawled on Goebbels' *Die Zeit Ohne Beispiel*, "Dear God, life is hell," is superseded by the statement of Father Zossima which the narrator appends to it. The horrendous social fact of our century and the outstanding spiritual motive of the age—genocide and love—are united in the history of a single American soldier, Staff Sergeant X. Thus the style of personal encounter in the first half of the story redeems the waste and anonymity of the second half. Thus may love overreach squalor as only love can, and the sound of two hands clapping may be heard the world around.

The Catcher in the Rye inevitably stands out as Salinger's only novel to date. As a "neo-picaresque," the book shows itself to be concerned far less with the education or initiation of an adolescent than with a dramatic exposure of the manner in which ideals are denied access to our lives and of the modes which mendacity assumes in our urban culture. The moving, even stabbing, qualities of the novel derive, to some extent, from Salinger's refusal to adopt a satirical stance. The work, instead, confirms the saving grace of vulnerability; its protest, debunking and indictments presuppose a willing responsiveness on the part of its hero.

On the surface, Holden Caulfield is Salinger's typical quixotic hero in search, once again, of the simple truth. Actually, Holden is in flight from mendacity rather than in search of truth, and his sensitivity to the failures of the world is compounded with his self-disgust. In comparison with his dear, dead brother, Allie, a kind of redheaded saint who united intelligence and compassion as no other member of the family could, setting for all a standard of performance which they try to recapture, Holden seems intolerant, perhaps even harsh. The controlling mood of the novel—and it is so consistent as to be a principle of unity—is one of acute depression always on the point of breaking loose. But despair and depression are kept, throughout, in check by Holden's remarkable lack of self-interest, a quality of self-heedlessness which is nearly saintly, and by his capacity to invoke his adolescent imagination, to "horse around," when he is most likely to go to pot. These contrary pressures keep the actions of the novel in tension and keep the theme of sentimental disenchantment on the stretch; and they are sustained by a style of versatile humor.

The action begins at a prep school from which Holden has flunked out, and continues in various parts of Manhattan; it covers some three days of the Christmas season. The big city, decked out in holiday splendor and gaudiness, is nevertheless unprepared for Holden's naked vision, and it seldom yields any occasions of peace, charity or even genuine merriment. From the moment Holden leaves Pencey behind, leaves its Stradlaters and Ackleys, its oafs, creeps and hypocrites, and dons his red hunting cap—why not, it's a mad world, isn't it?—we know that we are on to an adventure of pure self-expression, if not self-discovery.

In New York, it is once again the same story of creeps and hypocrites revealed in larger perspective. We hardly need to recapitulate the crowded incidents of the novel to see that Holden is motivated by a compelling desire to commune and communicate, a desire constantly thwarted by the phoniness, indifference and vulgarity that surround him. He resents the conditions which force upon him the burden of rejection. In protest against these conditions, he has devised a curious game of play-acting, of harmless and gratuitous lying, which is his way of coming to terms with a blistered sensibility, and of affirming his values of truth and imagination. But above all, he is continually performing the quixotic gesture. Thus he socks Stradlater, who is twice his weight, because he suspects the latter of having seduced Jane Gallagher, without any consideration of the fact that she is the kind of girl to keep all her kings, at checkers, in the back row. He gives money away to nuns. He can read a child's notebook all day and night. He furiously rubs out obscenities from the walls of schools. And when Phoebe asks him very seriously what he would like to be, he muses on Robert Burns's song, "If a body meet a body coming through the rye," which he had heard a kid hum in the street, and answers back: ". . . I keep picturing all these little kids playing some game in this big field of rye and all. Thousands of little kids, and nobody's around—nobody big, I mean—except me. And I'm standing on the edge of some crazy cliff. . . . That's all I'd do all day. I'd just be the catcher in the rye and all. I know it's crazy. . . ."

A closer look at *The Catcher in the Rye* might allow us to separate its real from its imaginary failings. Mr. Aldridge, for instance, taking his cue perhaps from Phoebe's comment to her brother, "You don't like *any*thing that's happening," has recently observed—Maxwell Geismar makes exactly the same point—that Holden "has objects for his contempt but no objects other than his sister for his love." It is true that Holden has *more* objects for his contempt than his love—this is the expense of his idealism and the price of his rebellion. But it is impossible to overlook his various degrees of affection for Allie, his dead brother, for James Castle, the boy who was killed because he wouldn't retract a statement he thought true, for the kettle drummer at Radio City, the nuns at the lunch counter, the kid humming the title song, or even the ducks in the park, without missing something of Holden's principal commitments. And his answer to Phoebe, "People never think anything is anything *really*. I'm getting goddam sick of it," may do for those who find these commitments rather slim. Nor can we disallow the feeling of pity which often modifies Holden's scorn, his pity for Ackley and the girls in the Lavender Room, or his confession to Antolini that he can hate people only part of the time, and that he quickly misses those whom he may have once hated. Holden, of course, is not in the least cynical; nor is he blind except to part of the truth which he can otherwise entertain so steadily. Still, there are those who feel that the novel accords no recognition to its hero, and that it fails to enlist our sense of tragedy. The lack of recognition, the avoidance of conversion and initiation, is almost as inherent in the structure of the novel as it is consonant with the bias of the American novel of adolescence. The action of the book is recollected by Holden, who is out West recuperating from his illness, and Holden only chooses to tell us "about this madman stuff that happened to me around last Christmas"—nothing more. He refuses to relate incidents to his past or to his character, and he refuses to draw any conclusions from his experience: "If you want to know the truth, I don't *know* what I think about it. . . . About all I know is, I sort of *miss* everybody I told about. Even old Stradlater and Ackley, for instance. . . . Don't ever tell anybody anything. If you do, you start missing everybody." This is an embarrassed testament of love, full of unresolved ambiguities, the only lyrical and undramatic recognition the novel can afford. The partial blindness of Holden, which has been correctly attributed to Holden's juvenile impatience with the reality of compromise, is made more serious by Salinger's failure to modify Holden's point of view by any other. In *Joseph Andrews,* for instance, the innocence of Adams is constantly criticized by the tone of the book and the nature of its comic incidents. There is also some danger that we may be too easily disarmed by the confessional candor of Salinger's novel. When Holden says time and time again, "I swear to God I'm crazy," the danger is equally great in taking Holden at his word as in totally discounting his claim. Holden does succeed in making us perceive that the world is crazy, but his vision is also a function of his own adolescent instability, and the vision, we must admit, is more narrow and biased than that of Huck Finn, Parson Adams, or Don Quixote. It is this narrowness that limits the comic effects of the work. Funny it is without any doubt, and in a fashion that has been long absent from American fiction. But we must recall that true comedy is informed by the spirit of compromise, not intransigence. Huck Finn and Augie March are both, in this sense, closer to the assumptions of comedy than Holden Caulfield. This once understood, we can see how *The Catcher in the Rye* is *both* a funny and terrifying work—

traditional distinctions of modes have broken down in our time—a work full of pathos in the original sense of the word. But suffering is a subjective thing, and the novel's sly insistence on suffering makes it a more subjective work than the two novels which relate the adventures of Huck Finn and Augie March. Adventure is precisely what Holden does not endure; his sallies into the world are feigned; his sacrificial burden, carried with whimsy and sardonic defiance, determines his fate. The fate is that of the American rebel-victim.

The view that Salinger's most recent work predicts something of a new trend is vaguely supported by the troubled, spiritualistic bent which the latest six narratives share. The content of these stories invites some comparison with the ideals of Mahayana Buddhism and primitive Christianity, and also invites the condemnation of those who feel that "mysticism" is out of place in literature. The trend, nevertheless, is a natural outcome of Salinger's earlier interests. For it is not difficult to imagine how protestant disaffiliation may lead to holy unattachment, and how mysticism may appear, beyond childhood or adolescence, the last resort of innocence. If love is to survive in a world where personal communication has signally failed, then it can at least survive in universal compassion: love betrayed into dumbness may still speak in silence. Such an argument, however, makes the best of a dubious case. All writers may not succeed, like Carlyle, in extolling the virtue of silence through twenty volumes. And one suspects that Chekhov spoke for all artists when he said that he who doesn't desire anything, doesn't hope for anything, and isn't afraid of anything cannot be an artist.

It is perhaps as impertinent to inquire into Salinger's personal convictions as it is profitless to reconsider, at this time, the relation between literature and beliefs. The pointed references to Buddhism which he has recently made are best viewed in a more general way. Two of the cardinal assumptions in Salinger's work find expression in the Buddhist ideas of tanha, or blind self-demandingness, and of moksha, a state of liberation achieved by the kind of impersonal compassion which "The Parable of the Mustard Seed" exemplifies. In Mahayana Buddhism particularly, a religion of the Middle Way which avoids the excesses of worldliness and asceticism, the characters of Salinger seem to find a gentle and practical ideal against which their actions may be gauged. The ideal is matter-of-fact rather than mystical, and its emphasis in the Zen Buddhist variant, to which Salinger refers most directly, is on effortless and continuous love, on the superrational insights of the koan exercises, on the poetic concreteness of haiku, on the virtues of silence and on the unmediated vision of nature. For Zen is essentially a condition of being in which, without losing our identity, we are at one with the universe, and it requires, as does haiku poetry, a certain harmony between our imaginative and spiritual responsiveness to all things. It becomes evident that these qualities of Zen define some of the interest which Salinger has constantly kept at heart, and that Zen itself, in Salinger's work, makes up to an odd way of criticizing contemporary failures. As William Barrett has observed in his introduction to the writings of D. T. Suzuki, the Radical Intuitionism of Zen may allow the West to experience its own opposite at a critical stage of its moral, scientific and historical development. "In this new climate," Barrett continues, "a concern with something like Zen Buddhism can no longer be taxed as idle exoticism, for it has to do with the practical daily bread of the spirit."

Art, unfortunately, sometimes falls short of the best spiritual intentions. This is evident in the two narratives which usher Salinger's "religious phase" in. "Teddy," the story of the strange boy who believes in Vedantic incarnation and detachment, and who vaguely foresees his death, is much less satisfactory because it draws on notions that are alien to the West than because it fails to relate, within the dramatic structure of its narrative, the egoism of Teddy's parents and the ambiguous malice of his sister to the peculiar source of his own repose. There is also in "Teddy," and much more in "De Daumier-Smith's Blue Period," an uneasy juxtaposition of aesthetic and spiritual motives which are sometimes blurred and sometimes too simply resolved. In the latter story, the central character recollects, in manhood, the guiding revelation of his adolescence. On the surface, the revelation takes a quasi-mystical form. De Daumier-Smith discovers that art is less important than the sacramental view of life, which can itself transform, better than the creative imagination, the objects of ugliness and misery—the enameled urinals and bedpans of an orthopedic appliance shop—into "a shimmering field of exquisite, twice-blessed enamel flowers." But as Gwynn and Blotner have argued in their pamphlet on Salinger, a sexual element enters into the story—witness the imagery—and brings to a religious situation the Oedipal complications of a young art instructor in love with a nun whose drawings—and only the drawings—he has seen. The piece serves to remind us that the power of sexuality is never directly acknowledged in Salinger's work, and that love, when it is not refined into a transcendent or artistic ideal, centers on relations from which sex is notably absent: the love of a woman for a dead sweetheart or a boy for his little sister, or the Glasses for one another.

The exasperating Glass family does indeed provide Salinger with the means to exploit the nonsexual forms of love. One is never quite sure whether the intensely spiritual web of relations they weave around one another betokens an incestuous or narcissistic motive— it is as if the same tortured ego were seeking to express itself in seven fractured Glass images. Of this we can be more sure: that in their separateness and cunning identity the Glasses tell us far more about the darkness of love and self-hate than about the conditions of an urban Jewish family in mid-century America. Wise, talented and quixotic as they all seem—their common background is defined not so much by a Jewish father and Irish mother as by the radio program which used to be called "It's a Wise Child"—they all deny themselves sexual preoccupations to lose themselves into an imaginative or altruistic ideal—Boo Boo is a Tuckahoe homemaker, Buddy a writer, Zooey an actor, Waker a monk, Seymour and Franny are "mystics" of a kind.

In "Franny," Salinger succeeds far better in rendering the *experience* of Smith's conclusion: "Everybody is a nun." The story reveals the lacerated bonds between human beings when the intellect is proud and the self insatiate, and it hints at the availability of mercy. The surface is that of the bright, sophisticated expectancy of a college weekend; the anguish is underneath. Almost entirely in dialogue, the narrative develops the rising antagonism between Lane, a somewhat cerebral college jerk, and his intuitive girl friend, Franny, the youngest and most engaging of the Glasses. The clarity and hysteria of Franny—she is capable of withering rejoinders—

derive from her aversion to the egomaniac principle in her environment more than the possibility, vaguely and ambiguously hinted at, that she may be illicitly pregnant. "Everything everybody does," she exclaims helplessly, "is so—I don't know—not *wrong*, or even mean, or even stupid necessarily. But just so tiny and meaningless and— sad-making." Like Holden Caulfield she is committed to intransigence; and it is characteristic that she can only practice her devotions—the incessant prayers of the starets and Nembutsu Buddhists —in the seclusion of a lavatory, huddled in a fetal position, a work of mysticism clasped to her heart. And it is characteristic, too, that Franny's desire to burst the ego's shell does not confine itself to the action of an adolescent who, for the first time, reaches out beyond himself in sexual love.

Less perfect, perhaps, but certainly more ambitious in its formal intentions—this is the beginning of Salinger's parenthetical and digestive dialogue with himself—"Raise High the Roof Beam, Carpenters" takes us a step further in the Glass history. In Seymour Glass, the fictional descendant of Babe Gladwaller, Raymond Ford and Vincent Caulfield, Salinger has no doubt created his fullest intelligence; in the story of his wedding and the record of his buried life Salinger has exercised his powers of spiritual severity and formal resourcefulness to their limit; and it is indicative of Salinger's recent predicament that in the story the powers of spirit overreach the resources of form. The ideas of normality and alienation, of imperviousness and vulnerability, of assertiveness and responsiveness, of squalid purpose and lovely inutility, of irreverent prejudice and holy indiscrimination are all released within an unwieldy frame of three concentric references. In the middle there are the actual characters, all strangers, crowded into a limousine on their way from a wedding which Seymour, the bridegroom, was "too happy" to attend, preferring later to elope with the bride. There is the formidable and indignant Matron of Honor, a "one-woman mob," raging away at the absent bridegroom; there is the narrator, Buddy Glass, taking refuge in anonymity till the burden becomes intolerable; there is the quaint, tiny relative of the bride, steeped in the saving silence of his deaf-muteness; and there are the other marginal characters which every society includes. But around this inhuman collocation of human beings press the organized forms of sentiment, cant and even hate which crush Seymour's quixotic gesture before it can ever translate itself into meaning—note the gaudy wedding, the vicious rumors about Seymour's homosexuality or his brutality to Charlotte Mayhew, the obstructions of a street parade and the very climate of the war which Salinger is anxious to preserve by referring often to the "crapulous" year of 1942. Between the private and the public response, between the impulse of love and the communal realization of it, language has traditionally acted as mediator. But it is Salinger's most final comment on our situation that language, in all its gradations, cannot fully redeem the tragic unavailability of the self. "It was a day, God knows, not only of rampant signs and symbols but of wildly extensive communication via the written word," Buddy says ironically. Thus the coarseness of the Matron's speech, the letters of Boo Boo or the Sapphic nuptial benediction she scrawls on the bathroom mirror, the diary of Seymour that Buddy reads, again, in the bathroom, and even the eternal silence of the bride's relative fall short of the spirit's ultimate intentions. In the end, it is only the holy indiscrimination of love that can be of any avail. "Followed purely," Seymour notes in his diary, ". . . it's the way of Tao, and undoubtedly the highest way. But for a discriminating man to achieve this, it would mean that he would have to dispossess himself of poetry, go *beyond* poetry." In the earlier stories Salinger had concerned himself with the *gesture* that is prior to poetry; in his latest work he is seeking, beyond poetry, beyond all speech, the *act* which makes communion possible. As action may turn to silence, so may satire turn to praise.

Praise is precisely what finally takes the place of satire in "Zooey." The novelette reverts to Franny's state of nausea with the world, and ends, via the action of Seymour on Zooey and Zooey on Franny, with her reconciliation to it. The story is narrated by Buddy Glass, official biographer of the family, who comes more and more to assume the persona of Salinger.

Buddy begins by confessing that his narrative is not a story at all but a "sort of prose home movie"; and in the process relieves himself of certain autobiographical remarks which identify him, in an arch and sophisticated way, with Salinger. But this tricky point of view is no sooner established than dropped; the rest of the story is told in the third person. The prologue ends, the curtain goes up on the

Glass apartment in New York and we see Zooey, the youngest brother, a beautiful and talented TV actor, sitting in a bathtub and reading a four-year-old letter of Buddy's who is now simply another invisible party in the play. By this device, the absent characters (Seymour, Buddy) and those present (Bessie, Zooey, Franny) are caught somewhat uneasily in a common perspective. The story continues in a witty dialogue of doting brutality, between Zooey and Bessie in the bathroom, between Zooey and Franny in the living room.

In the foreground of the action is Zooey, who intercedes between Franny—she has gone on a hunger strike as the result of her religious crisis—and a bowl of chicken soup her earthbound mother humbly wants to offer. Zooey's real purpose, however, is to mediate between Franny and the two elder brothers, Seymour and Buddy, who have acted as the spiritual conscience of the family, turning it, by their high and holy standards, as Zooey angrily feels, into freaks. The Four Great Vows on which the family is brought up read: "However innumerable beings are, I vow to save them; however inexhaustible the passions are, I vow to extinguish them; however immeasurable the Dharmas are, I vow to master them; however incomparable the Buddha-truth is, I vow to attain it." To which Zooey adds, "Yay, team. I know I can do it. Just put me in, coach." Zooey's compulsive wit, it becomes clear, questions the workaday wisdom of Bessie, the arrogant idealism of Franny and even the saintliness of the dead Seymour. He is in fact the most qualified member of the family to understand and rebuke his youngest sister because, like her, he holds in horror everything "campusy and phony," because, despite himself, he is forever sitting in judgment on his fellow men. (Does not this exaggerated terror of sham betray the self-hate men harbor for themselves?) When Franny objects to the tendency in our society to turn everything—knowledge, art, love—into "negotiable treasure," Zooey retorts that her own incessant use of the Jesus Prayer may not entirely escape the same stricture. He takes her to task for secretly preferring the engaging personality of St. Francis to the virile character of Jesus: "I *don't* see how you can go ahead with the Jesus Prayer till you know who's who and what's what. . . . You're constitutionally unable to love or under-*stand* any son of God who throws tables around. And you're constitutionally unable to love or understand any son of God who says that a human being, *any* human being . . . is more valuable to God than any soft, helpless Easter chick." And again: "You keep talking about *ego*. My God, it would take Christ himself to decide what's ego and what isn't. This is *God's* universe, buddy, not yours. . . ." Man's duty in this life cannot be easily repealed by piety or continuous prayer. Franny's "tenth-rate" religious breakdown comes to an end when, after a phone conversation in which Zooey pretends unsuccessfully to be Buddy, she realizes that desirelessness is the heart of prayer, and understands that Seymour's ubiquitous Fat Lady, the eternal vulgarian, is Christ himself.

This is high praise of life. It is the sound of humility, calling us to *this* world. The vulgarian and the outsider are reconciled, not in the momentary flash of a quixotic gesture, nor even in the exclusive heart of a mystical revelation, but in the constancy of love. The living room, cluttered to the ceiling with bric-a-brac, full of things perishable and enduring, profane and holy, betokens that mixed, quotidian quality of grace which is perhaps the only quality grace can assume in our world. We cannot but feel that in this novelette Salinger has come close to realizing the full contradictions of his vision. If these contradictions seem to be still unexorcised, it is because the form of the novelette—its internal shifts and spurts—does not appear entirely conscious of its purpose. The improvised "home prose movie" ticks on in the dark.

The steady concerns of Salinger in the last decade came to an unhappy focus in "Seymour: An Introduction," which a good many readers hope may also prove to be Seymour's sprawling epitaph. The novelette starts with quotations from Kafka and Kierkegaard which proclaim the author's "steadfast love" for his fictional creations and apologize for his inability to do them full justice. But what starts as an effort on the part of Buddy Glass to appease once again the impossible ghost of his brother in a labor of love and art turns out to be a monstrous amalgam of parenthetical remarks, a sermon in the form of description, a polemic autobiographical tract. The voice behind the piece is not entirely Buddy's nor exactly that of Salinger himself; it is a voice that can sound alternately rasping and contentious, engaging and coy; and it is one of the peculiarities of its tone that the reader sometimes gains the distinct impression he is being told to stop reading the author, to stop *bothering* him, since the author has nothing really to say. Prolixity born of irrelevance may be still another form of silence, it seems.

There is much in the piece to compound our discomfort. The autobiographical references to the reception of "Teddy," or the widespread rumor that Salinger had entered a Buddhist monastery—there is a variant which puts him in a mental institution—or to the speculations concerning the identity of Holden and Seymour seem more peevish than sly. Nor do the tirades, however justified, against critics, psychoanalysts, pedants, existentialists and cultists of Zen appear convincing. Salinger returns to the satirical stance—indeed, he never found the way to escape it completely—but in making his exposé through a voice so uncomfortably close to his own, he is actually saying, rather disingenuously, what he only feigns to be saying as a character in a work of fiction. On the whole, we are made too keenly aware that Salinger has permitted his consciousness of rumor and his awareness of a specific audience—his "fair-weather friends," as he genially calls them—to dictate to his art. The artist's material should have proved a better dictator.

Having said this, one should add that Salinger's awareness of his audience, to which the singular qualities of his reticence and popularity have contributed, translates itself into a significant, dramatic theme: the Poet in American Society. Art and Sickness, we know, have been allied for some time in the popular imagination, but the Sick Poet, as Buddy argues, is also a Seer, and the Seer, like Seymour (See-More), is a man who in penetrating the substance of life suffers through his *eyes*. The gift of true vision requires more than artifice. Buddy puts it thus: "I say that the true artist-seer, the heavenly fool who can and does produce beauty, is mainly dazzled to death by his own scruples, the blinding shapes and colors of his own sacred human conscience." True vision, we see, requires holiness; the artist is a saintly fool. In taking upon himself the burden of holiness, the artist also develops an attitude of holy indifference to his audience. Seymour's Chinese and Japanese poetry—haikus and "double" haikus—may not take its place in the American pantheon for decades to come. But this is immaterial. As Seymour reveals to Buddy during a game of marbles, the great Zen Master Archers are those who teach us not to aim at the target. Straining for aim is an invitation to chance; our willful involvement with ends blinds us to the means. And indeed, how can there be any goals to existence if, as Seymour maintains, "all we do our whole lives is go from one little piece of Holy Ground to the next." "Is he *never* wrong?" Buddy asks.

The novella does not add much to our knowledge of Seymour as a character. The endless supercilious descriptions of his hair, ears, nose, eyes, etc., the scattered bouquets of parenthetical anecdotes concerning his behavior, do not finally amount to a credible dramatic image of an incredible genius—saint, poet, linguist, athlete, mentor and Big Brother all in one. The piece, however, does show Seymour to be not only a *muktatma*, a God-knower and ring-ding enlightened man, but also the infallible spiritual center of the Glass clan. Inbred in a common history of Fancies, the Glasses seem capable of looking outward beyond their bright familial circle only through the eyes of their dead brother, who constantly mediates between their inner world and a world they find hard to endure. Because they are his brothers—"I can't be my brother's brother for nothing," Buddy exclaims—they are brothers to everyone. And because they give themselves wholly to his imagination, they become part of all that his imagination commands. Intricately attuned and calibrated, they communicate with one another, past death itself, by letters, diaries, phone conversations and a dialogue of deceptive simplicity. But their highest hope is to make language perform the impossible: to make it carry the full burden of love for which their family narcissism is only a guise. Seymour shoulders this burden. Scapegoat to vulgarians, the Seer is still to freaks a redeemer.

"It is the duty of the man of letters to supervise the culture of language, to which the rest of culture is subordinate," Allen Tate has said, "and to warn us when our language is ceasing to forward the ends proper to man. The end of social man is communion in time through love, which is beyond time." The style J. D. Salinger has created shows clearly what human ends may be considered proper, and it carries its own warnings about the ways language may come to fail man. Beneath the tingling surface, the constant play of humor and perception, the ebullience of emotions, which are all part of Salinger's generosity, there always lurks the sad reality of human failure; and it is much as if the responsiveness, both spiritual and imaginative, of Salinger's language is constantly trying not only to reveal but also to expiate the burden of these failures.

Thus whimsy and humor, when they are not simply forms of facetiousness, prove themselves to be quixotic modes of communion or understanding. Vincent Caulfield, for instance, hits it off immediately with little Mattie Gladwaller when he says to her: "If A has three apples, and B leaves at three o'clock, how long will it take C to row five thousand miles upstream, bounded on the north by Chile?" Seymour's funny comments on bananafish or Walt's quip about Uncle Wiggily—this is a standard Glass technique—are likewise little testaments of love. There are times, however, when Salinger's wit, itself a form of satiric awareness, seems more biting and hyperbolic—Franny describes a Bennington-Sarah Lawrence type of girl by saying that she "looked like she'd spent the whole train ride in the john, sculpting or painting or something, or as though she had a leotard under her dress." The source of humor can also be found in the intimate and disconcerting gesture which reveals actor to witness, and witness to reader, in a peculiar light—Howie Croft suddenly takes the shoulder pads out of his coat, in the middle of a delicate conversation with Corinne, and Spencer picks his nose, making out "like he was only pinching it," while doling out advice to Holden Caulfield. But of the different kinds of humor Salinger uses, humor of contrast and situation, of action and characterization, of sudden perception and verbal formulation—Salinger seems to be fond of strung expressions like "the God-and-Walter-Winchell section of the Stork Club"—of all these it may be said that their ultimate function is to sharpen our sense of the radical discrepancy between what is and what ought to be.

The discrepancy is apparent in the verbal nature of his style which itself attempts to convey the difficulty of communication between human beings. Adolescents as well as adults are constantly groping for the life-giving Word. Their recourse to such expressions as "Oh, I don't know," and "You know what I mean," to oaths and obscenities, to trailing, fragmentary speeches and fierce emphases on neutral syllables, to solecisms, repetitions, clichés, and asides, betrays both the urgency of their need and the compulsion to save their utterances from the fate of mere ejaculation.

Even the structure of Salinger's stories—the obsessive use of first person narration or intimate dialogue, of epistolary and diary

G

techniques, of the confessional tone—even the structure calls our attention to the tight, lucent caul from which the captive self seldom escapes. It is not accidental that the recording consciousness of the later stories, Buddy Glass, describes himself as "the odd man out," or that so many crucial experiences seem to take place within the tiled sanctum of the Glass bathrooms. The rambling, ranting, devotional forms of these narratives equally deny the classic precepts of the short story and the well-made novelette. As Buddy puts it, the short story form eats up fat little undetached writers like him whole. This is quite in keeping with Salinger's purpose, which is to discover the form of confession and communion, the way the self can be made available to another, the point at which the irrelevant fact and transcendental idea silently meet. The purpose is not easy to achieve. Two warring impulses of the soul distend the shape of Salinger's most recent fiction: one cries in outrage at a world dominated by sham and spiritual vulgarity; the other knows, as Seymour did, that Christ ordered us to call no man a Fool. Revulsion and holiness make up the rack on which Salinger's art still twitches.

In retrospect, the artistic identity of Salinger, which also may be called his limitation, appears clear enough. Despite his striking gifts for dialogue—Salinger had once expressed the hope of becoming a playwright—the broad sense of dramatic participation is lacking in his fiction. The lack is not occasioned by the refusal of Salinger's characters to engage reality; rather is it occasioned by their insistence to engage no more of reality than they can ultimately criticize. Their access to social facts remains limited. And their very identity, their recurrent types and their intransigence toward experience, often admits to their vision—and to ours, since no other vision qualifies theirs—such extremes of corruption and innocence as make the complex entanglements of life beyond their reach. Then, too, the cult they make of vulnerability, of amateurism in life, which is the very opposite of Hemingway's cult of professionalism, diffuses the pressure of Salinger's insight onto a rather thin surface. The quixotic gesture—Seymour searching for God by poking his finger into ashtrays—is made to carry a heavier burden of meaning than it can sustain. Love averts itself easily in whimsy or laughter. The highest candor requires us to praise things by adjectives no more complex than the word "nice."

But from the early search for innocence to the later testament of love, from the slick adequacy of his earlier style to the tense lyrical form of his later, if not latest, stories, Salinger has kept faith with the redeeming powers of outrage and compassion. His faith in these has not always allowed him to reconcile their shifting focus or to create the forms of dramatic permanence. When reconciliation is granted, when the rare, quixotic gesture, striking through, becomes the form of fiction, incarnate and ineluctable, we see Salinger at last for what he is: an American poet, his thin and intelligent face all but lost among the countless faces of the modern city; his vision, forever lonely and responsive, troubled by the dream of innocence and riddled by the presence both of love and of squalor. What saves Salinger's vision from sentimentality is the knowledge that no man can give an object more tenderness than God accords to it. His heroes, children, adolescents or adult victims to the affluence of their own spirit, play upon our nostalgia for a mythic American past. They also manage to raise nostalgia to the condition of hope.

VIII. Between Miracle and Suicide

A basically religious view is what the critics in this section bring to Salinger. Josephine Jacobsen's attitude may seem a little too devotional to many; the beatific smile may be preferable to the secularist sneer, but it is not necessarily any more accurate as literary criticism. In the end though, her notion of Salinger's work as a gift is disarming. Incidentally, the reader who savors contrast might, at this point, turn back to the essays of Misses Didion and Kapp. This is not to suggest that female critics tend to extremes of one kind or another more than men; the difference in tone and thought, however, will be exhilarating.

Donald Barr insists on the Beatitudes rather than on the Lonely Crowd with considerable force, and his quotation of the O'Sheel lines alone make this piece worth the price of admission. Dan Wakefield further develops what all these critics regard as Salinger's main theme—"the relationship of man to God, or the lack of God." Unlike Kazin and others, he regards the Salinger characters' dread of phoniness not so much as condescension toward the rest of humanity as a protest against lovelessness. And he makes an interesting point in saying that Holden is not so much saddened by what people do to him as by what they do to each other: perhaps the strongest answer to the notion that he is a mere adolescent rebel. The quotation from Marcel Arland ("between miracle and suicide . . .") is strikingly apt, and a passing delight is Wakefield's observation that age is moral, not chronological, which pleasantly brings to mind Bernard Shaw's dictum that every man over forty is a scoundrel.

The short Granville Hicks piece is included in this section because he, too, is sympathetic to Salinger's religious motif and particularly to what Salinger is trying to accomplish with "Seymour." Other critics guess that Salinger is attempting to create a contemporary saint; few, if any, say flatly: "In the end he convinces me."

BEATIFIC SIGNALS

by JOSEPHINE JACOBSEN

In one of his early stories, "De Daumier-Smith's Blue Period," the major direction of the best of J. D. Salinger's work is foreshadowed —from Holden Caulfield's query to the taxidriver about the winter refuge of the Central Park ducks, to Zooey's blurted confession that he doesn't even feel like going down to *lunch* with someone any more unless he thinks there's a good chance it's going to turn out to be Jesus . . . or the Buddha. It is difficult, and perhaps indefensible, to tear passages from their organic places, but so important do they seem as an indication of how consistently Salinger has seen the way of his own growth, that it will be risked.

> . . . As I was returning . . . after dark—I stopped on the sidewalk . . . and looked into the lighted display window of the orthopedic appliances shop. Then something altogether hideous happened. The thought was forced on me that no matter how coolly or sensibly or gracefully I might one day learn to live my life, I would always at best be a visitor in a garden of enamel urinals and bedpans, with a sightless, wooden dummy-deity standing by in a marked-down rupture truss. The thought, certainly, couldn't have been endurable for more than a few seconds.

The writer of this passage has exterminated any facile approach to joy. This vision, in the shop window, is of the world in which Samuel Beckett's prose moves, with a differing but equal horror; it is the world made familiar to us by the best of the literature of despair, which, in its turn, comprises most of our best contemporary writing. And it is this first passage which commands respect for the second—the note of felicity which is Salinger's deepest and rarest gift to us:

> . . . In the nine o'clock twilight . . . there was a light on in the orthopedic appliances shop. I was startled to see a live person in the shopcase, a hefty girl of about thirty, in a green, yellow and lavender chiffon dress. She was changing the truss of the wooden dummy. . . . I stood watching her, fascinated, till suddenly she sensed, then saw, that she was being watched. I quickly smiled—to show her that this was a non-hostile figure . . . but it did no good. The girl's confusion was out of all normal proportion. She blushed, she dropped the removed truss, she stepped back on a stack of irrigation basins—and her feet went out from under her. I reached out to her instantly, hitting the tips of my fingers on the glass. She landed heavily on her bottom, like a skater. She immediately got to her feet without looking at me. Her face still flushed, she pushed her hair back with one hand, and resumed lacing up the truss on the dummy. It was just then that I had my Experience. Suddenly . . . the sun came up and sped toward the bridge of my nose· at the rate of ninety-three million miles a second. Blinded and very frightened, I had to put my hand on the glass to keep my balance. The thing lasted for no more than a few seconds. When I got my sight back, the girl had gone from the window, leaving behind her a shimmering field of exquisite, twice-blessed, enamel flowers.

Salinger has struck his note. The sordid, soulless, hopeless, pointless has been fractured by the force of the delicate, irresistible infusion: the human exchange of beatific signals. The grotesquely clad, grotesquely occupied girl, separated from the watching boy by every barrier conceivable, has brought down upon him the bolt of revelation. But this moment sternly satisfies the mind. This is no maudlin positive-thinking about trusses and ugliness. Nor is it sentimental evasion. The sordidness, in this moment, is not compromised with; it is destroyed.

"I am . . ." says Salinger's protagonist, Buddy Glass, "unjolly, unmerry, to the marrow, but my afflatus seems to be punctureproof." And Seymour, just before his marriage, writes in his diary, "Oh God, if I'm anything by a clinical name I'm a kind of paranoiac in reverse. I suspect people of plotting to make me happy. . . ." He has written of the stigmata of joy: "I have scars on my hands from touching certain people. Once, in the park, when Franny was still in the carriage, I put my hand on the downy pate of her head and left it there too long. Another time . . . with Zooey during a spooky movie. He was about six or seven, and he went under the seat to avoid watching a scary scene. I put my hand on his head. Certain things, certain colors and textures of human hair leave permanent marks on me. . . ."

When the creator of characters as sensitive to suffering and forms of evil as are Salinger's can recur to the clear note of joy, and sustain it, something so rare in current literature has occurred that it had better be examined. And a beginning can be made by asking two questions.

First, why have the dominant forces of Salinger's work been by-passed with a nervous rush? Second, through what forms does his sense of joy express itself?

So far, public comment on Salinger's work is like the comments a panic-stricken, valiant Victorian-minded spinster might make in trying to discuss Dr. Kinsey's report without referring to sex. These critics are interested in Mr. Salinger's modulations of style, in his psychology, in his characterization, in the increasingly vertiginous path he has set himself; but their acknowledgment of the core of his work is absent. Even in *Franny and Zooey*, in which the author's own statement becomes explicit, if characteristic, the religious core is passed off as Salinger's method of proving his biographical or psychological point.

Detractors and admirers alike battle on grounds of a spectacular irrelevance. ("I do cavil," says Buddy ardently, "with . . . the current ruling intellectual artistocracy educated in one or another of the big public psychoanalytical schools. . . . They're a peerage of tin ears.") Salinger's methods, his style, his course, certainly, are extraordinarily interesting; but they are interesting most of all—perhaps, in the last analysis, exclusively—in the framework of an objective followed with an organized and meticulously logical determination. That objective is the pursuit of wisdom, and its core is religious.

One of the three most urgent preoccupations underlying the fable of the Glass family (the related stories by which the full stature of Salinger as a writer has been revealed) is that of incarnation; the revelation, through matter, of spirit. The urinals and bedpans, in the blinding sun of Daumier-Smith's revelation, became a field of beautiful and twice-blessed enamel flowers.

From here on the list grows: Esmé's watch, bringing sleep to a mind on the brink of disaster; the "perfectly innocent Blake lyric" pinned "like a poultice" to Sergeant X's shirt in the front lines; the little green clothbound book of the Pilgrim which rests on Franny's knees in the ladies' room at Sickler's; the use of Seymour's phone in Zooey's rescue of a floundering Franny; all these are the gift made flesh. This is the substructure of all the Glass stories, shading boundlessly into Salinger's second foundation—the illusion of classification.

Here again, the development is not random. Teddy says, at first, he would not have children told how an elephant is big, or grass green, but learn the classification after experiencing the substance. This is perfected and clarified when the four-year-old girl who tells Buddy she has two boy friends, answers his "What are their names?" with "Bobby and Dorothy"; more overtly, in Zooey's childhood comment on the identical houses in indistinguishable streets: "Zooey said they are 'nice.' He said you'd keep thinking everyone you met was your wife or your mother or father, and people would always be throwing their arms around each other wherever they went and it would look 'very nice.'" The unity essence projected through the distinction in persons.

One of Salinger's special gifts is the juxtaposition of the august and the trivial, in which the latter never deflates the former, but is instead mysteriously infused by it, while never losing its own nature. The vaudevillian's bicycle, the boy's marble, the shoes shined for the Fat Lady, expand and deepen before our eyes, suddenly congruous. These intimate and unevident relationships are an integral part of the way in which Salinger thinks and writes.

The third foundation of Salinger's work is poetry. A brief, elliptical glimpse of his view of poetry is dropped, as though accidentally, in Seymour's depressed, exalted, quasi-affectionate description of his unnerving mother-in-law to be. He marvels at her courage. She goes here and there, does this and that, when, he says, she might as well be dead. And what is Seymour's analysis of a person who

might as well be dead? "A person deprived for life of any understanding or taste for the main current of poetry which flows through
things, all things."

Salinger's preoccupation with poetry is intense. "They," Buddy
says, "couldn't see Seymour for what he was—a poet, for God's
sake." (And here the dependent phrase is not accidental.) "And I
mean a poet." "I know this much is all," Franny says. "If you're a
poet, you do something beautiful. I mean you're supposed to *leave*
something beautiful after you get off the page and everything."

Seymour, the poet, is aware that the path of poetry may cut across
another path and veer away in its passage. Seymour sees poetry as
at once a manner of life, and a crisis, ". . . and poetry surely is a
crisis, perhaps the only actionable one we can call our own."

On these bases—matter as incarnation of spirit; the unity of
essence, secret under its distinctions; and poetry as an implacable,
demanding kind of wisdom—Salinger constructs the dignity of his
joy. It is this dignity which is essential—that it be not a substitute,
cheap, spurious, full of false claims and lies, but instead, the pure
essence which has nothing to do with satisfactions, content or even
the presence of sorrow; invulnerable to the event. "My afflatus seems
to be puncture-proof."

It is a joy based on gratitude, and that gratitude demands the
incarnation, essence and poetry for its justification. It is a joy skillfully and inevitably clothed in contemporaneity, as our despair has
been clothed in contemporaneity. This is one of the things which
have made Salinger's chore difficult. The thought, speech, clothes,
setting, the very skin and bones of his people, are passionately
of a time, of a moment—a time and moment in which their time-
lessness and universal energy are released. Zooey *had* to be a television actor, to use mid-century idiom, to live in a New York apartment in *order* to say, "Not that anyone's interested, but I can't
even sit down to a goddam *meal*, to this day, without first saying
the Four Great Vows under my breath. . . . My God, I've been
mumbling that under my breath three meals a day every day of my
life since I was ten. I can't *eat* unless I say it. I tried skipping it once
when I was having a lunch with LeSage. I gagged on a goddam
cherrystone clam, doing it."

The theme of gratitude recurs. Zooey struggling not to make a misstep, during Franny's crisis, argues with his mother and himself: "For a psychoanalyst to be any good with Franny at all, he'd have to be a pretty peculiar type. I don't know. . . . He'd have to believe that it's through the grace of God that he has the native intelligence to be able to help his goddam patients at *all*. . . . If she got somebody . . . who didn't even have any crazy, mysterious, *gratitude* for his insight and intelligence—she'd come out of analysis in even worse shape than Seymour did. . . ."

The student of Salinger's work receives a gift—a gift which he may or may not value or decide to accept. In order to hear Salinger, there must be more suspension of disbelief than has often been accorded him. He himself has shown his consciousness of this in his prefatory remarks on Seymour: those who are unwilling or unable to listen can get off here. Those who accept his offering will, in turn and inevitably, offer gratitude.

SAINTS, PILGRIMS AND ARTISTS

by DONALD BARR

Breaking, sick with revulsion, a combat soldier reads a letter from his little sister, overcomes despair and falls asleep. A boy of sixteen, flunking out of prep school, runs gently amuck in Manhattan, talks to his little sister and ends in a sanitarium. A staff sergeant on occupation duty in Germany, just released from a neuropsychiatric ward, is shaking in black isolation in his billet, finds a letter from a little English girl who has befriended him and falls into a quiet sleep. A pretty college girl lunching with her date on a football weekend suddenly loses control, and after a sweating attempt to explain a religious book she has read, faints and lies ejaculating silently, "Lord Jesus Christ, have mercy on me," over and over.

Those who regard stories as symptoms will find a whole syndrome in the works of Jerome David Salinger. He is preoccupied with collapses of nerve, with the cracking laugh of the outraged, with terrifying feelings of loneliness and alienation. He seems to correspond peculiarly to the psychological aura of our moment of history. And since he appears chiefly in a slick magazine written for the urban upper and would-be-upper middle classes, it seems easy to find in his tormented souls the insulted psyche of the "other-directed man" of Professor Riesman's *The Lonely Crowd*. A recent article in the *Nation* was hopefully titled, "J. D. Salinger: Mirror of Crisis."

But this is wrong. First, Salinger, though he served an apprenticeship in the *Saturday Evening Post* and writes for *The New Yorker*, is an artist and art is not for diagnosis—not until we are through with it as art. Once we have made it a source of data, we cannot treat it as a source of wisdom. Second, Salinger does *not* write about the Lonely Crowd, the man made in the image of B.B.D.O., the Great American Oral Type, the consumer of love and Rauwolfia. He writes about saints, pilgrims and artists.

Salinger's first published work was a sketch in *Story* of a girl trying too hard at a party, done in the slice-of-life fashion, its very point lying in its seeming pointlessness. It is witty and concentrated, but it was followed by stories of army life in *Collier's* which are coy, maladroit, patriotic lies. The stories which appeared while Salinger himself was in training are different. Only thinly falsified, they show his special emphasis, the disclosure of character—not public character in its social relations or in questions of right conduct, but private character. The personality is always at grips with a problem which is almost too strong for it. The problem is always love. (By always, I mean, of course, usually. By love, I mean the willing exposure of the soul to pain, not the appetite.) They also show an ear trained to everyday speech and thought, preparing for the great bravura of *The Catcher in the Rye*. Few novels have been written throughout in so strongly marked an idiom, for that is essentially a short-story device. Yet through seventy-five-thousand words it does not pall; and for two reasons.

First, there is no insinuated laughter *at* Holden Caulfield's idiom, though it is very funny. This sort of narration is almost never intended to get an effect of ultimate dignity. Ring Lardner mixes parody with very little pathos. "Is *this* a human being?" we say. "Well, well, it takes all kinds." Nelson Algren, while he wishes us to feel the bitter pathos of freakishness, must also invite us to feel guiltily superior to it. "Is *this* a human being?" we say. "It is the tragic price of the System that supports me." But of Holden Caulfield we say, "*This* is a human being." He is troubled, lost, but in the image of God.

Second, Salinger has an ear not only for idiosyncrasies of diction and syntax, but for mental processes. Holden Caulfield's phrase is "and all"—"She looked so damn *nice,* the way she kept going around and around in her blue coat and all"—as if each experience wore a halo. His fallacy is *ab uno disce omnes;* he abstracts and generalizes wildly, and his closing words are, "It's funny. Don't ever tell anybody anything. If you do, you start missing everybody." Each experience fills the whole universe for a moment.

Let us put down some statements about Holden Caulfield. His terrible word of condemnation is "phony." He is kept celibate by compassion. ("I thought of her going in a store and buying [the dress] and nobody in the store knowing she was a prostitute and all. . . . It made me feel sad as hell—I don't know why exactly.") Even his anger is a twisted compassion. (To the pimp who beats him up he cries, "You're a stupid chiseling moron, and in about two years you'll be one of those scraggy guys that come up to you on the street and ask for a dime for coffee. You'll have snot all over your dirty, filthy overcoat, and you'll be . . .") He feels the injustices done others as done to himself. What he wants to be is "the catcher in the rye," the only big person in a field of playing children, with the job of catching them, keeping them from falling off "some crazy cliff." He wakes up a schoolmate to ask, "What's the routine on joining a monastery?"

Holden Caulfield is not a finished saint, but the Beatitudes apply to him better than Professor Riesman's valuable book does.

Some graduate-student girl in flats and a grown-out Napoleon cut, schlepping her *Finnegans Wake,* loose-leaf notebook with colored tabs and *Reporter* magazine around Columbia, could do a good master's essay on the sources of the *New Yorker* tradition in the short story. She would have chapters, of course, on Chekhov and Maupassant (ordinariness, and the unresolved cadence at the end); Joyce (the story turning on an "epiphany," a moment of awareness when some incident brings the inner meaning of experiences into clarity), with a well-hedged comparison to Zen Buddhism (enlightenment coming from sudden flashes of perception rather than from thought); Henry James (compassion, sensitivity and taste making their possessors terribly vulnerable to the world); Somerset Maugham and Aldous Huxley (neutrality toward passion, and the punishment of the characters' hubris or pride by the author's observation); and the immediate founders like Benchley, Dorothy Parker, Thurber, E. B. White, Perelman (variously: unmuscular agnosticism, fullback-hating, hatred of whimsy, laughing in a relieved way at one's lack of power, the use of pregnant trivialities, admiring people who have faith as if they were gamblers who had won and measuring oneself ruefully against the literature of competence and strength that flourished in the boyhood of the world before World War I).

It is during this last chapter that our girl would begin to have trouble with Salinger, for even when he wrote his classically *New Yorker* stories, he did not conform wholly to a certain sickish ethos which runs in the magazine's tradition, and which happens to be what Holden Caulfield's teacher describes as the "terrible, terrible fall" that awaits the merely sensitive, "where at the age of thirty, you sit in some bar hating everybody who comes in looking as if he might have played football in college."

Our graduate student could state the difference in terms of poems. For the magazine's ethos, she will, of course, turn to her well-loved *Collected Poems of T. S. Eliot,* to the overheard voices of the Waste Land, and to Prufrock, with his social obligations, his hospital metaphor to describe the world he lives in and his mermaid metaphor to describe the world he cannot live in, his "No! I am not Prince Hamlet, nor was meant to be." For Salinger's ethos, I would suggest the poem by Shaemas O'Sheel that begins: "They went forth to battle but they always fell," especially the lines from "It was a secret music that they heard," down to

Ah, they by some strange troubling doubt were stirred,
And died for hearing what no foeman heard.

I have been moving by heavy hints and preparations to a theological conclusion. In Salinger's early stories, a growing sense of a man's estrangement from his world and his kind, of his being marooned on the island of himself, is attributed to the war. Babe Gladwaller feels that those who have not shared his experience cannot really understand his mind. In the second phase, the Veteran gives place to the Lover: Holden Caulfield loves; Seymour Glass loves; the husband of the wanton girl loves; Sergeant X loves. Some love a single object, and it is inaccessible through coldness or coarseness or circumstance. Others love the whole world, and it is busy. A few are content in their lonely benevolence; but most suffer from the feeling that they have failed at loving.

Sergeant X in his German billet finds a book left by a Nazi woman who has been interned. She has written in it: "Dear God, life is hell." He writes a quotation from Dostoevsky underneath: "Fathers and teachers, I ponder 'What is hell?' I maintain that it is the suffering of being unable to love."

Most of Salinger's work, therefore, is about those who think they are in hell, a place where the soul suffers according to its qualities, and without escape.

Ordinarily, we all are interested in hell. Ten people have read and enjoyed the *Inferno* for every one who has read the *Purgatorio* or the *Paradiso*. It is fun; like looking at real estate, it gives us a sense of our own possibilities. But Salinger's hell is different. It is hell for the good, who can feel pain, who really love or hope to love. On the gate of this hell we do not read the words "*Lasciate ogni speranza, voi ch'entrate.*" Hope is not abandoned here—hope is the implement of torture, hope deferred. We identify ourselves both with the victims and the devils. And it is not strange real estate. It is home.

To the Christian hell is in the afterlife; to the atheist it is in this life; but to both hell is eternal, because it lasts as long as the soul does. But to the Mahayana Buddhist, for example, hell is not eternal. He does not admit the three laws of thought, that whatever is, is; that no thing both is and is not; and that a thing is or is not. In his Nirvana, the soul both is and is not; it exists egolessly. It has given up living and dying. What the body is doing meanwhile, I am not sure. Nirvana may be an oblivious afterlife, or a state of miraculous unconcern in the midst of this world. In any case, this—and not surprisingly, when we recall the stories in which sleep is the end of suffering—is the exit of hell which Salinger now sought.

In January, 1953, after a year and a half of literary fame and literary silence, Salinger published in *The New Yorker* a story called "Teddy," which began his latest phase. It reads *methodically,* as if the impulse had first been to write something that was not a story. It has dialogue of a kind then new to his work but now his standard: no longer seducing our belief and lighting up characters with things we had heard but not listened to, but expounding an ordered set of ideas as plainly as can be done without actually destroying the characters into whose mouths they are put. The ideas are mostly Zen. The direct, mystical glimpsing of God behind the identities of this world is the way. An unsentimental and unpossessive love is the practical result. But the God—one feels this—is not our God, only divinity in the abstract. The love—one could not prove it—is no longer our love, only benignity.

In the stories Salinger has published since then, "Franny," "Raise High the Roof Beam, Carpenters," and "Zooey"—poignant, beautifully managed philosophic dialogues, really—the doctrine is developed sometimes in the language of Christian mysticism (after Meister Eckhart) and sometimes as a rather highflying syncretism.

This mysticism aims not at a rejection of the world, a flight from life, but an affirmative feeling for life that transforms it to the terms of its essential godhead, and gives peace. It is the triumph of Salinger's third phase that he elevates almost into a bodhisattva, a Buddhist saint, the young man Seymour Glass, who nine years before had been given to us as a critically wounded soul.

What is definite in doctrine and what is definite in fiction are virtually opposite. Salinger's prose has not improved as he carries his answers to these many decimal places. No longer are the trivialities pregnant; they are delivered by Caesarian. When Buddy Glass overhears a lady say, ". . . and the next morning, mind you, they took a pint of pus out of that lovely young body of hers," the incident is worked up into a regular symbol. His characterizations are less telling. The Veteran became the Lover; now the Lover has become the Perfectionist.

Salinger's kind of mystic is a spiritual perfectionist, and the members of the Glass family who carry on his recent, immensely long dialogues are artist-perfectionists as well. Their standards are their author's, just as their learning is their author's. It is not a humble attitude. For no one was ever ashamed to admit that he was a perfectionist. As a self-accusation, it has everything; it diagnoses one's neurotic ailments, wraps one in a small but fetching mantle of mystery, implies great refinement and intense suffering, and even threatens one's audience a bit. For we all can love a little, but none of us is perfect.

Yet Salinger remains one of the most powerful talents now practicing the short story. For the many who are involved in an effort like his, his struggles are more meaningful than other men's successes.

THE SEARCH FOR LOVE

by DAN WAKEFIELD

Fathers and teachers, I ponder "What is Hell?" I maintain that it is the suffering of being unable to love.

—Dostoevsky

Late one night in a New York apartment a boy who has just been kicked out of his third prep school is trying to explain his troubles to a former teacher, and the teacher is struggling to give the boy some hope and advice:

> Among other things, you'll find that you're not the first person who was ever confused and frightened and sickened by human behavior. You're by no means alone on that score, you'll be excited and *stimulated* to know. Many, many men have been just as troubled morally and spiritually as you are right now. Happily, some of them kept records of their troubles. You'll learn from them—if you want to. . . . It's a beautiful reciprocal arrangement. And it isn't education. It's history. It's poetry.

The boy is Holden Caulfield, the teacher is Mr. Antolini and the author of the novel they live in, *The Catcher in the Rye,* is J. D. Salinger. The jacket of the novel tells us that Salinger was born in New York City, attended public schools, a military academy and three colleges, and the reader perhaps may imagine that Salinger himself was kicked out of school once and given such advice as Mr. Antolini gave Holden Caulfield. Whatever speculations may be, we know for certain that J. D. Salinger has "kept a record of his troubles"—a record it is possible to think of not as education but as history and poetry.

The record is essentially the record of a search, and some of the seeds of its later development can be found in the stories that Salinger began to write and publish at the age of fifteen. But the real beginning of the search was marked by the publication of Salinger's first and as yet his only novel and has continued through a series of stories, most of which have appeared in *The New Yorker* magazine. The search begins with the troubled odyssey of sixteen-year-old Holden Caulfield in *The Catcher in the Rye,* and has, through that one novel and a dozen stories, moved from the mere revulsion from "phoniness" to a concept of love so large that it enables Franny Glass and her brother Zooey to turn from the desire of withdrawal from the world to an entry, through love, into the midst of life.

Salinger's search has been followed by a great many people, for *The Catcher in the Rye* was acclaimed by book reviewers all across the country on its publication in 1951, made a Book-of-the-Month Club selection and, since then, along with his book of *Nine Stories,* has been selling steadily and well. The three latest stories, published in *The New Yorker,* were awaited with great anticipation and received as events of the first order by the growing group of Salinger's admirers. It has only been in the past few years, however, that professional literary critics have taken Salinger under their microscopes for examination. Even this belated inspection has been not so much out of interest in his search as it has in him as a species held in high regard by the "Young Generation." Surely this is of interest, but to make it the most important thing in considering Salinger is to distort the meaning of his work.

Out of my own personal experience, which is that of a student at Columbia College in the early fifties who has spent the last several years in New York, I know that Salinger is indeed regarded highly by many young people. I have heard his work discussed among my friends and acquaintances more than any other contemporary author, and I have heard enough speculation about Salinger himself to feel that there is indeed a "Salinger myth," as there was in the twenties, though in a different way, a "Fitzgerald myth." Certainly any myth alive in our fact-smothered era is of interest, and this one perhaps especially since its nature is so extremely different from the twenties myth. The Fitzgerald myth had its hero in Gatsby-like parties and dunkings in the fountain at Union Square; the Salinger myth has its hero living in a cabin in the woods or going to Japan to study Zen. But in both cases the work of the man is of far more importance than the myth. Limiting Salinger's work to its interest as some kind of "document" that appeals only to people of a certain age and social background is as sensible and rewarding as considering *The Great Gatsby* as a sociological monograph once enjoyed by a now extinct species known as "Flaming Youth."

And yet it seems to follow in the eyes of some older observers that if Salinger is indeed a myth and mentor of many young people, interest in his work is restricted to young people and that this is symptomatic of the fact that it is really childish, sentimental, adolescent and irrelevant.

Significantly enough, the only critical writer to speak at all in real understanding and appreciation of Salinger's search was one of the group in England labeled the "Angry Young Men"—a group of writers who feel the need for such a search themselves, and who are most inflamed by what they feel is the moral decay of their country. In the Angry Young Men's *Declaration*, London drama critic Kenneth Tynan asks:

> Do I speak for you when I ask for a society where people care more for what you have learned than for where you have learned it; where people who think and people who work can share the common idiom; where art connects itself instead of separating people; where people feel, as in the new Salinger story, that every fat woman on earth is Jesus Christ . . . ?

He speaks, surely, for all who have not lost hope—or even if they have lost hope, have not lost interest—in the search for love and morality in the present-day world. There is the need for such a search in any time, and certainly in our time. The need has not changed—and, if anything, has become more acute—since the young writers of the twenties discovered that they were "lost" in a time when, as Fitzgerald put it, all wars were fought, all gods

were dead. More wars have been fought, but they have become increasingly depersonalized wars, and the next one that threatens
offers the ultimate depersonalization. There have been no new gods,
and the old ones have sunk continually deeper in their graves. The
inheritors of the "lost" tradition have only produced variations on
the theme of being lost, and in attitudes described by the adjectives
"beat" and "silent" they have sunk deeper into that state, losing
interest even in the possibilities of a search to be "found." The anger
expressed by the young English writers is the first sign of interest
in revival of such a search, and we have to go back to the time
of the simply "lost" to hear a similar desire expressed. It was expressed by a young French writer named Marcel Arland in 1924
when he wrote a piece for the *Nouvelle Revue Française* which
better than anything I have read can serve to describe the search
going on in the writing of Salinger:

> Morality will be our first concern. I cannot conceive of literature
> without an ethic. No doctrine can satisfy us, but the total absence
> of doctrine is a torment to us. . . . Between miracle and suicide,
> and before one reaches resignation, there is room for an extremely
> individual literature, dangerous, to be sure, and sometimes lyric
> and abnormal. . . .

It is not men and women who happen to be past the age of thirty-
five who are automatically uninterested in such a concern, but men
and women who have, at whatever age, reached resignation. A
doctor who spoke at a recent convention of the National Geriatrics
Society said that "Age is physiological—not chronological." If we
can alter his judgment to read that "Age is moral—not chronological," I think we can better understand the nature of the "youthful" appeal of Salinger's work.

Moral senility can come at any age, or need not come at all, and
we have recently borne painful witness through the howls of the
writers of the "Beat Generation" that moral senility can afflict quite
young men and women. This group dismisses the search of Salinger
on the grounds that he is "slick" (he writes for *The New Yorker*,
and as any sensitive person can tell, it is printed on a slick type of
paper). But now that the roar from the motorcycles of Jack
Kerouac's imagination has begun to subside, we find that the highly
advertised search of the Beat has ended, at least literarily, not with

love but with heroin. The appropriate nature of the symbol can be seen in the fact that the physiological experience of heroin is one of negation (it is the ultimate tranquilizer), releasing the user during the duration of his "high" from the drive for sex, for love and for answers. Fortunately for the rest of us, the characters in Salinger's fiction have found no such simple formula as a "fix" for relief from their troubles.

Sixteen-year-old Holden Caulfield was (just like Jack Kerouac) sickened by the material values and the inhumanity of the world around him. That sickness, however, marked the beginning and not the end of the search of Salinger's characters to find an order of morality and a possibility of love within the world. The things that Holden finds so deeply repulsive are things he calls "phony"—and the "phoniness" in every instance is the absence of love, and, often, the substitution of pretense for love. Holden's revulsion is a meaningful one, for he does not, like the "Beat" thinkers, simply equate material values with some abstract social evil embodied by "Madison Avenue." Holden is repulsed because material values draw on what little store of love there is in the world and expend it on "things" instead of people.

> Take most people, they're crazy about cars. They worry if they get a little scratch on them, and they're always talking about how many miles they get to a gallon, and if they get a brand-new car already they start thinking about trading it in for one that's even newer. I don't even like *old* cars. I mean they don't even interest me. I'd rather have a goddam horse. A horse is at least *human*, for God's sake. . . .

Holden, through the course of his search, is repulsed and frightened, not by what people do to him (he feels sorry for the teacher who flunks him in history, and when accused of knowing nothing about the course, says, "I know that, sir. Boy, I know it. You couldn't help it") but rather by what people do to each other, and to themselves.

There is only pretense, and therefore lack of love, and therefore human injury, in the actions of the headmaster of one of his former boys' schools who charmed all the "best" parents on Sunday visits, but ". . . if a boy's mother was sort of fat or corny-looking or something, and if somebody's father was one of those guys that wear those suits with very big shoulders and corny black-and-white shoes," then "old Haas," the headmaster, paid no attention to them.

There is only the pretense of love in the rich alumnus undertaker who comes back to Pencey Prep to give a chapel speech and tells the boys that they shouldn't be afraid to pray to God:

> He told us we ought to think of Jesus as our buddy and all. He said *he* talked to Jesus all the time. Even when he was driving his car. That killed me. I can just see the big phony bastard shifting into first gear and asking Jesus to send him a few more stiffs. . . .

When Holden flunks out of school and goes to New York he tries to explain to a girl friend he meets for a date why he thinks all boys' schools are "full of phonies," and what he explains is the cruelty of pretense and of the separation that walls off the possibilities of love:

> . . . all you do is study so that you can learn enough to be smart enough to buy a goddam Cadillac some day, and you have to keep making believe you give a damn if the football team loses, and all you do is talk about girls and liquor and sex all day, and everybody sticks together in these dirty little goddam cliques. The guys that are on the basketball team stick together . . . the goddam intellectuals stick together. . . . Even the guys that belong to the goddam Book-of-the-*Month* Club stick together. . . .

In the course of his wanderings around New York, Holden is constantly running into walls that separate people—from each other and from themselves—and shut out love. He goes to Radio City Music Hall for the Christmas pageant, and there, as in so many other places, pretense has become institutionalized and emotion therefore paralyzed:

> It's supposed to be religious as hell, I know, and very pretty and all, but I can't see anything religious or pretty, for God's sake, about a bunch of actors carrying crucifixes all over the stage. When they were all finished and started going out the boxes again, you could tell they could hardly wait to get a cigarette or something. . . .

Holden can only find genuine love in children, who have not yet learned the deadening rituals of pretense. The only person he really can talk to is his ten-year-old sister, Phoebe, and when she listens to his troubles and says that he doesn't like anything, the only thing that he can think of that he really likes is the memory of his dead brother Allie and sitting there talking to Phoebe. As for something he'd like to be—there is no job in the world he can think of that fulfills his rigorous requirements of genuine love, and all he can do is create such a job in his imagination:

> . . . I keep picturing all these little kids playing some game in this big field of rye and all. Thousands of little kids, and nobody's around—nobody big, I mean—except me. And I'm standing on the edge of some crazy cliff. What I have to do, I have to catch everybody if they start to go over the cliff—I mean if they're running and they don't look where they're going I have to come out from somewhere and *catch* them. That's all I'd do all day. I'd just be the catcher in the rye and all. I know it's crazy, but that's the only thing I'd really like to be. I know it's crazy.

Later on, Holden imagines escaping to a cabin in the woods where "I'd have this rule that nobody could do anything phony when they visited me. If anybody tries to do anything phony they couldn't stay." But the cabin in the woods and the field of rye—those unspoiled places of love and refuge—are not to be found in the real world. Holden can find the world of love only within his imagination, and, finally breaking down from his strenuous search, ends the recitation of his story in a hospital where he is getting psychiatric care. It is not, however, the end of his search—or of Salinger's. It is the end of one leg of the journey, for Holden and for Salinger, and as far as the future is concerned, Holden perhaps was speaking for Salinger as well as himself when the psychiatrist asked him if he was going to apply himself when he went back to school in the fall and Holden said:

> "It's such a stupid question, in my opinion. I mean how do you know what you're going to do till you do it? The answer is, you don't."

What Salinger did was carry on his record from sixteen-year-old Holden's search to the world of adults, as well as children and adolescents, in *Nine Stories*. Here, too, is the suffering from the lack of love, from the inability to feel love, and the torment of it drives the characters to answers of suicide, immersion in memory and alcohol and, finally, mysticism. It is in one of these stories, "For Esmé—with Love and Squalor," that the inability to love first becomes specifically articulated as the ailment that is plaguing the pilgrims of Salinger's search. The soldier in the story (Sergeant X) has come out of battle and the hospital that treated his physical wounds, and is quartered in a house in Bavaria that had, until a few weeks before, belonged to a family whose daughter was a low official in the Nazi party. The soldier, able only to smoke a continuous series of cigarettes that quiver between his fingers, picks up a book by Goebbels that belonged to the Nazi girl, and, for the third time that day, reads the inscription on the flyleaf:

> Written in ink, in German, in a small, hopelessly sincere handwriting, were the words "Dear God, life is hell." Nothing led up to it or away from it. Alone on the page, and in the sickly stillness of the room, the words appeared to have the stature of of an uncontestable, even classic indictment. X stared at the page for several minutes, trying, against heavy odds, not to be taken in. Then, with far more zeal than he had done anything in weeks, he picked up a pencil stub and wrote down under the inscription, in English, "Fathers and teachers, I ponder 'What is Hell?' I maintain that it is the suffering of being unable to love." He started to write Dostoevski's name under the inscription, but saw—with fright that ran through his whole body— that what he had written was almost entirely illegible. He shut the book.

Having seen his suffering—human suffering—as the inability to love, Sergeant X is shortly afterward, unexpectedly, saved by love. He finds a package for him from a thirteen-year-old girl he had briefly talked with in England before being sent to the front. The girl's father had been killed in the war, and she proudly wore his wrist watch that was much too big for her. She had sent it as a gift to Sergeant X with a note expressing the hope "that you will use it to greater advantage in these difficult days than I ever can and accept it as a lucky talisman." For the first time in a long time, Sergeant X feels that he may be able to sleep.

The unspoiled love of children is found throughout the course of Salinger's fiction, but only in this story does it actually provide a resolution to the problems of any of the characters.

From the sudden salvation by love of a child, Salinger moves to the sudden salvation of a "transcendent"—or, if you wish, "religious" or "moral"—vision in the story "De Daumier-Smith's Blue Period." The nineteen-year-old hero of the story has managed through a wonderful fabrication to get himself installed as an instructor in a correspondence art school in Canada, and is there but a few days when the whole thing, which had seemed such a fine plan, seems now as hopeless and depressing as his study in the art school he had just come from. One day when he is walking alone down the unfamiliar streets of the town he comes upon an orthopedic appliance shop, and while staring at its window is struck with the awful fear that "no matter how coolly or sensibly or gracefully I might one day learn to live my life, I would always at best be a visitor in a garden of enamel urinals and bedpans with a sightless, wooden dummy-deity standing by in a marked-down rupture truss." But the story does not end with this picture. The boy passes by the shop a few days later, in the depth of his depression, and stops to stare in the window again where a shopgirl is changing the display, when

> Suddenly (and I say this, I believe, with all due self-conscious-ness), the sun came up and sped toward the bridge of my nose at the rate of ninety-three million miles a second. Blinded and very frightened—I had to put my hand on the glass to keep my balance. The thing lasted for no more than a few seconds. When I got my sight back, the girl had gone from the window, leaving behind her a shimmering field of exquisite, twice-blessed enamel flowers.

This revelation that saves the boy from his downward spiral of depression was not preceded by any mystic study or contemplation, and is not the reward or fruit of such study. The narrator of the story describes it as a "transcendent" experience but quickly avows that it was not a case, "or even a borderline case, of genuine mysticism." But the next and last of the nine stories, "Teddy," is precisely that.

Teddy is a ten-year-old child prodigy who has his first mystical experience at the age of six, when

> "I saw that everything was God, and my hair stood up, and all that. . . . It was on a Sunday, I remember. My sister was only a tiny child then, and she was drinking her milk, and all of a

sudden I saw that *she* was God and the *milk* was God. I mean all she was doing was pouring God into God, if you know what I mean."

Teddy is a genuine mystic with the Oriental religious vision, which sees "Logic" as the apple eaten in the Garden of Eden and the beginning of man's concern with material life and separation from real, spiritual, life. He believes that he fell from grace before final Illumination in his last life and so had to come back again to earth, but this time, he feels, for a much briefer time. He foresees his own death, which he regards not with Western logic as the end of his life but rather as the final fulfillment and reunion with life. The story ends with that fulfillment, precisely the way that Teddy foresaw it.

The fulfillment by death that comes to Teddy through his genuinely mystic vision of life is not a fulfillment that many mortals of the Western world—we avid apple-eaters of logic—are equipped to experience. Seymour Glass, the war veteran who commits suicide in the first of the *Nine Stories* ("A Perfect Day for Bananafish"), is probably better equipped than any of the other inhabitants of Salinger's world besides the fully equipped Teddy. We learn in a later story that Seymour was a student of the Eastern religions whose understanding at the age of sixteen enabled him to shock the American radio audience of the "It's a Wise Child" show with what was essentially a Zen critique of the Gettysburg Address ("I'd said that 51,112 men were casualties at Gettysburg, and that if someone *had* to speak at the anniversary of the event, he should simply have come forward and shaken his fist at the audience and then walked off. . . .") and that he had a lifelong record of "transcendent" experience—but even he cannot reach the purely mystical conclusion of Teddy. Seymour does not die by some foreseen accident that he feels will reunite him with God, but rather, in a hotel room which "smelled of new calfskin luggage and nail-lacquer remover," presses a pistol to his head and commits suicide. Though many of Salinger's characters are concerned with mysticism, Teddy is the only real mystic, and his particular answer is not the answer for any other characters and does not provide an answer to Salinger's search.

Salinger has sometimes been accused of "retreating" into mysticism, and yet in reality the search of his fiction moves from

Teddy's mystical withdrawal from the mortal world to three long stories that chronicle a pilgrim's progress into that world. It is almost as if, at the conclusive end of "Teddy," the author looked back upon the characters left in the suspended life of the other stories and, in love, brought them together to create a family whose record he could write to carry them forward in their life and their search. The latest stories concern the history of the Glass family, whose seven children include Seymour, the ·man who committed suicide in "A Perfect Day for Bananafish"; Boo Boo, the young mother in "Down at the Dinghy"; Walt, who was killed in the war but still remained the only love in the life of Eloise in "Uncle Wiggily in Connecticut"; and, we may guess, Buddy, the writer who appeared as Sergeant X in "For Esmé." The three other children in the family are Waker, a Roman Catholic priest; Zooey, an actor and Franny, the youngest of the family and a student in college. The parents are retired vaudevillians, the father Jewish and mother Irish, and their home and family headquarters is a large and memento-marked apartment in the fashionable Upper East Side of New York.

The Upper East Side, the Ivy League schools and colleges, are probably the world that Salinger knew, and therefore the world that provides the setting for these stories. The setting is real and convincing and yet it is not the subject of the stories. Their overhanging question is not whether the heroine moves to Westport or the hero gets into Harvard. No one hurls himself out of a window as a result of the Buffalo Drop Forge and Tool Company's amalgamation with Hercules Steel Products. Salinger's fiction is not what we have come to identify as "sociological."

It is precisely because Salinger is more concerned with something beyond these considerations that his fiction differs from that of any new writer in America today—and perhaps why it is more interesting. Salinger is the only new writer to emerge in America since the Second World War who is writing on what has been the grandest theme of literature: the relationship of man to God, or the lack of God.

Marcel Arland, in speaking of the kind of moral literature that he felt was so sorely needed, wrote that all problems boil down to the single problem of God:

God, the eternal scourge of men, whether they are intent upon creating Him or destroying Him! Virgil's work is explained by His permanent presence; Rousseau's by the search for Him; Stendhal's by the attempts of passion to cover up His absence.

We are living in a time, as Arland did, in which men are "no longer feeling within themselves the idol but still feeling the altar," and the question of what replaces the idol which once provided a set of answers for human conduct, the question of how men act with morality and love if there is no idol which prescribes the rules, is a central and vital question. It is a question which stands, as the last three Salinger stories stand, "between miracle and suicide, and before one reaches resignation. . . ." The question is a vital one for anyone who has not yet reached resignation. It is probably met most violently when it first becomes a question, in adolescence (where Holden Caulfield met it), and then again when the formal ritual of education is about to end. It is then that a person is confronted with the questions which are casually stated in all the immensity of their meaning: What are you going to *do?* What are you going to *be?* There are possibilities of resignation, suicide, miracle and search, and it is at the beginning of such a search that we meet Franny Glass.

Franny is a pretty and intelligent young girl who is down for the weekend of the Yale game with her boy friend, Lane Coutell, who is heady with the triumph of a paper attacking Flaubert which got an A from a professor who is "a big Flaubert man." But Franny, listening to this and to the plans which are the plans of every other Yale game weekend with every other character who always has a part in the cast, becomes progressively depressed and begins to ridicule "Wally Campbell," the fellow who is giving the inevitable cocktail party. Her complaint, though, is not a personal one against Wally Campbell, but the resignation he represents:

> "It's *ev*erybody, I mean. Everything everybody does is so—
> I don't know—not *wrong*, or even mean, or even stupid necessarily. But just so tiny and meaningless and—sad-making. And the worst part is, if you go bohemian or something crazy like that, you're conforming just as much as everybody else, only in a different way."

The only thing that Franny can find that seems worth thinking or talking about is a small green book she is carrying in her purse called *The Way of a Pilgrim*. It records the search of a Russian peasant who sets out to learn what it means in the Bible when it says you should pray incessantly. He learns about the "Jesus Prayer" —"Lord Jesus Christ, have mercy on me"—and that if you say it long enough with your lips it becomes "automatic," a continual prayer. She tells Lane, who is skeptical of the "psychological" value of such an experiment, that "you do it to purify your whole outlook and get an absolutely new conception of what everything's about." Lane, however, is anxious to make it over to the cocktail party. Franny tries to put her questions aside to go on with "the weekend" but instead she becomes sick to her stomach, and faints, in the restaurant where she and Lane are having lunch. She apologizes and says she is fine when she wakes up with Lane looking over her in the back room of the restaurant. But the story ends as Lane goes off to get the car and Franny lies in the room, alone, with her prayer: "Her lips began to move, forming soundless words, and they continued to move."

Franny, like all the children of the Glass family, is concerned with the possibility of mysticism as an answer to her search, but she is not, nor are any of her brothers or her sister, a mystic who finds a mystical answer. The closest that any of the family comes to true mysticism is Seymour, but his experiences which might be described as mystic are the kind that Salinger rightly distinguishes earlier (in de Daumier-Smith) as "transcendent" rather than mystic experiences. We hear about them through Seymour's diary in the second of the Glass family stories, "Raise High the Roof Beam, Carpenters," which reaches back in the family record before Seymour's suicide to give an account of his wedding day. We hear about how as a child he threw a rock at a girl "because she looked so beautiful sitting there in the middle of the driveway . . ." and, through his diaries, how

I have scars on my hands from touching certain people. Once, in the park, when Franny was still in the carriage, I put my hand on the downy pate of her head and left it there too long. Another time, at Loew's Seventy-second Street, with Zooey during a spooky movie. He was about six or seven, and he went under the seat to avoid watching a scary scene. I put my hand on his head. Certain heads, certain colors and textures of human hair, leave permanent marks on me. . . .

If anything, Seymour was too close to being a mystic for his own survival. He was close enough to be unsatisfied with anything less than perfection—close enough to be unable to find perfection in the Western world of "things," and yet not close enough to achieve perfection through the mystical fulfillment of Teddy. He wrote in his diary that

> I'll champion indiscrimination till doomsday, on the ground that it leads to health and a kind of very real, enviable happiness. *Followed purely* it's the way of the Tao, and undoubtedly the highest way. But for a discriminating man to achieve this, it would mean that he would have to dispossess himself of poetry, go *beyond* poetry. That is, he couldn't possibly learn or drive himself to *like* bad poetry in the abstract, let alone equate it with good poetry. He would have to drop poetry altogether. I said it would be no easy thing to do. Dr. Sims said I was putting it too stringently—putting it, he said, as only a perfectionist would. Can I deny it?

Seymour was beyond the possibility of resignation to imperfection, but short of the possibility of a miracle; he ends in suicide.

Although neither mysticism nor religion in the narrow sense of the words provides an answer to the search of any of the members of the Glass family, a concern with mystic and religious experience provides a path to Zooey's and Franny's conception of perfect love in "Zooey." That conception includes, embraces and goes beyond the ordinary conceptions of religion and morality (and in its humanness, stops short of mysticism) and can properly be called by no other name than the simple and profound name of love.

"Zooey" begins a little beyond where "Franny" left off, with Franny Glass at home on the verge of a breakdown and in complete withdrawal from everything except the "Jesus Prayer." She says she has given up her ambitions to become an actress, and at the moment her only ambition is to find through the prayer that "new conception of what everything's about." The old conception, the conception she is living with, is one of revulsion from the world, from its "phoniness"—its lack of love and emphasis of "ego" and sham. She can feel no love for it, and see no hope of her living in it without the awaited, transforming, mystic miracle of the prayer —"Jesus Christ, have mercy on us."

But it is nothing so "simple" as a sudden mystic miracle that gives her any answer. It is rather a human conception of love—compound, multiple, pure and complicated love, wrought in the struggle of her brother Zooey to bring her out of withdrawal and into the world. Zooey is a twenty-five-year-old television actor who participates in a constant battle with himself to remain in action and find in his work the possibility of perfection and the justification of love. He, like Franny, was brought up on the perfectionist principles of their older brothers Seymour and Buddy, and understands Franny's retreat from the world and hope for a miracle. He argues against her withdrawal, argues against her "misuse" of the Jesus Prayer; but it is only toward the end of his long telephone conversation of persuasion that she begins to respond, when he tells her that "The only thing you can do now, the only *religious* thing you can do, is *act*. Act for God, if you want to—be *God's* actress, if you want to. . . . One other thing. And that's all. I promise you. But the thing is, you raved and you bitched when you came home about the stupidity of audiences. . . . You have no right to think about those things, I swear to you."

Zooey explains that he, too, has had these complaints. He had them in fact as a child when he took his place with the older children on the family radio program, and didn't want to shine his shoes before going to the studio. He told his older brother Seymour that the people in the audience were morons, the sponsors were morons and the announcer was a moron, and he didn't see why he had to shine his shoes for them. But Seymour "said to shine them for the Fat Lady. . . . This terribly clear, clear picture of the Fat Lady formed in my mind. I had her sitting on this porch all day, swatting flies, with her radio going full-blast from morning till night. I figured the heat was terrible, and she probably had cancer, and—I don't know."

Franny, becoming excited and involved in the conversation now for the first time, says that Seymour had told her, too, about the Fat

Lady, and that she, too, had pictured her nearly as Zooey had. Zooey quickly goes on to say:

> "I don't care where an actor acts. It can be in summer stock . . . it can be over *tele*vision, it can be in a goddam Broadway theatre, complete with the most fashionable, most well-fed, most sunburned-looking audience you can imagine. But I'll tell you a terrible secret. . . . There isn't anyone *any*where who isn't Seymour's Fat Lady. . . . And don't you know—*listen* to me, now—*don't you know who that Fat Lady really is?* . . . Ah, buddy, ah, buddy. It's Christ Himself. Christ Himself, buddy."

For joy, apparently, it was all Franny could do to hold the phone, even with both hands. . . .

Fitzgerald has said that "in a real dark night of the soul it is always three o'clock in the morning, day after day." But a real dark night does not, after all, come often, and perhaps it is more important to know what Salinger has told us—that in the everyday weather of the soul it is always three o'clock on a hot afternoon. And behind our sunburns, behind our bright disguises, we are all of us the Fat Lady, wedged in our wicker rocking chairs, swatting the flies away.

It is easy to despise and ridicule the Fat Lady, to rage against the façades that separate us and shut out love, and that is what many of our writers, often very eloquently, have done. Salinger has broken through those façades and told us who the Fat Lady really is. That is what his search has given us already, and, as Mr. Antolini explained the possibilities of such a search to Holden Caulfield, "it isn't education. It's history. It's poetry." It is the history of human trouble and the poetry of love.

THE SEARCH FOR WISDOM

by GRANVILLE HICKS

Recently I taught a course in contemporary fiction at a large university. When I was drawing up the reading list, a veteran teacher whom I consulted mildly questioned the inclusion of J. D. Salinger's

The Catcher in the Rye. "It's the one book," he said, "that every undergraduate in America has read." I think he was pretty nearly right about that, but, for my own sake, I'm glad I decided to teach the book. To most of my students, I discovered, Holden Caulfield meant more than Jake Barnes or Jay Gatsby or Augie March or any other character we encountered in the course, and in the discussion of the novel there was a sense of direct involvement such as I felt on no other occasion.

For the college generations of the fifties, Salinger has the kind of importance that Scott Fitzgerald and Ernest Hemingway had for the young people of the twenties. He is not a public figure as they were; on the contrary, his zeal for privacy is phenomenal; but he is felt nevertheless as a presence, a significant and congenial presence. There are, I am convinced, millions of young Americans who feel closer to Salinger than to any other writer. In the first place, he speaks their language. He not only speaks it; he shapes it, just as Hemingway influenced the speech of countless Americans in the twenties. The talk of his characters is, so to speak, righter than right. The voice of Holden Caulfield is a voice we instantly recognize, and yet there is just that twist of stylistic intensification that always distinguishes good dialogue.

In the second place, he expresses their rebellion. Most of my undergraduates, so far as I could tell, were as nonpolitical as Holden Caulfield. They spoke of the lack of interest in political and social problems as characteristic of their generation, a phenomenon to be neither praised nor condemned but simply accepted. Yet they were far from complacency, and they delighted in Holden's attacks on meanness, stupidity and especially phoniness. They admired his intransigence, too, which he so often refers to as his craziness, and rejoiced in his gestures of defiance.

But Holden is not merely a rebel, and this also my students understood. What is strongest in him, as is indicated by the passage that gives *The Catcher in the Rye* its title, is compassion. He is not only full of tenderness toward his sister Phoebe and all children; he is touched by persons casually met on his pilgrimage—by the woman on the train, by the girls in the night club, by the nuns in the station —and wants to make them happy. In the end he feels sorry even for those who have hurt him.

I have been talking seriously about a book that on page after page is wildly funny, but it is fundamentally a serious book, as its younger readers know. Holden Caulfield is torn, and nearly destroyed, by the conflict between integrity and love. He is driven by the need not to be less than himself, not to accept what he knows to be base. On the other hand, he is capable of understanding and loving the persons to whom his integrity places him in opposition. The problem of values with which Salinger so persuasively confronts his sixteen-year-old is not exclusively a problem of adolescence.

It is a problem that has continued to engage Salinger. Between 1953 and the present he has published only four stories, all of them, to be sure, quite long. As everyone knows, they are all concerned with members of a family by the name of Glass. He had introduced the family in earlier stories, but it was not until "Franny" that he made a full-length study of one of the seven Glass children—Franny is the youngest of them—and it was not until "Raise High the Roof Beam, Carpenters" that he gave his readers an idea of the family as a whole. In "Zooey" he was even more informative, and in "Seymour: An Introduction" he has gone on building his structure higher and higher.

There are many things to say about "Seymour," but I want to concentrate on two. The story is told in the first person by Buddy, the second oldest of the Glass children, and Salinger has chosen to identify himself completely with Buddy: for instance, Buddy describes three stories he has written, and they are three stories written and signed by J. D. Salinger. This does not entitle us to assume that Salinger had four brothers and two sisters or appeared on a quiz show or teaches in a women's college, but we cannot avoid the conclusion that when Buddy speaks on literary matters he speaks for Salinger. What we discover is that Salinger is acutely self-conscious, about his writing, about his philosophy, about his reputation. (Buddy alludes to "the bogus information that I spend six months of the year in a Buddhist monastery and the other six in a mental institution.") Indeed, self-consciousness gives the story its peculiar quality, and although the tone is beautifully sustained, as always in Salinger's later work, the self is exceedingly obtrusive.

H

Buddy was prominent in "Raise High the Roof Beam, Carpenters," but he wasn't constantly talking about himself as a writer, and I think that was a better story than this. (So was "Zooey," if only by virtue of the wonderful bathroom conversations between Zooey and his mother, which "Seymour" has nothing to equal.)

On the other hand, as a piece of stylistic virtuosity, the story does make the reader's hair stand on end, and, what is more, the reader begins to see Seymour as Salinger wants us to see him. He was interesting and likable in "A Perfect Day for Bananafish," but no more than that. In "Raise High the Roof Beam, Carpenters" and "Zooey" we felt that he was a man of unusual powers, but we saw him only from a distance. Now, in brief glimpses but in the most concrete way, Salinger makes us feel Seymour's brilliance, his high poetic gifts and above all his capacity for love. "What was he, anyway?" Buddy asks. "A *saint?* Thankfully, it isn't my responsibility to answer that one." But that is exactly what Salinger is trying to create—a contemporary saint—and in the end he convinces me.

Salinger doesn't make things easy for his readers as he moves along his chosen path, but I imagine that the devotees are still with him. The Glass saga can go on for a long time: Salinger intimates that he may do more with Seymour, and about Waker, Walt and Boo Boo we so far know only enough to be sure we should be glad to know more. On the other hand, Salinger may grow tired of the Glasses, or may be led in a new direction by his constant experimentation with technique. For myself, I shall be glad if he moves away from Buddy's self-consciousness, but, whatever he writes, I look forward to reading it.

When we were discussing *The Catcher in the Rye* in class, there was one dissenting voice, one student who felt that Holden Caulfield's rebellion was too immature and ineffectual to be worth serious consideration. Most of the students loudly disagreed, and I went along with the majority. Holden is not rejecting maturity but is looking for a better model than his elders by and large present. Like the Glasses, though in a less ostentatious way, he is a seeker after wisdom. That Salinger can make the search for wisdom seem important to large numbers of young people is not exactly cause for alarm.

IX. Holden and Huck: A Quest

Arthur Heiserman and James Miller, unlike the critics in the preceding section, do not see Salinger in religious terms so much as
in epic ones; they place him in the great tradition of the Quest.
They see his heroism in his refusal to compromise with "phony
adultism," and they recall the Wiegand diagnosis of banana fever
when they remark that Holden "does not suffer from an inability
to love but he does despair of finding a place to bestow his love."
Yet for all their insight, one does get a feeling that matters are
a little out of control when Holden appears in the company, however remotely, of Aeneas and Ulysses (both the original and the
Joycean), and when there are allusions to the Grail. Holden and
Salinger can probably defend themselves against their detractors,
but one wonders whether they can long carry the burden of such
praise. Messrs. Heiserman and Miller are on much safer ground
when they reduce their Quest to Huck Finn's, as does Edgar
Branch. Of all the comparisons between Holden and Huck, Branch's
is the most detailed and, despite touches of pedantry, the most
satisfying as it traces these two "parallel myths." Branch is surely
right in contrasting Huck's essential victory over life with Holden's
defeat by it.

SOME CRAZY CLIFF

by ARTHUR HEISERMAN and JAMES E. MILLER, JR.

It is clear that J. D. Salinger's *The Catcher in the Rye* belongs to an ancient and honorable narrative tradition, perhaps the most profound in Western fiction. The tradition is the central pattern of the epic and has been enriched by every tongue; for not only is it in itself exciting but also it provides the artist a framework upon which he may hang almost any fabric of events and characters.

It is, of course, the tradition of the Quest. We use the medieval term because it signifies a seeking after what is tremendous, greater than the love of a woman. The love of a woman may be part of the seeking, part even of the object sought, for we have been told that the Grail has gender and Penelope did wait in Ithaca. But if the love of woman is essential to the seeking or to the object sought, we must call the search a romance. These two terms (quest and romance) distinguish thematic patterns, and have nothing to do with tragic or comic effects. Furthermore, the same plots, characters and idioms might be employed inside either pattern. But somewhere upon the arc of the Quest, the love of woman must be eschewed or absorbed: the hero must bind himself to the mast, or must seek his Ducalinda because she is Virtue, not because she is Female.

There are at least two sorts of quests, depending upon the object sought. Stephen Dedalus sought a reality uncontaminated by home, country, church; for like Eugene Gant and Natty Bumppo he knew that social institutions tend to force what is ingenious in a man into their own channels. He sought the opposite of security, for security was a cataract of the eye. Bloom, on the other hand, was already an outcast and sought acceptance by an Ithaca and a Penelope which despised him. And, tragically enough, he also sought an Icarian son who had fled the very maze which he, Bloom, desired to enter. So the two kinds of quests, the one seeking acceptance and stability, the other precisely the opposite, differ significantly, and can cross only briefly to the drunken wonder of both heroes. Bloom, the protagonist of *The Waste Land*, the Joads, Alyosha Karamazov, Aeneas, Ulysses, Gatsby—these heroes seek acceptance, stability, a life embosomed upon what is known and can be trusted. Dedalus, Huck Finn, Ishmael, Hans Castorp, Huxley's heroes, Dostoevsky's Idiot—these protagonists place themselves outside the bounds of what is known and seek not stability but a Truth which is unwarped by stability.

American literature seems fascinated with the outcast, the person who defies traditions in order to arrive at some pristine knowledge, some personal integrity. Natty Bumppo maintains his integrity out of doors only, for upon the frontier a man must be a man or perish. For Huck Finn both sides of the Mississippi are lined with fraud and hatred; and because the great brown river acts as a kind of sewer, you're liable to find murderers and thieves afloat on it— even the father whom you fled might turn up dead in it, as though the river were a dream. But in the middle of the great natural river, when you're naked of civilization and in company with an outcast more untarnished and childlike than yourself—*there* is peace. And in northern Mississippi, in the ante-Snopes era, frontiersmen conquer the wilderness using only their courage and their fury; and they behave, even when civilization has almost extinguished them, with the kind of insane honor that drives Quentin Compson outside of society and into suicide. And the hunter, as he tracks the great mythic bear or the incredible whale, must leave behind whatever is unnatural or convenient. Similarly, when the bull charges, you are faced with the same compulsion for integrity as is required by the wilderness, the whale, the bear, the river; and very often, the world so botches things that you must "make a separate peace" in order to maintain your moral entity intact.

All the virtues of these American heroes are personal ones: they most often, as a matter of fact, are in conflict with home, family, church. The typical American hero must flee these institutions, become a tramp in the earth, cut himself off from Chicago, Winesburg, Hannibal, Cooperstown, New York, Asheville, Minneapolis. For only by flight can he find knowledge of what is real. And if he does not flee, he at least defies.

The protagonist of *The Catcher in the Rye*, Holden Caulfield, is one of these American heroes, but with a significant difference. He seems to be engaged in both sorts of quests at once: he needs to go home and he needs to leave it. Unlike the other American knights-errant, Holden seeks Virtue second to Love. He wants to be good. When the little children are playing in the rye field on the cliff top, Holden wants to be the one who catches them before they fall off the cliff. He is not driven toward honor or courage. He is not driven toward love of woman. Holden is driven toward love of his fellow man, charity—virtues which were perhaps not quite virile enough for Natty Bumppo, Ishmael, Huck Finn or Nick Adams. Holden is actually frightened by a frontier code of masculinity—a code which sometimes requires its adherents to behave in sentimental and bumptious fashion. But like these American heroes, Holden is a wanderer, for in order to be good he has to be more of a bad boy than the puritanical Huck could have imagined. Holden has had enough of both Hannibal, Missouri, *and* the Mississippi; and his tragedy is that when he starts back up the river, he has no place to go—save, of course, a California psychiatrist's couch.

So Salinger translates the old tradition into contemporary terms. The phoniness of society forces Holden Caulfield to leave it, but he is seeking nothing less than stability and love. He would like nothing better than a home, a life embosomed upon what is known and can be trusted; he is a very wise sheep forced into lone wolf's clothing; he is Stephen Dedalus and Leopold Bloom rolled into one crazy kid. And here is the point; for poor Holden, there is no Ithaca. Ithaca has not merely been defiled by a horde of suitors: it has sunk beneath waves of phoniness. He does, of course, have a Penelope who is still intact. She is his little sister Phoebe whom he must protect at all costs from the phantoms of lust, hypocrisy, conceit and fear—all of the attributes which Holden sees in society and which Huck Finn saw on the banks of the Mississippi and Dedalus saw in Dublin. So at the end, like the hero of *Antic Hay,* Holden delights in circles—a comforting, bounded figure which yet connotes hopelessness. He breaks down as he watches his beloved little Phoebe going round and round on a carousel; she is so *damned* happy. From that lunatic delight in a circle, he is shipped off to the psychiatrist. For Holden loves the world more than the world can bear.

Holden's Quest takes him outside society; yet the grail he seeks is the world and the grail is full of love. To be a catcher in the rye in this world is possible only at the price of leaving it. To be good is to be a "case," a "bad boy" who confounds the society of men. So Holden seeks the one role which would allow him to be a catcher, and that role is the role of the child. As a child, he would be condoned, for a child is a sort of savage and a pariah because he is innocent and good. But it is Holden's tragedy that he is sixteen, and like Wordsworth he can never be less. In childhood he had what he is now seeking—nonphoniness, truth, innocence. He can find it now only in Phoebe and in his dead brother Allie's baseball mitt, in a red hunting cap and the tender little nuns. Still, unlike all of us, Holden refuses to compromise with adulthood and its necessary adulteries; and his heroism drives him berserk. Huck Finn had the Mississippi and at the end of the Mississippi he had the wild west beyond Arkansas. The hero of *The Waste Land* had Shantih, the peace which passes human understanding. Bloom had Molly and his own ignorance; Dedalus had Paris and Zurich. But for Holden, there is no place to go.

The central theme of Salinger's work is stated explicitly in one of his best short stories, "For Esmé—with Love and Squalor." Salinger quotes a passage from Dostoevsky: "Fathers and teachers, I ponder 'What is Hell?' I maintain that it is the suffering of being unable to love."

The hero of "For Esmé" is an American soldier who, driven too near psychosis by five campaigns of World War II and a moronic jeepmate, is saved in an act of childish love by two remarkable English children. Just as surely as war and neurosis are both manifestations of the lack of love, the soldier discovers peace and happiness are manifestations of love's presence. This Love must be spelled with a capital; for it is not the alienated, romantic love of the courtly romances and "Dover Beach"—a love which is tragic because it is founded upon Eros; but rather it is the expansive, yea-saying love of all Creation which we find in the saints and which is never tragic because it is founded upon Agape. This love is the dominant trait of all Salinger's heroes, and when it is thwarted the hero either shoots himself, as does the veteran with "battle fatigue" in "A Perfect Day for Bananafish," or goes berserk or melancholic as do the heroes of *The Catcher in the Rye* and

"Uncle Wiggily in Connecticut." But when, on the other hand, a person finds a way to love the world, then that person is saved from madness and suicide as is the soldier in "For Esmé." Salinger thus diagnoses the neurosis and fatigue of the world in one simple way: if we cannot love, we cannot live.

Childhood and the loss of innocence have obsessed much of Western literature at least since the Enlightenment, when man was declared innately good, corrupted only by his institutions. If we could return to childhood, or to noble savagery; or if we could retain the spontaneity of childhood, our social and personal problems would disappear. Emile, Candide, the young Wordsworth, Huck Finn, Holden Caulfield—all lament or seek a return to a lost childhood for precisely the same reasons that one is forced to make peace with one's childhood on the analyst's couch, or that the Marxist must look with a sigh upon Eden, where the fruits of production were consumed entirely by their tenders. Each of us does indeed carry an Adam inside us, whether he be Original Sin or Innocence: and the modern world has for the most part judged him innocent. Yet the clouds of glory which we trailed dwindle and turn back in adulthood; for when the world was new, before the pimples appeared, it was with us not too much but utterly and we could love it innocently, without fear. Of course, what Wordsworth remembered above Tintern Abbey, what Clemens recalled in New York, what Rousseau attempted to breed in France, what modern art attempted to re-create from Negro and Oriental models, never really existed in pure form in the first place. How horrified Wordsworth would have been had he learned what romanticism's dank blossom, Freud, discovered in the dictum that "the child is father of the man"! Nevertheless, as Freud made Childism clinical he also made it rampant; and the initiation story, the fable of Innocence Lost, has developed into a dominant motif in contemporary fiction.

The flight out of the world, out of the ordinary, and into an Eden of innocence or childhood is a common flight indeed, and it is one which Salinger's heroes are constantly attempting. But Salinger's childism is consubstantial with his concern for love and neurosis. Adultism is precisely "the suffering of being unable to love," and it is that which produces neurosis. Everyone able to love in Salinger's stories is either a child or a man influenced by a

child. All the adults not informed by love and innocence are by
definition phonies and prostitutes. "You take adults, they always
look lousy when they're asleep with their mouths open, but kids
don't. . . . They look all right." Kids like Phoebe shut up when they
haven't anything to say. They even say "thank you" when you
tighten their skates, and they don't go behind a post to button their
pants. The nuns expect no swanky lunches after standing on a
corner to collect money. Young James Castle would not go back on
his word even though he had to jump from a window to keep it.

Holden is the kind of person who feels sorry for the teachers who
have to flunk him. He fears for the ducks when the lagoon freezes
over, for he is a duck himself with no place to go. He must enter
his own home like a crook, lying to elevator boys and tiptoeing past
bedrooms. His dad "will kill" him and his mother will weep for
his incorrigible "laziness." He wants only to pretend he is a deaf-
mute and live as a hermit filling-station operator in Colorado, but
he winds up where the frontier ends, California, in an institution
for sick rich kids. And we can see, on the final note of irony in
the book, that that frontier West which represented escape from
"sivilization" for Huck Finn has ended by becoming the symbol for
depravity and phoniness in our national shrine at Hollywood.

The most distinctive aspect of Salinger's humor is its invariable
effect of intensifying poignance and even horror. At the end of
"A Perfect Day for Bananafish," Seymour Glass, the sensitive young
protagonist, is unable to reconcile himself to the evil adult world
into which he has been thrust, with its brutal wars and sordid
and even hateful relationships with a shallow-headed wife and
her self-centered family. Even the steadying influence of the
genuine innocence of little Sibyl Carpenter is not sufficient to
deter Seymour from his will to self-destruction. As he is on his
way to his room at the end of the story, he boards the hotel
elevator and believes that one of his fellow passengers is scrutiniz-
ing him. "I see you're looking at my feet," he says, and the startled
woman with zinc salve on her nose replies, "I *beg* your pardon?"
But the young man has become acutely sensitive: "If you want to
look at my feet, say so. . . . But don't be a God-damned sneak
about it."

The story at this point is simultaneously at its funniest and its

most poignant. In less than one brief page the young man is dead:
"Then he went over and sat down on the unoccupied twin bed,
looked at the girl, aimed the pistol, and fired a bullet through
his right temple." The close juxtaposition of these two passages,
the one a height in comic incongruity, the other a depth in tragic
action, works a unique effect. The comic element intensifies rather
than relieves the tragic. As we observe the young man raise the
pistol to his head, we are horrified that we have just been laughing
at his extreme sensitivity about his feet. Perhaps we even have
the guilty feeling of having ridiculed a deformity—a deformity of
the spirit. In any event we are stunned into a keen realization
of the tragic human plight.

It is this poignance which characterizes all of Salinger's humor,
this catch in the throat that accompanies all of the laughs. Holden
Caulfield is no clown nor is he a tragic hero; he is a sixteen-year-
old lad whose vivid encounter with everyday life is tragically
humorous—or humorously tragic. At the end of the novel, as we
leave Holden in the psychiatric ward of the California hospital,
we come to the realization that the abundant and richly varied
humor of the novel has re-enforced the serious intensity of Holden's
frantic flight from Adultism and his frenzied search for the genuine
in a terrifyingly phony world.

Holden Caulfield, like Huckleberry Finn, tells his own story
and it is in the language of the telling in both books that a great
part of the humor lies. In the nineteenth century, Huck began,
"You don't know about me without you have read a book by
the name of *The Adventures of Tom Sawyer:* but that ain't no
matter." The English of Huck's twentieth-century counterpart,
Holden Caulfield, is perhaps more correct but none the less distinctive: "If you really want to hear about it, the first thing you'll
probably want to know is where I was born, and what my lousy
childhood was like, and how my parents were occupied and all
before they had me, and all that David Copperfield kind of crap,
but I don't feel like going into it, if you want to know the truth."

The skepticism inherent in that casual phrase, "if you want to
know the truth," suggesting that as a matter of fact in the world of
Holden Caulfield very few people do, characterizes this sixteen-
year-old "crazy mixed up kid" more sharply and vividly than pages

of character "analysis" possibly could. In a similar manner Huck's "that ain't no matter" speaks volumes for his relationship to the alien adult world in which he finds himself a sojourner. But if these two boys lay their souls bare by their own voices, in doing so they provoke smiles at their mishandling and sometimes downright mangling of the English language.

Huck's spelling of "sivilization" gives the word a look which makes what it stands for understandably distasteful. Holden's incorrectness frequently appears to be straining after correctness ("She'd give Allie or I a push. . . .") which suggests a subconscious will to nonconformity. But the similarities of language of Huck and Holden are balanced by marked differences. Both boys are fugitives from education, but Holden has suffered more of the evil than Huck. Holden's best subject in the several schools he has tolerated briefly is English. And, too, Holden is a child of the twentieth century. Mark Twain himself would probably be startled not at the frankness of Holden's language but at the daring of J. D. Salinger in copying it so faithfully.

But of course neither J. D. Salinger nor Mark Twain really "copied" anything. Their books would be unreadable had they merely recorded intact the language of a real-life Huck and a real-life Holden. Their genius lies in their mastery of the technique of first person narration which, through meticulous selection, creates vividly the illusion of life: gradually and subtly their narrators emerge and stand revealed, stripped to their innermost beings. It is a mark of their creator's mastery that Huck and Holden appear to reveal themselves.

It is not the least surprising aspect of *The Catcher in the Rye* that trite expressions and metaphors with which we are all familiar and even bored turn out, when emerging from the mouth of a sixteen-year-old, to be funny. The unimaginative repetition of identical expressions in countless situations intensifies the humor. The things in Holden's world are always jumping up and down or bouncing or scattering "like madmen." Holden always lets us know when he has insight into the absurdity of the endless absurd situations which make up the life of a sixteen-year-old by exclaiming, "It killed me." In a phony world Holden feels compelled to reenforce his sincerity and truthfulness constantly with, "It really is" or "It really did." Incongruously the adjective "old" serves as a term of endearment, from "old" Thomas Hardy to "old" Phoebe. And many of the things Holden does, he does ambiguously, "like a bastard."

Holden is a master of the ludicrous irrelevancy. Indeed, a large part of *The Catcher in the Rye* consists of the relevantly irrelevant. On the opening page, Holden says, "I'm not going to tell you my whole goddam autobiography or anything. I'll just tell you about this madman stuff that happened to me around last Christmas. . . ." By the time we have finished *Catcher* we feel that we know Holden as thoroughly as any biography could reveal him, and one of the reasons is that he has not hesitated to follow in his tale wherever whim and fancy lead him. For example, in the early part of the novel, Holden goes at some length into the history of the Ossenburger Memorial Wing of the new dorms, his place of residence. Ossenburger, we are told, was the Pencey alumnus who made a "pot of dough" in the undertaking business, and who, after giving money to Pencey, gave a speech in chapel "that lasted about ten hours." "He told us we should always pray to God— talk to Him and all—wherever we were. He told us we ought to think of Jesus as our buddy and all. He said *he* talked to Jesus all of the time. Even when he was driving his car. That killed me. I can just see the big phony bastard shifting into first gear and asking Jesus to send him a few more stiffs." Ossenburger, of course, has nothing to do, directly, with the "madman stuff" that happened to Holden around Christmas; but Holden's value judgment of the phony Ossenburger is certainly relevant to Salinger's purpose, the revelation of Holden's character.

When Holden refuses to express aggressive dislike of the repulsive Ackley, the pimply boy whose teeth "looked mossy and awful," he is not being facetious nor is he lying. He is simply expressing an innocence incapable of genuine hatred. Holden does not suffer from the inability to love, but he does despair of finding a place to bestow his love. The depth of Holden's capacity for love is revealed in his final words, as he sits in the psychiatric ward musing over his nightmarish adventures: "If you want to know the truth, I don't *know* what I think about it. I'm sorry I told so many people about it. About all I know is, I sort of miss everybody I told about. Even old Stradlater and Ackley, for instance. I think

I even miss that goddam Maurice. It's funny. Don't ever tell anybody anything. If you do, you start missing everybody." We agree
with Holden that it is funny, but it is funny in a pathetic kind of
way. As we leave Holden alone in his room in the psychiatric ward,
we are aware of the book's last ironic incongruity. It is not Holden
who should be examined for a sickness of the mind, but the world
in which he has sojourned and found himself an alien. To "cure"
Holden, he must be given the contagious, almost universal disease
of phony adultism; he must be pushed over that "crazy cliff."

MARK TWAIN AND J. D. SALINGER:
A STUDY IN LITERARY CONTINUITY

by EDGAR BRANCH

In J. D. Salinger's *The Catcher in the Rye* Holden Caulfield reflects
on Mr. Antolini, his former teacher, from whose homosexual pet-
tings he has just fled in panic: ". . . I started thinking that even
if he was a flit he certainly'd been very nice to me. I thought how
he hadn't minded it when I'd called him up so late, and how he'd
told me to come right over. . . . And how he went to all that trouble
giving me that advice about finding out the size of your mind
and all. . . ." Huckleberry Finn, in his "close place" a century
earlier, muses on his best teacher, Jim: "I . . . got to thinking over
our trip down the river; and I see Jim . . . standing my watch on
top of his'n . . . so I could go on sleeping; and see him how glad
he was when I come back out of the fog . . . and such-like times;
and would always call me honey, and pet me and do everything he
could think of for me . . ." Huck can always depend on Jim; their
physical relationship is consciously innocent. But Mr. Antolini is
Holden's last adult refuge in his disintegrating world. Huck, resolving his inner conflict by a free moral decision, takes immediate
bold steps to help Jim. But Holden becomes "more depressed and
screwed up" than ever after fleeing Mr. Antolini. Ominously, as
he walks down Fifth Avenue, he feels he is disappearing. He
retreats to the Museum of Natural History, the "place where the

mummies were" and a favorite childhood haunt that he remembers
as "so nice and peaceful"—like Huck's raft. But even there life-
obscenity intrudes—Huck's raft has its Duke and Dauphin too—
and he learns that "You can't ever find a place that's nice and
peaceful, because there isn't any." Each of these experienced boys
knows all about fraud and violence but retains the charity of an
innocent heart. Each is a measure of the need and possibility for
human love in his society.

Holden's society differs as dramatically from Huck's as does a
Broadway traffic jam from a raft drifting down the Mississippi a
long century ago. Yet a flight down the river and a flight through
New York streets turn out to be not so different after all. The
pattern of Holden's experience is essentially Huck's. Salinger's
writing carries familiar rhythms and attitudes. The creative imagina-
tions of these two authors who fuse given fact and boyish consciousness into expressive, dramatized narrative are strikingly similar.
The Catcher in the Rye, in fact, is a kind of *Huckleberry Finn* in
modern dress. This paper does not propose to reveal any direct,
"real" or conscious "influences"—if these exist at all—that *Huckleberry Finn* had upon Salinger's novel. Nor is its purpose to compare
the "then" and "now" of American society through the illustrative
use of these books. Rather, it attempts to bare one nerve of cultural
continuity in America by dissecting some literary relationships
between the two novels.

Consider first the narrative patterns and styles.

Huck initially flees conventionalities, constraint and terror. On
the river he meets murderous thieves, a treacherous fog, Negro
hunters and a steamboat that rips through the raft and thrusts him
among feuding country gentility. He lives with professional crooks
who fatten on "greenhorns" and "flatheads." He sees a harmless
drunk shot dead and a Southern colonel almost lynched, observes
some theatrical obscenities and at great personal risk saves the
inheritance of three innocent girls. Experience teaches Huck that
truth is usually weak, trouble best avoided and evil often inevitable.
It confirms his love of beauty and peaceful security. But notably in
his greatest struggle, over Jim, he acts spontaneously and defiantly
for goodness. Huck eventually comes to the Phelps plantation, the

homelike place where Jim finds freedom and where Huck will take leave of "sivilization" by going west.

Holden Caulfield, intensely troubled, escapes initially from the stupid constraints and violence of his prep school life. Like Huck, he enters a jungle world, New York City, where he knows his way around but from which he is alienated. There for two hectic days and nights he steers his course through battering adventures with fearsome "dopes," "fakers," "morons" and sluggers. On this journey Holden's Jim is primarily the recurring image of Jane Gallagher, an old friend who needs love and whom he loves with strange unawareness. Holden's Jim is also all little children, whom he would save from adult sexuality. Like Huck, Holden has a conflict. His adolescent sexual urges are somehow entangled with what is predatory in the "mean guys" he hates. They befoul his sense of the fine and good. Although not as self-sufficient as Huck, Holden is usually as realistic, and he too loves beauty and peace. Yet he values goodness above know-how, sophistication, style, success. After a secret visit home, he plans to lead a hermit's life in the West, but is reconciled to the city by the love of his little sister Phoebe. Physically weakened and psychically wounded, he is last seen recuperating in a sanitarium. Clearly Mark Twain and Salinger present parallel myths of American youth confronting his world—Huck Finn over many months, when time was expendable; Holden over two days when, Salinger seems to imply, time is rapidly running out.

Each novel employs an appropriate first person vernacular. Holden has the more "educated" vocabulary; he speaks with a modern schoolboy's idiom and slang and he can spell. Also he can swear. Both boys observe accurately and swiftly. Both are artists of deadpan, yet can subtly convey the interplay of feeling and scene. Huck arrives at the Phelps farm:

> When I got there it was all still and Sunday-like, and hot and sunshiny—the hands was gone to the fields; and there was them kind of faint dronings of bugs and flies in the air that makes it seem so lonesome and like everybody's dead and gone; and if a breeze fans along and quivers the leaves, it makes you feel mournful, because you feel like it's spirits whispering—spirits that's been dead ever so many years—and you always think

they're talking about *you*. As a general thing it makes a body
wish *he* was dead, too, and done with it all.

Holden observes New York's streets from a taxicab:

What made it worse, it was so quiet and lonesome out, even
though it was Saturday night. I didn't see hardly anybody on the
street. Now and then you just saw a man and a girl crossing a
street, with their arms around each other's waists and all, or a
bunch of hoodlumy-looking guys and their dates, all of them
laughing like hyenas at something you could bet wasn't funny.
New York's terrible when somebody laughs on the street very late
at night. You can hear it for miles. It makes you feel so lonesome
and depressed. I kept wishing I could go home. . . .

Huck's speech, usually dispassionate and matter-of-fact, is relaxed
and flexibly rhythmical. Holden, frequently conscious of the
smothering omnipresence of sex, draws most things taut. Nervous,
jerky reiteration often points up his emotional tensions. His speech
is sometimes raucous and jarring. He tends to rail and condemn.
Huck's direct apprehension gives us an objective recording rich in
implication. His version etches an open world, clear, solid, real, with
living characters moving autonomously in it. Holden's tense out-
pouring is a convincing expression of his psychological unrest and
of the release he is finding in psychiatric treatment. His speech
carries hints of the frantic overtones of a Poe character speaking
from a madhouse (humanized by delightful comedy), and his
world and its people, though violently alive, revolve in the whirl-
pool of his egocentricity. Both styles are effectively ironic and
humorous.

Perhaps Huck's profoundest relation to life is an animal faith, an
acceptance of reality that assimilates the irrational and cruel even
while it condemns them through exposure. That acceptance pro-
motes a classic simplicity of style, the more dignified for the dark
undertones present. But Holden's rejection and disgust create a
feverish modern dissonance. Alienation is expressed by obsessive
revelation, sometimes more suggestive of Theodor Fischer in Mark
Twain's *The Mysterious Stranger* than of Huck Finn. Holden's
speech is indeed suited to his neurotic experience of the all-
engulfing modern city. Huck's speech is equally well suited to
his personality and to what Mark Twain had to say about a vanished

era, a time permitting Huck's hard-won victory over self and circumstance. Salinger's adaptation of the language to his hero's
speech habits, character and times points up the stylistic continuity
between the two books. . . .

Especially in its characterization of the hero, *The Catcher in
the Rye* is a haunting reminder of *Huckleberry Finn.*

Holden wants to shepherd the young, to be the only big person
around; but Huck is the youthful liberator of a grown man, and
whether he knows it or not his effort is directed toward making
maturity possible. Holden is a conscious idealist who yet says, "I
kept wishing I could go home." Huck lives humbly and prudently
to get what he wants, but for *his* future home he chooses hell. Mr.
Antolini is warning Holden when he says that the immature man
wants to die nobly for a cause, while the mature man wants to live
humbly for one—but he might have been approving Huck. The
hope in Mark Twain's novel is that a ragamuffin preadolescent
acts maturely for what is good in an open society. The underlying
despair of Salinger's book is that a privileged adolescent wants
to act immaturely for what he believes is good in a society thickened
into vulgarity.

Yet Holden is truly a kind of latter-day, urbanized Huck. He is
acutely sensitive to places and times, whether groping through a
dark foyer in the early morning hours or relaxing in the cozy
auditorium of the Museum of Natural History, where it "always
smelled like it was raining outside, even if it wasn't. . . ." He knows
the uniqueness of things: the feel of a roller-skate key is unforget-
table, everlasting, shimmering with human meaning. With every
nerve he feels the moral character of others. He sharply registers the
unguarded phrase or facial expression—the prostitute Sunny's
childish "Like fun you are," or the beauty of Phoebe's open-mouthed
sleep. Although Huck can easily spot "phonies"—witness the Widow
Douglas, who approved of taking snuff "because she done it herself"—Holden is violently allergic to them: Carl Luce, a specialist
in extracting intimate sex confessions from young boys but a sore-
head "if you starting asking *him* questions about *himself*"; or the
popular entertainer Ernie who, when playing the piano, "*sounds
like the kind of a guy that won't talk to you unless you're a big
shot.*" But the kettle drummer in the Radio City orchestra, whom

Holden had observed closely for years, never looked bored even though he might bang the drums only twice during a piece. "Then when he does bang them, he does it so nice and sweet, with this nervous expression on his face." The drummer is what "Jesus *really* would've liked" in all the lavish Radio City Christmas pageant.

Holden has Huck's judicious mind and his respect for fact and knowledge. Huck "studies," Holden "analyzes." Both will generously grant any person his particular points. Harris Macklin, for instance, is the biggest bore Holden knows, but Harris is an inimitable whistler—"So I don't know about bores. . . . They don't hurt anybody, most of them, and maybe they're secretly all terrific whistlers or something." But Holden is not equally generous with himself. He is the "only really dumb one" in his family, "very yellow" and a "sacrilegious atheist." His relentless self-criticism is alerted by the slightest stirring of "phoniness" within. As with Huck, his humility ironically reveals his goodness and integrity. . . .

In this corrupt world Holden miraculously keeps the uncorrupted heart that most reminds us of Huckleberry Finn. He genuinely loves natural beauty and the socially unspoiled. Freer than Huck from conventional responses, he is an instinctive moralistic democrat whose feelings recall Whitman's "By God! I will accept nothing which all cannot have their counterpart of on the same terms." He sympathizes with the kindhearted, the suffering and the helpless. He lies outrageously to protect a mother from the knowledge that her son's basic character is displayed in his passion for snapping, with his soggy knotted towel, the backsides of boys emerging from the shower. In a touching flashback he comforts unhappy Jane Gallagher, whom he values for her human eccentricities and her real quality—her "muckle-mouthed" way of talking, her curious way of playing checkers and her love of poetry. He best conceives peace and virtue in the imagery of physical and mental cripples— the Bible "lunatic . . . that lived in the tombs and kept cutting himself with stones," and the "poor deaf-mute bastard" Holden himself would like to be. He is haunted by the peace of two nuns he met, and in several of his actions he unconsciously imitates the compassion of Jesus.

Holden, in short, like Huck, respects human personality and hates whatever demeans it. He knows that snobbery is aggression, and that subordinating people to ideas and things destroys fruitful human intercourse. . . . Unselfish love and spontaneous joy— Holden values these expressions of the uncontaminated spirit above all. So rarely are they found and so often thwarted in adult life that their slightest appearance saddens him. As he prepares to leave Pencey and packs the brand-new ice skates his mother had just bought him, he can see her "going in Spaulding's and asking the salesman a million dopey questions—and here I was getting the ax again. It made me feel pretty sad." Later on, Sunny, who sells her love at so much a throw, wants Holden to hang up her new dress to prevent wrinkles. Again he feels sad as he thinks of her buying it and "nobody in the store knowing she was a prostitute and all. The salesman probably just thought she was a regular girl when he bought it." But the little boy singing "Coming Through the Rye" is a regular kid, happy, fulfilled, innocently insulated from the disagreeable. "He had a pretty little voice, too. . . . The cars zoomed by, brakes screeched all over the place, his parents paid no attention to him, and he kept on walking next to the curb and singing 'If a body catch a body coming through the rye.' It made me feel better." Holden is happy in the world of innocence that creates its own conditions. Desperately lonesome, he reveals his need for human intimacy by using the word "catch."

Clearly Holden and Huck, who so often shape their experience in similar patterns, have similar qualities. Holden's acute self-consciousness and his evident neuroticism do not diminish the reality or worth of what he is and feels. Nor do they invalidate the comparison between the two boys. Rather, by appropriately distinguishing a typically modern personality from Huck Finn, still predominantly one of the "Divine Inert" but already, in his extreme and sensitive youth, bearing the scars of harsh experience, they help define the direct descent of Holden from Huck.

Huckleberry Finn and *The Catcher in the Rye* are akin also in ethical-social import. Each book is a devastating criticism of American society and voices a morality of love and humanity.

In many important matters, as we have just seen, Huck and Holden—not to speak of others like Jim and Phoebe—affirm goodness, honesty and loyalty. Huck does so almost unconsciously, backhandedly, often against his conventional conscience, and Holden does so with an agonizing self-consciousness and a bitter spirit. In each the perception of innocence is radical: from their mouths come pessimistic judgments damning the social forms that help make men less than fully human. "Human beings *can* be awful cruel to one another," observes Huck after seeing the Duke and Dauphin tarred and feathered. And Huck assumes his share of the guilt. Holden, with searingly honest insight that gets to the root of sadistic practices and class jealousies, remarks: "I can even get to hate somebody, just *looking* at them, if they have cheap suitcases with them . . . it's really hard to be roommates with people if your suitcases are much better than theirs. . . . You think if they're intelligent . . . they don't give a damn whose suitcases are better, but they do. They really do." To Aunt Sally's question whether anybody was hurt in the steamboat accident, Huck replies, "No'm. Killed a nigger," and the blindness of a civilization is bared with terrible casualness. The same ironic exposure comes in Holden's apology for having to like a girl before he can get sexy— "I mean *really* sexy"—with her. So he remarks, "My sex life stinks." And Carl Luce, the modern expert on love, answers: "Naturally it does, for God's sake."

Such examples might easily be multiplied: the vision is often identical. Yet we must grant that the reliability and quality of Holden's vision are complicated, far beyond Huck's straightforward objectivity, by the loss he has sustained. As Holden recognizes, he is mentally ill. "I don't get hardly anything out of anything. I'm in bad shape. I'm in *lousy* shape." Bad as the modern world is, his view of it adds a distortion not found in Huck's picture. Almost everyone in Holden's world is "phony"—headmasters, students, alumni, bartenders, movie actors, moviegoers, people who say "Glad to've met you" or "Good luck!" or "Grand!", virile hand-shakers, Holy Joe ministers, even partially bald men who hopefully comb their hair over the bald spot. The book reeks with Holden's revulsion and nausea. He experiences things in an aura of disgusting physical details. The park is "lousy" with "dog crap, globs of spit and cigar butts." A chair is "vomity" looking. A cab smells as though someone had "tossed his cookies in it." Moreover, although Holden keeps his innocent heart, his adolescence has riddled the innocence of mind, that naïveté, which Huck in good measure still possesses. What Holden's heart seeks and responds to, his mind sees is violated everywhere by the mere fact of human maturity. Adult activities become expressive masks for adult sexuality. The four-letter word he reads with horror—and erases—on the wall of Phoebe's school follows him wherever he goes. In the quiet tomb of Pharaoh in the museum, he feels at peace for the first time—until suddenly he sees the same word in red crayon on the wall. Despairingly, hysterically, he thinks that even in death he will not escape that word which someone surely will write on his tombstone. A great difference between the two boys is measured by Huck's sensitive but reserved opinion of the obscene words on the wall of the abandoned house floating down the June rise: "the ignorantest kind of words . . ."

Certainly if Huck's vision reveals both the limitations and promises of democracy—the hope and despair—Holden's, in direct descent from Huck's, focuses upon the despair. In the predatory wasteland of the city, Holden can foresee no future refuge or good. (Is it by accident that some lines of weary futility from "The Love Song of J. Alfred Prufrock" are echoed in Holden's words to Sally Hayes: "It wouldn't be the same at all. You don't see what I mean at all"?) If he and Sally were married, Holden knows he would be an office worker "making a lot of dough, and riding to work in . . . Madison Avenue buses, and reading newspapers, and playing bridge all the time, and going to the movies and seeing a lot of stupid shorts and coming attractions and newsreels." He accurately describes the commercialized Christmas spirit as something over which "old Jesus probably would've puked if He could see it." He damns the competitive drive for status. Even the cab drivers, primitives of the city, are suspicious, raw-nerved. And nowhere is there peace. Holden's view of modern war concludes: "I'm sort of glad they've got the atomic bomb invented. If there's ever another war, I'm going to sit right the hell on top of it. I'll volunteer for it. . . ." Neurotic or not, Holden's criticism often hits home.

Like Holden, Huck knows the meaning of respectable routine, competition and violence, but the difference is that what is organized nightmare in Holden's world is merely nascent in Huck's. Everyone can remember the brutal and degenerate persons Huck encounters and some of the dozen or more corpses that bloody up his story. Holden's society holds far more possibilities for horror and depravity, and on a massive scale. Feverishly, obsessively on the move, it has more irritants and fewer profound satisfactions than does Huck's. Holden's cherished memory of one little duck pond in Central Park replaces Huck's Jackson's Island and lazy days on the Mississippi. The three or four lights Huck sees, "twinkling where there were sick folks, maybe," are not so much, compared to the health, the beauty, the freedom of the river. The sparkling metropolis Holden sees looming over the forlorn duck pond is inescapable, portentous. The life Huck explores, despite its evil and treachery, is still daring and redemptive, not just sodden, mean and self-destructive.

Given such contrasting conditions, what moral destiny confronts the individual in the worlds Salinger and Mark Twain create? Like the Central Park ducks in winter, Holden is essentially homeless, frozen out. But Huck, although an outcast, is a true homemaker wherever he is. Allie's baseball mitt is all that is left to Holden of Allie's love, and unlike Huck, he seems unable to break through the ring of hostility to find new sources of affection. Deprived of real opportunity for the sort of soul-shaking sacrifice Huck makes for Jim, Holden expresses his love for Phoebe by the gift of a phonograph record—which breaks. Of greater significance, Huck has Jim; but Holden, so desperately in need of love, is one of the loneliest characters in fiction. Obviously Huck is not as critically wounded as Holden. He has far more resilience, a stronger power of renewal. Necessity shows him the wisdom of prudence, and his natural environment provides therapeutic primal sanities. Both boys are rebels—with a difference. Huck can often go naked, but Holden can defy convention only by wearing his "corny" red hunting cap. Capable of making a free choice, Huck outwits his enemies and rises above the compulsions within. He is a practical rebel like Thoreau. He runs away to confront and modify reality, and thereby he proves, for his day, the explosive force of individual ethical action. Holden runs off too, but his actions are usually ineffective, and the path of escape leads him deeper into the mire of his personal difficulties.

Huckleberry Finn, in short, recognizes both necessity and freedom, the restrictions limiting moral accomplishment and its possibility. *The Catcher in the Rye* leaves us doubtful that the individual, even assisted by the analyst's best efforts, can ever truly escape the double trap of society and self. How well the two concluding scenes contrast these moral outlooks! Throughout *The Catcher in the Rye* Holden makes, and is, a telling criticism of our civilization: his "madness" in itself is a damning fact of our times; yet, doubly damning, what the "madman" says is often true, what he feels often unimpeachable. Supremely ironical, then, is our last glimpse of Holden making recovery and adjustment in the sanitarium—a prelude to compromise in the outside world—as Father Peter in Mark Twain's *The Mysterious Stranger* cannot do. Holden says: "I sort of *miss* everybody I told about. Even old Stradlater and Ackley, for instance. I think I even miss that goddam Maurice. It's funny. Don't ever tell anybody anything. If you do, you start missing everybody." Modern therapy takes over; Holden will return. For Holden's sake we wouldn't have it otherwise, even though it's a return to the big money and the dopey newsreels. But we remember Huck with admiration and with confidence in his personal future as, Jim freed and the Duke and Dauphin in limbo, he says: "I reckon I got to light out for the Territory ahead of the rest, because Aunt Sally she's going to adopt me and sivilize me and I can't stand it. I been there before."

No wonder Holden wants to remain forever the catcher in the rye—*his* free Territory—oblivious to the trap that maturity finally springs. His recessive traits suggest that the logical, perhaps desirable, end for him and his civilization is the pure silence of death, the final release from imperfect life. *Huckleberry Finn*, as Philip Young has recently realized, appeals to rescuing death in the series of escapes—gliding, still and dark—made by Huck and Jim as the raft slips into the flowing, mythic river. Huck, too, has guilt feelings that, if sufficiently intensified, could conceivably lead to self-destruction. But such suggestions are muted in Huck's story, for Huck is committed to life. In Salinger's book death symbols are more pronounced, and death openly fascinates Holden not only for its horror but for the peaceful refuge it offers from the consciousness of life. Beneath the appealing and often hilarious humor, comparable to some of the best of Mark Twain's, life is felt in this book fundamentally as a ceaseless, pushing round of activity that one would be well rid of. Holden carries with him a dim sense of the eternal and transcendental. He is something like a soul unknowingly striving to rise from the muck of this world to the peace of nirvana. Jane Gallagher is always beyond his reach; he must settle for Sally Hayes, the "queen of the Phonies." Like Teddy McArdle in Salinger's story "Teddy," Holden might have called his contemporaries a "bunch of apple-eaters." Like Jean in Salinger's "De Daumier-Smith's Blue Period," Holden might have felt that in this life he "would always at best be a visitor in a garden of enamel urinals and bedpans, with a sightless, wooden dummy-deity standing by. . . ." But for Jean, "the sun came up." Sudden spiritual insight transforms that garden into a "shimmering field of exquisite, twice-blessed, enamel flowers." Nirvana is here and now. Holden, of course, has hardly begun to find the peace and illumination inherent in a full understanding of the Zen koan inscribed in Salinger's second book, *Nine Stories:*

> We know the sound of two hands clapping.
> But what is the sound of one hand clapping?

but the urge to find them works deeply within him. Salinger's social criticism, it would seem, has a mystical base, a support more profound than mere belief in Holden's Christian virtues, though that belief is present too. It constantly implies a religious feeling, possibly a conviction, that dimly hints a way out of the life-trap. Mark Twain's social criticism in *Huckleberry Finn* is more simply that of the rational democrat and humanitarian who has not lost faith in the practical effectiveness of the good heart on this earth.

We have seen that *Huckleberry Finn* and *The Catcher in the Rye* share certain ethical and social attitudes. Yet Salinger's critical view assumes a cultural determinism that in Huckleberry Finn, although always present, permits freedom through self-guidance. Salinger's viewpoint also draws upon a mystical sense merely inchoate in Mark Twain's imagination. We have seen too that Holden's neuroticism is both literary cause and social effect. It is Salinger's means of etching the modern picture the more deeply, and a product of the culture it so sweepingly condemns on moral grounds. But Mark Twain's moral vision is projected through the prevailing normality of Huck's temperament. It is eminently central; fundamentally there is nothing rigged about Huck's experience or eccentric in his responses. So Huck on a raft, as profoundly symbolic today as Thoreau in his cabin, is ever more meaningful as our national experience hurtles us along routes more menacing than the Mississippi. *The Catcher in the Rye,* always cautionary, often horrifying in moral tone, creates an overwhelming sense of that hurtling. The point is not that Salinger's moral vision is therefore defective. Rather, because his vision is lit by the sick lamps of civilization, *The Catcher in the Rye* is as appropriate to our age as *Huckleberry Finn* is to an earlier America. Salinger's novel, in fact, suggests great truths about our times, as Whitman's *Democratic Vistas* did, in polemic form, about an earlier age that was cankered, crude, materialistic, depraved. *The Catcher in the Rye* has the same awesome relevance to our collective civilized fate that more subtly pervades Mark Twain's masterpiece. Nowhere is its literary descent from *Huckleberry Finn* more clearly seen than in its critical modern dramatization of moral and social themes.

To conclude, the two novels are clearly related in narrative pattern and style, characterization of the hero and critical import—the three areas discussed in this paper. The relationship argues the continuing vitality of Huck's archetypal story, absorbed by generations and still creatively at work in contemporary thought and art. *The Catcher in the Rye* takes its place in that literary tradition—spreading beyond Anderson, Lardner, Hemingway, Faulkner—that has one of its great sources in *Huckleberry Finn.* But the literary kinship of these two novels presupposes a type of cultural continuity more basic than the dynamics of literary tradition or than the persistence of Huck's story in the popular imagination. We have seen that each author responds sensitively to the times he depicts, appropriately choosing his facts and shaping his language and meaning to portray the social and moral realities clustered in and about his hero. Yet the resulting differences do not obscure the similarity in the conformations of character and social relationships that emerge. Fundamentally these books are brothers under the skin because they reflect a slowly developing but always recognizable pattern of moral and social meaning that is part of the active experience of young Americans let loose in the world, in this century and the last. Independently and in his own right, each author has probed beneath surface facts—so dramatically contrasted in Huck's and Holden's environments—to the experiential continuity of American life.

x. Against the Cult of the Child

This essay, somewhat abridged, by Leslie Fiedler is not directly concerned with Salinger, but it touches on his work at many points and builds a rather dazzling structure of generalization into which Salinger fits along with the rest of America. To what has already been said about this piece in the introduction, one might add that Fiedler seems to see the world as a sexual conspiracy: perversion lurks everywhere, and innocence is merely a front for the unspeakable. But Fiedler is a prophet among critics, and the prophet must see all evil, hear all evil: it is his job. Despite his touch of monomania, Fiedler is a remarkably subtle and flexible theorizer, whose tone is much crasser than his philosophy. Whether one agrees with him or not, one must admire his courage in tackling so sacred a subject as childhood and emerging on the opposite side of the angels.

THE EYE OF INNOCENCE

by LESLIE FIEDLER

We move through a world of books in which the child is so accepted a feature of the landscape that we are aware of him chiefly when he is absent. There he is (or she—it scarcely matters), his eye to the keyhole, his ear to the crack in the door, peering, listening, observing in his innocence our lack of it. He is the touchstone, the judge of our world—and a reproach to it in his unfallen freshness of insight, his unexpended vigor, his incorruptible naïveté. Or he is the hero himself: Tom Sawyer or Huck Finn or Holden Caulfield, the Good American, the unrecognized saint, living in a hogshead or thrown out of fashionable bars: the cornerstone the builders rejected, Christ as a J.D.

So ubiquitous and symbolic a figure is, of course, no mere reproduction of a fact of existence; he is a cultural invention, a product of the imagination. But what have we invented him *for*, and out of what stuff have we contrived him? There is something both ambiguous and unprecedented about the Cult of the Child; indeed, the notion that a mere falling short of adulthood is a guarantee of insight and even innocence is a sophisticated view, a latter-day Pastoralism, which finds a Golden Age not in history but at the beginning of each lifetime. The invention of special clothing, special books, a special role in literature for children belongs to a late, a perhaps decadent phase of our culture.

In Greek art, to be sure, the icon of the downy-cheeked boy is caressed in a thousand tender works of sculpture. The undraped adolescent, bent to remove the thorn in his foot or lying with his back to the beholder, becomes the Aphrodite of the pederast; but he is considered a love object only, not a small prophet or a guide to a lost innocence. In the Judaeo-Christian tradition, such erotic trifling with the image of childhood stirs only hostility; "he who offends the least of my little ones" is promised a fate which would make it better that a millstone were round his neck and he cast into the sea.

There is, however, no pious counteridealization of the child to replace the rejected image of the Greeks. In the Old Testament, indeed, there seems a willful, to us almost perverse, resolve not to exploit the possibilities of the child, even in stories which demand for him a central role. Isaac, who, in our reimaginings of the fable of the Sacrifice, has an outward shape and a psychology, is in Genesis a cipher. The rabbis when they commented on the story said that he was thirty when he submitted to his father's knife. Thirty! The revolution in imagination which lies between the Biblical account and our response to it is implicit in our difficulty in conceiving a middle-aged Isaac or making the legend come to life around him.

In the New Testament, there are other forces at work; and in the Gospel according to Luke, the Nativity story opens up what strike us as irresistible opportunities for creating images of appealing babyhood, the pure infant symbolically situated between beasts and Wise Men. It is not, however, until the Renaissance that the Babe escapes from the text to its mother's pearly breast, fulfills itself as a significant image: innocence as infancy, the infant as Innocence itself. Earlier, the Christian imagination does not know what to do with the paradox of the child as Savior; one recalls the rigid Christ Child of Byzantine mosaics, his tiny hand raised in a gesture of command and blessing—not an infant at all, only a miniature Emperor of the Universe. Indeed, not until the Renaissance blossoms into the baroque does the Christ Child come fully into his own; it is then that the prototypes of sentimental religious art are established once and for all: playing on the appeal of motherhood and babyhood in a maudlin upsurge of self-deception which ends by making quite good Christians (and parents of actual children) incapable of granting the possibility of infant damnation.

The orthodox and patriarchal Trinity of Father, Son and Holy Ghost is at this point replaced by a popular matriarchal anti-Trinity of Virgin, Cuckold and Infant; a group derived, the experts tell us, from ancient portrayals of Venus, Vulcan and Cupid, the antique form of the fatherless family. The dimpled Babe of the baroque tableau is still quite different, however, from the modern notion of the child as spokesman for the unfallen ego, still a part of the theatrical-sentimental attempt of the Counter Reformation to wash away Protestantism—that rigid reassertion of Fatherhood as an all-sufficient principle—in a flood compounded of mother's milk, the tears of the Magdalene and the blood of Jesus' circumcision.

Expectedly enough, so liquid and maternal a revolt, reducing the male to infant size, a helpless burden in the lap of his adoring mother, stirred little response in the paternalistic Protestant North, particularly in the Anglo-Saxon world. There child witches continued to be hanged; while infant damnation continued to seem probable to those remembering in a colder clime Augustine's observation that the innocence of childhood is more a matter of weakness of the limbs than of purity of the heart.

Even in the Catholic South, no fundamental change in the view of childhood was possible, despite the exploitation of its painterly appeal, so long as the orthodox theory of Original Sin was unchallenged. If one began by believing that an originally corrupted nature must be trained (cajoled and beaten) into the semblance of orderly virtue, he ended by being convinced that an adult had some chance of attaining goodness, the child little or none. Similarly, so long as maturity and virtue were identified, so long as goodness was considered the function of conscience rather than impulse, no adult could consider postulating the child as a moral touchstone. The occasional use of abused and suffering children for the sake of pathos, in Dante, say, or in Shakespeare, was necessarily peripheral. Children were, symbolically speaking, beside the point. It was no more possible to conceive of a child as hero than of a peasant in the same role.

One of the major shifts in modern thinking involves moving the child from the periphery to the center of art—and, indeed, to the center of life. Child-worship may begin as one of those pieces of literary hypocrisy (like the courtly adulation of woman), a purely theoretical gesture of compensation by those who, in real life, neither spared the rod nor spoiled the child (and felt a little guilty about it somehow); but it ends in a child-centered society, where the parent not merely serves but emulates his immature offspring. This revolution is, of course, merely the by-product of a much larger one, of the shift from a belief in Original Sin to one in Original Innocence—or, to put it more precisely, to a belief that the same original disposition once called "sin" was more properly labeled "innocence."

The time of that major revolution is the mid-eighteenth century and its prophet (however many statements to the contrary scholars extract from his utterly contradictory works) is Jean Jacques Rousseau, whose waking on the road to Vincennes, his waistcoat wet with tears, marks the moment of a New Revelation. It is told that on the day Christ was born, certain sailors off the coast of Illyria heard a wailing from the woods and a terrible voice crying, "The God Pan is dead!" If on the day of Rousseau's vision no one heard the countercry, "The God Pan is reborn!" that is because no one any longer listened.

The West that had for more than seventeen hundred years deified its superego turned again to making the id its god. The scholars have many names for the New Revelation in its various stages and aspects: Pantheism, Deism, *Sturm und Drang*, Sentimentalism, Romanticism, etc. In the light of depth psychology, which is one of the products of the movement and can be considered its "theology," let us call it the Psychic Breakthrough, the Re-emergence of the Id. We who are its children and its heirs live in an age characterized by the consciousness of the unconscious and by a resolve to propitiate and honor that dark force, so long surrendered to the auspices of unlettered witches and shabby wizards.

The keynote of such an age is revolution and its not-so-secret motto: "Whatever is up shall be down! Whatever is down shall be up!" In a very few years, the archetypal villains of the European mind, Don Juan and Faust, are transformed into heroes; "to make a pact with the Devil" becomes the hallmark of a real man and true artist. Since Hell had become the official name of the forbidden world of impulse and unreason, it is hailed by the poets as their natural home.

Images of impulse and natural virtue were found readily enough, where one would expect them, in the virgin forests of the newer worlds: in dark-skinned natives in general and Indians in particular. But there were noble savages closer to home; one did not have to go abroad for counterimages to set against the corrupt figure of the European courtier. The peasant could be glorified over the city dweller; the idiot or the buffoon over the philosopher; woman over man—and within the female sex, the whore over the bourgeoise. All such oppositions are dangerous, however; no matter how abstractedly, how theoretically indulged, they threaten a disruption of the social values by which bourgeois society lives; and bourgeois society was, in fact, consolidating its greatest triumphs at the moment of the Psychic Breakthrough. The sons of the burghers, indeed, were precisely the dreamers and insatiable revolutionaries who were extending the Psychic Breakthrough; and though their fathers had approved, while they were down, the slogans of reversal, it was quite another matter when they were up.

Where the artist is most firmly committed to bourgeois values, especially where there is no surviving artistocratic tradition with which he can identify himself (in the Anglo-Saxon world, for instance), there is available to him one safely genteel symbol of protest and impulse: the Child. It is possible to insist that the child is father of the man, that he comes "trailing clouds of glory" which are dissipated in a world of duty and work, without seeming seriously to threaten the middle-class ethos, without, indeed, revealing to oneself one's own revolutionary intent. Do not all decent people, after all, love children?

The holiest icon of the Cult of the Child, of the Dream of Innocence in its pristine Anglo-Saxon form, is the Good Good Girl, the blond asexual goddess of nursery or orphanage, reincarnated from Little Nell to Mary Pickford. In this single figure are satisfied the middle-class desire to idealize womanhood; the Protestant resolve to celebrate premarital chastity; the North European wish to glorify the fair and debase the black; as well as the sentimental need to deliver childhood from the odor of diapers and the implications of Original Sin. Only the girl child seems a sufficiently spotless savior to the imagination of the North, which rejected the austere orthodox Trinity and the gaudy baroque one, the Son of the Father and the Virgin's Babe. The Son and his Sacred Mother (corrupted by "Papist Mariolatry") are reserved for other uses.

The new Holy Family is centered not around the Divine Boy but the Good Good Girl, imagined not in the arms of the mother but in those of the father, and not at the moment of birth but at that of death. The basic image is what has been called the Protestant *Pietà* (foreshadowed by Shakespeare in the final scenes of *King Lear*): the white-clad daughter, dying or dead, in the arms of the Old Man, tearful papa or grandfather or woolly-haired slave. It is the unendurable Happy Ending, as the white slip of a thing too good for this world prepares to leave for the next, while we, abandoned, sob into our handkerchiefs. The Good Good Girl must die, not only so that we may weep (and tears are, for the sentimentalist, the way to salvation), but also because there is nothing else for her to do—no course of action which would not sully her. Allowed to grow up, she could only become (forbidden the nunnery of the Protestant ethos) wife, mother or widow, tinged no matter how slightly by the stain of sexuality, a sexuality suffered, perhaps, rather than sought, but one in any case *there*.

It is notorious that Dickens exploited all his life a version of
the class struggle quite different from that of Marx. Not the proletarian but the child was his innocent victim; and his readers,
convinced with him that all of adult society was a conspiracy
against childhood, could sigh, wipe away the furtive tear and return
to their ordinary tasks indescribably satisfied. "We are all child
murderers!" his admirers were able to tell themselves, quite unaware that the realization titillated as much as it horrified them.

In Dickens, the dwarfish, albino monsters of forbearance and piety
are not only Little Nells; his symbols of offended innocence include
boys, too: Tiny Tim or Paul Dombey, who first asked what the
wild waves were saying, and learned at last that they whispered
the death, *his* death, necessary to redeem his father from pride and
wealth; even Oliver Twist, who does not ever quite die, little tease
that he is, but is in and out of the sickbed, constantly flirting with
the final consummation. In America, however, such figures are
somehow not quite acceptable; for in this country, genteel primitivism, like all else, must learn to abide by the double standard.

Little Lord Fauntleroy is an import once much admired by Euro-
peanizing females but always scorned by rugged nativists no matter
how sentimental. The Good Good Girl is naturalized without a
qualm, for she is Daisy Miller's younger sister, "America's Sweetheart," whether in bottle curls or bangs; but the Good Good Boy
seems the juvenile reminder of a tradition of aristocratic culture
we left behind. He is the "little gentleman," which is to say, the
villain: an insufferable outsider who wears his Sunday clothes
during the week and would rather walk shod than run barefoot.
Sometimes the "little gentleman" is called the "mama's boy," but
this is misleading in the extreme, since all American boys belong to
mother. Tom Sawyer, who sets the pattern, is fatherless by definition, born into a world presided over only by Aunt Polly; and he
melts with shame at the thought of her believing him faithless to
the maternal principle.

To betray the mother—to deny her like the young rogue in *The
Prince and the Pauper*: this is for Mark Twain, who speaks here
for all of America, the only unforgivable sin. What then is the
difference between the Good Good Boy and the Good Bad Boy,
between Sid Sawyer and Tom? The Good Good Boy does what his

mother must pretend to the rest of the world (even to herself) that she wants him to do: obey, conform; the Good Bad Boy does what she *really* wants him to do: deceive, break her heart a little, so that she can forgive him, smother him in the embrace that seals him back into her world forever. No wonder we can never have done pillorying the Good Good Boy in our books; no wonder we insist that no matter how he enters our fiction, he must exit whimpering, whipped, exposed as an alien and an impostor, no Saviour at all, though he may be the minister's son. Even his death does not shock us; and he is therefore chosen to play the part of the victim in *The Bad Seed* (even as Leopold and Loeb once chose him in real life), just the sort of little monster we have all righteously longed to kill, though we have not, of course, yielded to the temptation.

The Good Bad Boy, on the other hand, we all understand and love—at least feel obliged to pretend to understand and love. For a long time he was merely the "bad boy" without further qualification —his goodness needing no adjective to declare it to those who *really* knew him, his proud title almost enough in itself to ensure a best seller: *Confessions of a Bad Boy, Peck's Bad Boy,* etc. The male reader not enterprising enough to have been actually "bad" as a child himself could persuade himself as he read that this was, indeed, the true shape of his childhood; and his wife beside him could nod comfortably, believing, too, that her husband had been just so untamed before she had imprisoned him in the gentle bonds of her love. "Oh, you bad thing!" cries Becky Thatcher to her small noble savage, Tom, and the epithet is revealed as the supreme term of endearment. It is the fate of Good Good Girls to love such boys precisely because they play hooky, lie, cuss, steal in a mild sort of way, act the part of Robin Hood—refuse in short to be "sissies." Where taboos forbid the expression of sexuality except once removed in the form of aggression, such delinquency is the declaration of maleness. Besides, the Good Good Girls know all the time (what, of course, they never tell) that their young lovers are rugged individualists in embryo, boy Philistines in training.

In quite the same way, the modern Bad Good Girl (no longer permitted to flaunt her virtue, but expected to preserve it in some sense all the same) knows that the young radical or bohemian she loves is *playing* at being bad; will, like Tom Sawyer before him, end up as judge or bank president, senior editor at Random House —at the least as author of some latter-day *Confessions of a Bad Boy: Memoirs of a Revolutionist*, perhaps, or *The Naked God, An End to Innocence* or *On the Road*. Our American bad boys are, alas, examples of natural virtue, and must not be confused with the monstrous little villains of exemplary British books for children— or even with the Katzenjammerish projections of infantile sadism whom the Germans find so amusing and satisfactory.

Still less are they the horny adolescents of Mediterranean fiction, bedeviled by desire, and falling via sex to adulthood. No American boy hero is, in the classic tradition at least, devirginated into participation in the moral ambiguity of life. At best he is *terrified* into it; at worst he grows away from it into the safety of respectability. The Tom Sawyer archetype, the junior Robin Hood, can only grow into goodness, *i.e.*, success; for his "badness" is his boyhood and he cannot leave one behind without abandoning the other. His fantasies of revolt are oral not genital, his dreams of indulgences the stolen slab of bacon and the forbidden pipeful of tobacco. Grown older he will alternately diet and grow fat, honor his dreams of rebellion on the Sunday picnic or over the built-in Jackson's Island in his back yard.

The Good Bad Boy is, of course, America's vision of itself, is authentic America, crude and unruly in his beginnings but endowed by his creator with an instinctive sense of what is right; sexually as pure as any milky maiden, he is a roughneck all the same, at once potent and submissive. That the image of a boy represents our consciousness of ourselves and our role is scarcely surprising. We are, to the eternal delight and scorn of Europeans, inhabitants of a society in which scarcely anyone is too grave or mature to toss a ball around on a warm afternoon. Where almost every male is still trying to sneak out on Mother (whom he demands *make* him sneak his pleasures); where, as Geoffrey Gorer has made quite clear, mothers are also fathers—that is, embodiments of the superego—growing up is for the male not inheriting the superego position, but shifting it to a wife, *i.e.*, a mother of his own choice. No wonder our greatest book is about a boy and that boy "bad"!

The book is, of course, *Huckleberry Finn* (with its extension back into *Tom Sawyer*), an astonishingly complicated novel, containing not one image of the boy child as a symbol of the good life of impulse, but a series of interlocking ones: boys within boys.° Tom Sawyer exists as the projection of all that Sid Sawyer, pious Good Good Boy, presumably yearns for and denies; but Huck Finn in turn stands for what Tom is not quite rebel enough to represent; and Nigger Jim (remade from boy to adult between the two books) embodies a world of instinct and primitive terror beyond what even the outcast paleface boy projects. In most ways, Huck is closer to Jim than to Tom—that is, closer to what the white world of gentility fears and excludes than to what it condescendingly indulges in the child. He can *play* with Tom at being an outlaw and runaway, counterfeit the anguish of the excluded, but he is playing on the square as Tom is not.

But the novel *Huckleberry Finn* exists on two levels: as the tragic book Mark Twain half-unwittingly had to write, and as the comic one he was content to have most readers believe he had written. Twain himself confuses the two books hopelessly at the end, when Huck, calling himself Tom, *becomes* Tom; when Tom himself appears and reveals his whole role as fiction, a lie; and the tragic moral problem of Jim's freedom is frittered away in a conventional Happy Ending celebrated in the midst of furious horseplay. It is to this Happy Ending that we owe our idyllic vision of Childhood on the Mississippi.

Partly because of Twain's uncertainty, partly because of its own inability to accept his tragic vision of childhood, America has kept alive in its collective memory a euphoric series of illustrations to the comic novel Twain did not really write. In our national imagination, two freckle-faced boys arm in arm, fishing poles over their shoulders, walk toward the river; or one alone floats peacefully on its water, a runaway Negro by his side. They are on the lam, we know, from Aunt Polly and Aunt Sally and the Widow Douglas and Miss Wilson, from little golden-haired Becky Thatcher, too, whose name Twain forgot between books: from all the reduplicated female symbols of religion and "sivilization."

They live in a mythicized rural hinterland of America, in the antebellum small town, in America's childhood; and they pass through

° Some of these notions were suggested to me by James Cox's essay, "The Sad Initiation of Huckleberry Finn."

a landscape based not so much on memory and fact as on an urban nostalgia for the countryside and the village, the rich man's longings for the falsified place of his poverty. It is these kidnaped images which the popular imagination further debases step by step via Penrod and Sam or O. Henry's "Red Chief" to Henry Aldrich or the insufferable Archie of the teenage funny books. They become constantly more false in their naïveté, in their hostility to culture in general and schoolteachers in particular; and it scarcely matters whether they are kept in the traditional costume of overalls and bare feet or are permitted jeans and sweaters decorated with high-school letters. On the riverbank or in the Coke shop, afoot or in a stripped-down hot rod, they represent the American faith in the boy who will not go to school willingly, who will not learn anything except what his heart whispers to him, who is always ready to hang up the sign: GONE FISHIN'; but who charms away our distrust, turning on us the shy grin of innocence that can still elect a President of the United States.

The one realm of childhood experience almost completely excluded from the sentimental world bounded by the Good Good Girl and the Good Bad Boy is sex. Yet surely boys and girls even before the Civil War giggled at the sight of each other's underpants, crept off into private corners for intimate examinations, even played "doctor"; nor was all of this unknown to their elders. Indeed, Freud once complained that, despite all the protests raised over his theories of infantile sexuality, it was his dull duty merely to make public facts known to every nursemaid. If childhood is innocent to the Anglo-Saxon world of the nineteenth century, it is innocent by definition, pure by virtue of its symbolic function, sexless because the novelist in flight from sex demanded it be so.

In the genteel era, the Good Good Girl is more and more protected from contamination by sex; not only is she portrayed as innocent in herself; after a while, she is not even permitted to stir lust in the most ignoble heart. In America in particular as the nineteenth century wears on, Seduction, which as accomplished fact or omnipresent threat had been the staple of female fiction for a hundred years, is banned; and the heroine is moved back in age across the dangerous border line of puberty. Only Lewis Carroll (who wept when the young girls he loved put up their hair and let down their dresses) was able to rescue the prenubile heroine from pious insipidity. His Alice moves through a fantastic landscape where the symbols of sexuality seem mere magic or nonsense, and the threat of puberty is waked from as from a bad dream. But the main line of female fiction, after its retreat back behind pubescence, leads inevitably to Elsie Dinsmore! The Good Good Girl expires in the sanctimonious bathos of juvenile fictions presented by maiden aunts to their nieces in a desire to teach them that a woman must weep, without really revealing to them for what. Even boys' literature cannot entirely escape the stereotypes and taboos; and *Huckleberry Finn* is like *Alice in Wonderland* an evasion rather than a breakthrough, an acceptance however devious of the genteel decree that *all* literature must be fit for the eye of the sexless child.

It is not only that Twain deprives Huck of the prostitute sisters who helped define the lot of his real-life prototype; he cannot even (beneath the comic high jinks and realistic dialogue) avoid creating him in the image of the child heroines of contemporary best sellers: an orphan adopted by widows and old maids, an outcast, harried by his own father, and misunderstood by the respectable community—and, of course, an irreproachable virgin. One of the reasons it is so hard to tell Huck Finn's age (Twain *says* he's fourteen!) is Twain's unwillingness to confess that, capable as he is of shifting for himself, he is also sexually mature. Huck is permitted, it is true, to move in the world of the raree show; but he is not allowed to respond to the sexuality of such spectacles with the same awareness that he brings to the world of lynchings and cruelty which is its twin. Twain's scruples work in almost precisely the opposite way from those of our own latter-day sentimentalists: he is squeamish about sex, utterly frank about violence.

Yet his unwillingness to grant that Huck is physically a man makes it hard to assess the impact on him of the alienation he endures. Genteel taboos do not prevent Twain from rendering the brutal predicament of the child (adolescent?) buffeted between his own imaginary fears and the real terrors of the society that rejects him. We find it disturbingly easy, however, to forget the isolation out of which Huck comes and to which he returns: the fate of all those excluded from the comfortable, empty world of Aunt Sally.

So much is he the "poor, motherless" boy, the "child of nature," that we confuse him with the barefoot boy with cheek of tan— demote him to the moral imbecility of early childhood. Twain takes advantage of this ambiguity to make us approve his antisocial, "satanic" behavior, before which we might at least have hesitated were his hero, say, unequivocally portrayed as old enough to desire a woman. Though we recall that Huck (in his innocence and ig- norance) stole Jim, perpetrated, that is to say, what in terms of his world's values was a crime and sin, we smile smugly. The child is right, we tell ourselves, childhood is always right, intelligence and experience always wrong. But we have forgotten (because Huck is "only a boy") that he has performed precisely the arrogant act of Raskolnikov or Oppenheimer or Leopold and Loeb, has appointed himself the lonely arbiter of morality.

Huck Finn is, then, in one sense the really Bad Boy, a projection of insolence and contempt for authority; but he is also the perse- cuted orphan (blurring into the figure of Oliver Twist), a nonresist- ing rebel, gentle and scared and (alas!) cute. He emerges out of the earlier stereotypes of Abused Innocence and fades back into their later versions, one more forerunner of the grubby little boy and his dog, but also one more ancestor of the Juvenile Delinquent, whose badges of innocence are the switch knife and the hot-wiring kit. Before our own Hucks, the young hoods of the mid-twentieth century, we are disabled still by literature: unable to tell fact from myth, the real child from the projection of our own moral plight. The guilt of the J.D. seems to us somehow only one more sign of his innocence, of *our* guiltiness in failing to protect and cultivate his original purity with enough love and security. The "child of a broken home" replaces the orphan among our current stereotypes, as "psychic rejection" replaces old-fashioned bullying and flogging. We are, however, still attempting to appease the same unappease- able anguish which once wailed with Dickens over poor Oliver in the hands of Fagin or with Twain over poor Huck trapped in Pap's cabin; though now the villain is no longer projected as the evil Jew or the fishbelly-white village drunk, but as the harried bourgeois father oozing baffled good will.

It is difficult for us to consider the plight of our children as if they had independent existence and free will, and were not merely projections of our unconscious. We permit that unconscious (and the child) more sexual freedom now and are deeply troubled that this has made no difference, that each still blindly rebels. Perhaps, we sometimes think, we are paying a price for having restricted the child's range of aggression in return for his erotic freedom. The Good Bad Boy can get himself laid these days even in the fiction of Anglo-Saxondom, but he is no longer permitted to glory in beating up on the Jewish kid next door, or the minister's son or the overdressed stranger from the big city. It is all a little like the joke in which the mother calls to her son, "Jakey! Jakey!" and he answers, "Here I am, Mama, behind the fence with Shirley." "And what are you doing, son?" she asks. "Screwing, Mama." "All right, all right. As long as you don't fight."

It is easy to exaggerate the difference a few generations have made in the basic concept of the Good Bad Boy. He is not to our moral imagination less innocent, merely permitted a new innocence, that of sex. Yet even though he is allowed now a certain amount of good clean sex (not as the basis of a relationship but as a kind of exhibition of prowess) and forbidden in return an equivalent amount of good clean violence, his standard repertory of permitted crimes remains pretty much the same. What are winked at still as permissible expressions of youthful exuberance are crimes against school and against property. The hood can mock his teacher and play hooky like Tom Sawyer before him, though in our days of prosperity and the indefinite extension of adolescence, he runs away (like the protagonists of J. D. Salinger or the speaker in Allen Ginsberg's poems) not from grade school, but from prep school or the university.

Recently a group of writers in their late youth and early middle age have appeared, who not only project in literature the image of the Good Bad Boy but even act out in life this standard role, as if they had just invented it. They think they are emulating Huck Finn, though in reality their model is Tom Sawyer, and even at times (so dewy and starry-eyed is their naïve acceptance of all experience) they rather resemble Becky Thatcher! Such writers range all the way from a suburban, upper-middle-class wing repre-sented by Salinger and his image Holden Caulfield to Allen Gins-berg and Jack Kerouac with their transparent, not-quite-fictional

representations of themselves. Rural no longer in their memories or
nostalgia, they yearn still for boyhood, and submit in their books
to speaking through their masks, in a language which simulates
that of the Good Bad Boy himself whether in his prep-school or
pseudo-hipster form. Unlike Twain, who makes poetry of inarticu-
lateness, his latter-day imitators produce only slick parodies of the
silent generation pretending to talk—or are content with exclama-
tory noises: "And I said to myself, Wham, listen to that man.
That's the West, here I am in the West. . . . Whooee, I told my soul,
and the cowboy came back and off we went to Grand Island."

In *Catcher in the Rye,* Holden comes to the dead end of ineffectual revolt in a breakdown out of which he is impelled to fight his
way by the Good Good Girl, in the guise of the Pure Little Sister,
from whose hands he passes directly into the hands of psychiatrist.
In *On the Road,* whose characters heal themselves as they go by
play-therapy, the inevitable adjustment to society is only promised,
not delivered; we must wait for the next installment to tell how the
Square Hipster makes good by acting out his role (with jazz ac-
companiment) in a New York night club, or even, perhaps, how he
has sold his *Confessions of a Bad Boy* to the movies. In the book
itself, all the stigmata of Tom Sawyer are already present except the
return to Aunt Polly; Paul Goodman has, without recalling the
stereotype, identified them precisely: "One is stunned by how conventional and law-fearing these lonely middleclass fellows are. They
dutifully get legal marriages and divorces. The hint of a gang-
bang makes them impotent. They never masturbate or perform
homosexual acts. . . . To disobey a cop is 'all hell.' Their idea of crime
is the petty shoplifting of ten-year-olds stealing cigarettes or of
teenagers joyriding in other people's cars. . . . Their behavior is
a conformity *plus royaliste que le roi.*"

Typically enough in our time, such boys are also *plus religieux
que le pape,* insisting on their dedication to God, their assumption
of the Christ role (unlike poor Huck, who chose to "go to hell")
in a way that would have made the anticlerical Twain wince. To be
sure, it is Zen Buddhism rather than Unitarianism or neo-Orthodoxy
which attracts the Square Hipster and *New Yorker* contributor alike,
binding together as improbable coreligionists Salinger and Kerouac;
indeed, if James Dean had not yet discovered this particular kick

before he smashed up in a sports car, it is because he died just a little too soon. Past the bongo drums and the fiddling around with sculpture it was waiting for him, the outsider's religion in a day when there is room inside for the outsider himself, provided he, too, goes "to the church of his choice."

The fact that one is tempted, even impelled to speak of, say, Jack Kerouac at thirty-five as a Boy, the fact that he writes as one of the Boys, is symptomatic of the degree to which the image of Good Bad Boyhood has impinged upon adult life itself, has become a "career" like everything else in America. The age of Kerouac's protagonists is just as ambiguous as that of Twain's, though for quite the opposite reasons. Twain blurred adolescence back into boyhood to avoid confronting the problem of sex; the newer writers, accepting the confusion of childhood and youth, blur both into manhood to avoid yielding up to maturity the fine clean rapture of childish "making out." The fictional counterparts of the provincial Hipsters have crossed the border line of genital maturity, but in all other respects they have not left Jackson's Island. *Plus ça change, plus c'est la même chose*, we sigh, capable only of banality in the face of such banality; and the American translation is, "Boys will be boys!"

Though the treatment of the child in twentieth-century fiction is often merely an up-to-date adaptation of sentimental prototypes, this is by no means universally true. The influence of depth psychology has not always stopped at the superficial level; on occasion it has gone beyond providing useful tags for the stage of infantile sexuality or making explicit insights already implicit in earlier fiction. Most crucially, it has helped undercut the moral optimism of sentimentalism by restoring a concept of the child (and of the world of impulse he represents) more like that of Augustine than that of Rousseau. Yet the child remains for us, less sanguine about the "natural" though not less concerned with it, still a fascinating literary theme; indeed, writers have come to depend rather more than less on the child's eye, the child's fresh vision as a true vision, a model of the artist's vision itself.

This child is, however, considered an example not of the innocence of the spirit but of the eye. Implicated in aggression and sexuality, he projects nonetheless an unfallen way of perceiving the world; and his ambiguous unfallenness is used ironically to portray the implication of us all in the guilt he shares but about which he has not yet learned to lie. The confrontation of adult corruption and childish perception remains a contemporary subject, though we no longer believe in the redemption of our guilt by the innocence of the child. His act of perception is portrayed as the beginning of his initiation into full-blown, self-conscious evil— the start of normal life. "Initiation" is the favorite word of an age which aspires not to "salvation" but to "maturity"; and the initiatory story has become popular almost to the point of triteness.

In its sentimental form, the fable of the encounter of the child and adult represents, it must be remembered, a bowdlerized version of the seduction theme. Just as in, say, *Pamela* and *Clarissa* the question is posed: will the Seducer seduce the Redeemer before the Redeemer redeems the Seducer, will the conflict end in the victory of the (good, female) Heart or the (evil, male) Head, in marriage or death; so in the more genteel, apparently asexual terms of Child-Adult fiction, the same question is posed: will Fagin win out or Oliver, Tiny Tim or Scrooge? Up to the very last moment, it is possible for Scrooge to find grace through Tiny Tim and Tiny Tim to be spared; or, as we have seen, redemption may be bought by the death of the Redeemer, Dombey ransomed by the sacrifice of Little Dombey; or the Redeemer may live and the Seducer die unredeemed as in the case of Oliver and Fagin. Beyond these comic and tragicomic resolutions, neither Dickens nor his more genteel American followers were prepared to go; in no case, at any rate, is the child-redeemer won over to evil.

Even Melville in *Moby-Dick* is unwilling to portray the corruption of a child; though every other crew member on the *Pequod* is committed temporarily to Ahab's diabolic quest, the cabin boy Pip is unseduced. True, he cannot, though he is endowed with *all* the symbolic attributes of natural virtue (he is a child and a Negro and mad to boot), redeem Ahab to the "humanities," and he dies with the rest; but he dies pure, the innocence of his vision only refined by his suffering. J. D. Salinger (the last reputable exploiter of the sentimental myths of childhood) pushes the redemption theme a step further into blackness; in "A Perfect Day for Bananafish" he shows how Seymour Glass, a not entirely vicious adult, is awakened by the innocence of a child to enough awareness of the lost world he inhabits to kill himself! Yet we are asked apparently to accept the act of self-destruction as a kind of salvation.

The *ambiguity* of the attraction to childhood remains as unperceived in Salinger as in any nineteenth-century Anglo-Saxon Dickensian. In Dostoevsky, however, leading Russian disciple of Dickens, the lesson of the master had long since been translated out of sentimentality into horror. Only he was capable of understanding the secret to which Dickens obliquely alluded when he spoke of Quilp (the deformed, grotesque persecutor of Little Nell) as a self-portrait. True to his preceptor, Dostoevsky sees the world as a conspiracy against the child. His works are full of child victims, typified by Ilusha in *The Brothers Karamazov*, infant martyrs whose death redeems those who crush them; while his childlike saviors go out to the children, Myshkin rescuing the little Swiss girl from her small persecutors and Alyosha becoming the hero of the pack of boys who cheer him at the novel's close. In the dream of Dmitri in *The Brothers Karamazov*, the vision of Russia as a wasteland is explained by the cry, "The child is weeping!" And Dostoevsky himself in his journal reminds himself over and over, "Do not torment the children, do not soil or corrupt them."

Yet Dostoevsky boasted at least once in public that he had raped a thirteen-year-old girl in the bath, and the image of the violated child appears again and again in his works. This is the crime which haunts Svidrigailov in *Crime and Punishment* and Stavrogin in *The Possessed*; according to surviving notes, it was originally to have been one of the sins of Dmitri, too; and it was certainly a fantasy that possessed the author all his life, an obsession he was driven to confess as fact and rewrite continually as fiction. Child-lover and child-rapist: these are two sides of a single coin, the sentimental and demonic aspects of the Cult of the Child, which elsewhere in the nineteenth century is presented as if it possessed only a single, benign side.

Implicit in the fable of the love affair of Seducer and Redeemer is the barest hint that the child seeks out evil not only to transform it, but also out of a dim, unconfessed yearning for it. Eventually this underground perception will develop into the revelation of the moral coquetry of the child, in a sense of how his flaunted innocence is an invitation to violation. In nineteenth-century literature, particularly in England and America, this ambiguous insight is somewhat naïvely projected as the Innocent Flirtation. In such fiction, the child in his simplicity finds himself attracted to adult evil rather than adult good; for the former seems to him to possess a spontaneity and grace more like his own than anything in the safe, dull world of grown-up virtue. There is a hint of such a flirtation with evil in Huck Finn's apparent choice of the Duke and Dauphin over the Widow Douglas; but he is more their prisoner than their accomplice, and in the end he feels for them not love but pity.

Clearer examples are to be found in the standard American story in which the Good Bad Boy enters into an alliance with Rip Van Winkle, the town idler or drunk (William Faulkner's "Uncle Willy" is a classic instance) against the world of conscience and womanhood.

The Seduction-Redemption theme is not easily surrendered. In various forms its victimized small saviors survive: as the Salinger girl heroines of *Catcher in the Rye* and "For Esmé—with Love and Squalor"; as the protagonist of *Poil de Carotte,* whose motion-picture success has ensured his survival beyond that of the novel in which he first appeared; as the poisoned, tormented children of the Reggie Fortune mystery stories; and most lately as the child mutants (telepaths, teleports, superhuman monsters of virtue as well as intelligence) who in a score of science-fiction tales struggle with the dull world their merely human parents have made. *Childhood's End,* the most successful of such fictions is called; and, indeed, its author, Arthur C. Clarke, has reached the end of a much exploited myth of childhood. It is tempting to read the conclusion of his book, in which the superchildren he has imagined desert this world utterly, as a symbolic prophecy that we are through with them as they are with us; but the social scientists caught in a cultural lag will take up what fiction has outlived, the Dr. Werthams of our society talking about the *Seduction of the Innocent* long after the Dickenses of our time have turned elsewhere for pathos.

Most serious writers in the twentieth century, however, have given up the notion of seduction as well as that of redemption; they are no more moved by the concept of corruption than they are by that of salvation, substituting for the more traditional fable of a fall to evil that of an initiation into good-and-evil. In a sense, this represents a transition from the worship of innocence to that of experience, from a concern with the latency period of the child to a concentration of the moment of adolescence. *Huckleberry Finn* is sometimes thought of as the prototype of this newer kind of fable; and one of the most perceptive recent interpretations of that novel is James Cox's "The Sad Initiation of Huckleberry Finn." But it is hard finally to believe in Huck's having been initiated into anything; if he is at all different at the end of the book from what he is at its start, it is only in possessing a few more nightmares; but in such treasures he was rich enough to begin with. Sympathy he does not learn; for he has as much when he sets out as when he returns, and always it alternates with an astonishing callousness. The original innocence of Huck is not his ignorance of evil (he is the son of his father, after all) but his immunity to experience, his resistance to responsibility; and these preclude the fortunate fall we call initiation.

An initiation is a fall through knowledge to maturity; behind it there persists the myth of the Garden of Eden, the assumption that to know good and evil is to be done with the joy of innocence and to take on the burdens of work and childbearing and death. Yet typically, in Anglo-Saxon literature at least, the child is not a participant in the fall, but a *witness*, only vicariously inducted into the knowledge of sin. In the modern version of the Fall of Man, there are four participants, not three: the man, the woman, the serpent and the child (presumably watching everything from behind the tree). It is Henry James who sets the pattern once and for all in *What Maisie Knew*, in which the details of a particularly complicated and sordid adulterous tangle are presented to us as refracted through the half-ignorance of a preadolescent girl. The fictional working out of the Vicarious Initiation presupposes the invention of a technique (the famous Jamesian point of view) which leaves no doubt in the reader's mind about who is witnessing the events related; and so the perfection of a formal device makes possible the development of a new theme.

Once James has achieved the convention and the image, once he has established the Child as Peeping Tom, it is adapted everywhere, on every level of literature from highest to lowest. Eye to the crack in the door, ear attuned from the bed where he presumably sleeps, curious or at idle play, the innocent observer stumbles upon the murderer bent over the corpse, the guilty lovers in each other's arms, the idolized jockey in a whore house, a slattern on his knee. Such children are the presiding geniuses of modern fiction, reborn in a hundred guises: as Hemingway's Nick Adams overhearing the gossip about his Indian girl; as the baffled boy of Sherwood Anderson's "I Want to Know Why"; as the little Jew of Salinger's "Down at the Dinghy" hearing the cook call his father a "kike"; as the upper-class child confronted with the vulgar sin of servants in Graham Greene's "Basement Room," or Walter de la Mare's "The Perfect Craftsman." Even in drama, where point of view is hard to maintain, in Inge's *The Dark at the Top of the Stairs,* for instance, writers are driven to emulate the prototype, to render the experience of evil in terms of *what the child sees.*

But *why* have our writers welcomed so indirect an evocation of the child's passage from innocence to experience? In a way, it seems the last genteel reticence; a refusal to portray the child as an actual sinner, though it is no longer possible to postulate his innocence as absolute. In the fiction of France and Italy, indeed, the initiation of the boy into manhood is portrayed in frankly sexual terms; he is *devirginated* into maturity by the kindly, aging whore, who is the high priestess of this *rite de passage* in the stories of writers like Colette or Alberto Moravia; and he may even, released from the burden of innocence (as in the recent movie *The Game of Love*) then induct the young girl into the world of experience he has entered. Sometimes, even in European fiction, the initiation is the sexual experience fumbled rather than fulfilled, the visit to the whore house which ends in impotence or even in flight at the very threshold, as in Flaubert's *A Sentimental Education.* This quasi-devirgination, the fall via sexual queasiness rather than sexual satisfaction, has become a cliché in stories both here and abroad; but the *typical* American convention, where the Vicarious Initiation is spurned, is quite different.

In the United States it is through murder rather than sex, death rather than love that the child enters the fallen world. He is not asked, to be sure, to kill a fellow human, only an animal, deer or bear, or even fish, some woodland totem, in slaying whom (some-

times he is even smeared with the blood of his victim) he enters
into a communion of guilt with the natural world in which hitherto
he has led the privileged existence of an outsider. Hemingway and
Faulkner are, of course, the leading serious exploiters of this theme,
and "The Bear" its classic expression; but in pulp fiction and outdoor
books it is repeated over and over on the level of the stereotype.
The boy with "buck fever," the kid trembling over the broken body
of his first rabbit or the first bird brought down with a sling, is the
equivalent in the world of violence to the queasy stripling over the
whore's bed in the world of passion. But even as the sexually in-
experienced boy is redeemed by the old tart, so the child unused
to death is initiated by the old Negro or Indian, the dark-skinned
primitive who mediates between him and the world of wild beasts
and prepares him for this bloody First Communion.

Yet even this last device, so implicated in the cult of nature which
everywhere influences American life, cannot replace completely the
theme of the Vicarious Initiation; for that theme is *more* finally than
an evasion. Indeed, the stories which it informs embody in various
disguises one or another of the two major crises of preadolescent
emotional life: the stumbling on the Primal Scene, mother and father in the sexual act (or less dramatically the inference of it from
creaking springs and ambiguous cries); or the discovery of heterosexual "treachery" on the part of some crush, idolized in innocent
homosexual yearning. *What Maisie Knew* is ultimately the same old
scandal that brought her into being; and *The Fallen Idol* is inevitably
the desexualized substitute father caught out in turn in the primal
defection. "At the track the air don't taste as good. . . ." Sherwood
Anderson makes his disillusioned Peeping Tom declare. "It's because
a man like Jerry Tilford . . . could see a horse like Sunstreak run,
and kiss a woman like that the same day . . . it spoils looking at
horses and smelling things and hearing niggers laugh and everything.
. . . What did he do it for? I want to know why!" But he does know
why already and it is what Maisie knew before him; the knowledge
that was to make us as gods and taught us only that we die.

The fate of the child after his vicarious initiation can be variously
portrayed; the work of William Faulkner provides a paradigm of
all the possibilities. For the earlier Faulkner, the fall to sexual

knowledge is a fall to inevitable corruption and death; but the later Faulkner, plagued perhaps by declining powers and certainly converted to more "positive" attitudes, has revised his views of these matters, as he has revised his tragic view of life in general. The more serious successors of Faulkner, the homosexual-gothic novelists who have, unexpectedly enough, inherited his symbolic Southern landscape and his concern with evil, have ignored his later versions of the plight of the child in favor of the earlier ones. Their preadolescent protagonists confront still the decaying plantation house, the miasma-laden swamp, the secret lives of the Negro. They serve as symbols of exclusion as well as innocence, though no longer (as in Faulkner's case) merely of the exclusion of the fallen aristocrat and the unsuccessful writer. Like the circus freaks, the deaf and dumb, the idiots also congenial to their authors, they project the invert's exclusion from the family, his sense of heterosexual passion as a threat and an offense; and this awareness is easily translated into the child's bafflement before weddings or honeymoons or copulation itself.

Such child figures are ambiguous, epicene, caught at the indeterminate point where the charm of boy and girl are scarcely distinguishable. Truman Capote is a notable contributor to this gallery of ephebic forms; but it is Carson McCullers who has adapted it to the popular imagination, breaking out of the bounds of the novel (with the help of Julie Harris) to stage and screen; so that her boy-girls, with their jeans and chopped-off hair and noncommittal first names, have made familiar to us all the fantastic image of the Good Bad Boy as Teenage Tomboy, Huck Finn as F. Jasmine Adams. It is turn and turn about, for Huck once played the girl as these now ape the boy; but if his exigencies were similar Mark Twain did not know it. Much has remained the same, the Negro, for instance, still providing comfort for these transvestite Hucks in their moments of misery; though Jim, too, has been transformed from male to female.

The *Harper's Bazaar* Faulknerians remain faithful at least to the tragic implications of the initiation story; certainly, they are not tempted by the sentimental fables so popular with their British opposite numbers and recently worked by Angus Wilson into his *Anglo-Saxon Attitudes*. Once the child has been remade by homosexual sensibility into the image of an ambiguous object of desire, the lust for the child is revealed as a flight from woman, the family, maturity itself; and unless the writer sentimentalizes pederasty on some romantic, English public-school model, he finds himself confronting a theme as dark and terrible as Dostoevsky's evocation of the child rapist. Hints of this theme are everywhere in fiction of the McCullers school, but nowhere does it seem to me to be treated with full awareness. Oddly enough, J. D. Salinger (elsewhere more grossly sentimental about children than any contemporary writer of similar stature) comes once to the very verge of expressing it in "A Perfect Day for Bananafish," when Seymour Glass trifles erotically with the child Sybil, playing with her fingers, kissing her feet in an appalling demonstration which the author will not quite let us accept as pathological. Actually, he demands that we accept this ambiguous lovemaking as a moment of sanity before suicide, that we read the child as the embodiment of all that is clean and life-giving as opposed to the vulgar, destructive (*i.e.*, fully sexual) wife. To have made the little girl a little *boy* would have given the game away; but this Salinger refused to do, clinging like a good American to little Eva even on the verge of the tragic.

In two European novellas by Ronald Firbank and Thomas Mann, however, the final step had already been taken, long before the time of Salinger, of McCullers or Capote. Indeed, it had been anticipated before Firbank and Mann by Ibsen in *The Master Builder*; but he had projected the elusive image of youth teasing the artist toward his own destruction as a half-mad girl already past puberty. The not-quite-mature boy, dimly aware of his own homosexual allure, seems finally an apter, certainly a more sinister embodiment of the Romantic drive toward self-immolation. At any rate, in *Death in Venice* and *The Eccentricities of Cardinal Pirelli*, Mann and Firbank have created with great tenderness but even greater truth portraits of boy coquettes; on the literal level, they are callow flirts, cruel without any deep sense of the real pleasures or the true threat of cruelty; on a symbolic level, images of death itself. The last mad pursuit in which the naked Cardinal chases Don Skylark around the empty Cathedral, the "cage of God," and the final vision of the great writer von Aschenbach, painted and hectic at his shameful end, indicate the same thing: that what they have all along desired, known all along that the child really figured forth, was self-destruction. What such poetic treatments have once established, no later

version of the lust for childhood can quite ignore. Like all sophisticated yearnings for the primitive and inchoate, the nostalgia for
innocence and the child is suicidal.

The dis-ease with Romantic primitivism that underlies the tragic
statements of Mann and Firbank is at work, though less profoundly,
elsewhere in our culture. Even at the level of popular literature,
certain antistereotypes of the child begin to establish themselves.
Little Annie Rooney and Little Orphan Annie play out latter-day
versions of the Good Good Girl as outcast and wanderer, while
Dennis the Menace revives the image of Peck's Bad Boy. The Small
Angel in the House and the Little Devil survive side by side. For
a long time, however, quite serious writers have suggested that
children may indeed be instruments of the diabolic rather than
embodiments of innocence. In some liberal quarters any such suggestion, especially if associated with New England Calvinism, is
considered as absurd as asserting that some government officials may
have been Communists; and, indeed, Arthur Miller managed to
make a play whose two layers of meaning depended on associating
charges of witchcraft against children with "McCarthyism." But
ever since Henry James's *Turn of the Screw*, subtler writers have
presented as objects of horror children possessed, children through
whom the satanic attempts to enter the adult world. After all,
"satanic" is merely another word for the impulsive, unconscious life
otherwise called "innocent."

How equivocal our attitudes toward that subrational life in fact
are is best portrayed by the popular reception of *Peter Pan*, a fictional diatribe against adulthood and paternal authority, disguised
as a tract in favor of fairies. The most ordinary Broadway producer
knows these days the poor papa in his doghouse and the evil Captain
Hook ought to be played by the same actor; but the Oedipal slaying
(the triumph of boy over man, the father figure fed to the *vagina
dentata*!) with which the play reaches its climax is sufficiently disguised in sticky cuteness to make its reading a nursery ritual, and
the trip to see it in the theater a Holy Pilgrimage of the bourgeois
family! Barrie's protagonist is Pan in a real sense; and therefore not
only a callous, amoral, vain boy, but a *devil*, against whom all
windows must be shut. But Barrie, sentimentalist and popular entertainer, equivocates before he is through, making Pan only a Good

Bad Little Devil, who must be sewed for and told stories—although he will not abide mothering contaminated with sex, and in the end lights out for his territory!

Barrie's story is finally a "fantasy" (capable of being transformed by Disney's vulgar touch into a mere dream) and even Henry James's tale a "ghost story," an entertainment to which one condescends a little. Realer monsters, child demons implicated in the actual world we inhabit are to be found in Saki's story of the small boy rejoicing in the killing of his evil governess by a pet mongoose, and especially in Walter de la Mare's "The Perfect Craftsman." The boy protagonist of the latter, stumbling on a murder, helps in icy calm the rattled killer arrange all the evidence so that it looks like a suicide—then runs in panic through the dark passageways of a house haunted by imagined terrors. Two larger-scale attempts at creating counter-stereotypes of the child are Richard Hughes' *The Innocent Voyage* and *Lord of the Flies*, by William Golding. In each, we are presented not with a single child but a gallery of children ranging in age from just out of infancy to just short of full adolescence; in each (in Hughes's nostalgic evocation of the end of piracy, by a typhoon; in Golding's more recent book, by an atomic bombing) a group of children is removed from the constraints of normal adult society; and in each the innocent protagonists are shown as reinventing the evil of which the sentimentalists had considered them the passive victims. The Hughes book portrays a society in which girls play a leading part (Golding's island community is all male); and its fourteen-year-old Margaret, who becomes the forecastle whore, as well as its younger Emily, who kills a bound man, stabbing him in a dozen places, are profanations of the Good Good Girl—not mere antistereotypes but blasphemies. Emily's crime is not only unsuspected; it does not even bring her to self-awareness. Unlike Golding's Ralph, she sinks back into innocence without regret or self-reproach, is lost in a crowd of schoolgirls.

Emily has not remained an isolated case. In Faulkner's *Absalom, Absalom!*, the young girl Judith is discovered, leaning over the edge of a loft and screaming with the blood-lust her brother does not share (he trembles, nauseated), while her father wrestles naked and bloody with one of his field Negroes. Faulkner is as interested in profaning the myth of the Good Woman as he is in debunking that of the Innocent Child—and the image of the Child Witch serves for him a double purpose. Judith, after her first scene, he cannot quite make come alive; but in *The Hamlet* he tries again, on a less Gothic, more comic level, with Eula Varner, more Girl Bitch than Child Witch this time, but equally terrifying. The scene in which the schoolmaster Labove, helpless with the desire that an eleven-year-old girl has stirred in him and will not satisfy, chases her mindless, quivering flesh round and round the classroom comes closer than anything in American literature to the horrific vision of *Cardinal Pirelli*. Eula finally knocks him down. " 'Stop pawing me,' she said. 'You old headless horseman Ichabod Crane.' " She is magnificent at that ridiculous point, a prematurely developed temptress, more myth than fact, fit symbol for all Faulkner's ambivalence toward the flesh; and nothing in his vapid later novel, *The Town*, can convince us that so monstrous a figure was all along only a Good Bad Woman in embyro.

Eula belongs not with her adult namesake whom an aging Faulkner tries to redeem, but with Hughes's Emily or the child-murderer of William March's *The Bad Seed*, reading *Elsie Dinsmore* and acting out for unsuspecting adults the role of winsome innocent she has learned from such literature. The avowed "serious" themes of March's book (the question of whether criminal traits can be inherited, and the decision of a mother to kill her own child) scarcely matter before the evocation of the sweet young thing as diabolical killer. It is the latter theme which filled the theaters and movie houses with middlebrow, middle-class beholders eager to participate in the defilement of their own sacred images. That defilement is carried even further in Vladimir Nabokov's *Lolita*, whose subject is the seduction of a middle-aged man by a twelve-year-old girl.

The subject involves multiple ironies; for it is the naïve child, the female, the American who corrupts the sophisticated adult, the male, the European. In a single work, Richardson, Dickens and Henry James are controverted, all customary symbols for the encounter of innocence and experience stood on their heads. Nowhere are the myths of sentimentality more amusingly and convincingly parodied, and it is surely for this reason that the book was, for a time, banned. True enough, the child's manipulation of her would-be seducer's excitement is documented, as it must be, physiologically and step by step, but Bowles's story is by all odds "dirtier"; and it is undoubtedly as an irreligious book rather than a pornographic one that *Lolita* was forced under the counter. It is the final blasphemy against the Cult of the Child.

Lolita and the tradition to which it belongs represent a resolve to reassess the innocence of the child, to reveal it as a kind of moral idiocy, a dangerous freedom from the restraints of culture and custom, a threat to order. In the place of the sentimental dream of childhood, writers like Faulkner and Nabokov have been creating for us a nightmare in which the child is no longer raped, strangled or seduced, but is himself (better herself!) rapist, murderer and seducer.

Their books reflect a growing awareness on the part of us all that our society has tended (at least aspired) to become not the conspiracy against the child against which our ancestors raged—but a conspiracy in his favor, against the adult. Certainly, in a permissive, family-oriented, servantless America, whose conscience is forged by popularizations of Freud, a new tyranny has become possible. If in the comics the baby sitter cowers in terror before Junior and in Nabokov the grown man trembles in passion before the prepubescent coquette, the causes are the same. We begin to feel that we are the slaves of our anxiety about our children, guilt-ridden by our fear of rejecting them, not giving them enough security or love, robbing them of spontaneity or creativeness; and like slaves everywhere, we grow sullen and resentful.

But the appeasement of the child is only one form of the appeasement of the id, a resolve to give the (former) devil his due. The child remains still, what he has been since the beginnings of Romanticism, a surrogate for our unconscious, impulsive lives; and the pattern of the family (at least as we dream it) is *a* symbolic representation of the way in which we have chosen to resolve certain persistent conflicts of what used to be called the Heart and the Head. The work of recent writers for whom tales of childhood are inevitably tales of terror, in which the child poses a threat, represents a literature blasphemous and revolutionary. Such writers have come to believe that the self can be betrayed to impulse as well as to rigor; that an Age of Innocence can be a tyranny no less terrible than an Age of Reason and that the Gods of such an age if not yet dead must be killed, however snub-nosed, freckled-faced or golden-haired they may be.

XI. The Phoenix

Placing these two pieces jointly at the end is not entirely arbitrary They are, in a sense, both by noncritics, and it seems fitting that they should constitute the last word (or nearly so) in a volume almost entirely given over to critics. Although Martin Green is a very good critic indeed, he has earned his place in this category by a particularly charming admission. When he asks how Salinger does it—how he manages to give his characters such an extraordinary degree of life —he answers himself: "Heaven knows how!" Surely most professional critics would do almost anything, even join the Book-of-the-Month Club along with the Fat Lady, rather than admit that they do not know how an author achieves his effects. Green calls Salinger a celebrator, not a depicter; perhaps Green himself is at heart a celebrator, not a critic. At any rate, he celebrates the right thing: the life of Salinger's characters, not merely their much-emphasized lovability but their plausibility.

From his English point of view, Green may exaggerate when he calls the identification of the young with Salinger's characters a "cultural miracle." But if a miracle of sorts is involved, Christopher Parker is a participant. He is one of the young Green speaks of: he has dabbled in acting, has attended Illinois Institute of Technology and has at times been "between colleges." He was asked why he liked *The Catcher in the Rye* and obliged with an answer that seems worth hearing: in its own way, it recognizes the courage that is needed for growing up and, sometimes, for not growing up.

THE IMAGE-MAKER

by MARTIN GREEN

It seems to me that, in the nexus of relationship between the individual and the culture in which he develops, there is one most important factor, the cultural image, which I have never seen defined or discussed to my satisfaction. In fact, the cultural image seems to me *the* most important single mode of connection between the two, and therefore of mutual creation, for by means of it the society creates an individual, and the individual creates his society —an image being a concrete and dramatic version of an achieved life, in which you recognize yourself as you could be, your powers developed in some sense fully and harmoniously, dealing with your problems and responsibilities on the whole triumphantly; for—this is the crucial point—you respond to, revel in, *love* this mode of being.

Looking back on my own period of greatest growth, I think I can now trace all kinds of surprisingly personal frustrations and failures to the fact that my society, England, provided me with no adequate images. None good enough, that is, to excite me, arouse me, set me moving inside, growing, reaching out. For if there is no adequate image, if one cannot excitedly want to be the kind of man on whom, for instance, T. S. Eliot or J. B. Priestley sheds the greatest glamour, one may not want to be anything at all; one's most valuable energies, that is, may remain quiescent; one may not want to *be* at all—not, that is, with the intensity one is capable of, and unused intensities easily become perverse.

[Green discusses the relative thinness of Anglo-Saxon "cultural images" as compared to those of other races, and the relative thinness of British images as compared to those available in America. As an example of this, he cites various "images of 'authority' and 'innocence,' which are crucial and polar possibilities in America as well as in Britain, and perhaps in all Western culture."]

The image of innocence in America is a very brilliant one; it takes disparate forms, in *From Here to Eternity*, J. D. Salinger, Marlon Brando, "Billy Budd," Mark Twain, James Dean, Fitzgerald and

Henry James; but all, in their different ways, are mourning over the moment of adjustment to the adult word of compromise and insincerity. Huck Finn's innocence has a character of ignorance set beside Holden Caulfield's, but it is sophistication that is the great evil for both of them, and it is the purest innocence they both cling to in the figures of Jim the slave, Holden's sister Phoebe and the nuns. It is the problem of corruption and their relation to it that tortured James Dean and Marlon Brando, in some of their best scenes, just as much as Isabel Archer and other of James's heroines. It is the moment cynicism becomes comfortable and unconscious they are all weeping over, fighting off, protesting against. This image of innocence is characterized by a great splendor of vitality, and intelligence, and positive achievement.

By contrast, the British image seems all the more frail, requiring protection on every side in order not to suffer. They can live only among each other, the most sensitive and beautiful, and even then life is too rough for them. Middleton Murry's life with Katherine Mansfield is a tragicomic example. It is not that such people are weak; they are genuinely fine-drawn, but to the point of uselessness. This kind of thing is perhaps nearer to Blanche Dubois in *A Streetcar Named Desire* than to Huck Finn. American innocence differs above all because it can include toughness—without ceasing to be innocence. Its figures suffer from the corruption of the world, but they can handle its crudities. You need only set Holden Caulfield beside L. P. Hartley's Eustace, or Brando beside Gielgud, to be convinced. The Americans' relation with the world is much less predominantly aesthetic.

In short, the American images, of both innocence and authority, are whole men, whole lives, and the waking mind responds to them with some thrust of enthusiasm. The British images—and perhaps the same is true of most European cultures—are mutilated. Response to them must be feebler, and imitation a disaster.

This is no doubt the effect, but I think it is also the cause, of a generally inferior vitality.

America is better off than Britain; and is in a generally healthy condition culturally, from this one, and very important, point of view. Nevertheless she is impoverished, in having only fragmentary

THE PHOENIX 249

images. Fragmented images are like diffracted light, diffuse, comparatively ineffective. Huck Finn, for example, embodies his innocence in a form almost as irrelevant to our immediate needs as Anna Magnani's passion. A boy cannot long grow upward into Huck Finn—or into Marlon Brando. Faulkner's Dilsey and the Marshal are self-conscious aesthetic devices; while you are reading their speeches and actions you are aware that it is the author who is telling you something by means of them; they themselves do not fill the eye and absorb the attention, and I could not respond to them as I did to Paul Morel.

The truly rich culture offers its members some choice of images that are whole in themselves, magnificently real and keenly relevant to the time and place and situation of the young reader. The supreme examples of such images and of an image-maker are the two great novels of Tolstoy and Tolstoy himself. The heroes, Bezuhov and Levin, and the families they marry into, the Rostovs and the Shtcherbatskys, embody a way of life that is not so much depicted as celebrated. Other characters are depicted, as in Flaubert and George Eliot; figures like Vronsky and Bolkonsky, whom the author admires, and marvelously "understands," but who don't have the special Tolstoyan glamour; even Anna herself remains half within an aesthetic dimension Bezuhov escapes. And the central characters and their family lives are presented as not merely good but "natural," "Russian." There are sharp *pictures* of the Frenchman, and the German, and the Englishman. And somehow we are made to feel that Alexey Karenin, and Alexey Vronsky, and Sergey Koznishev are less "Russian" than Levin—the "Russian" man being big, enthusiastic, simple, clumsy, stammering, manly, fatherly, loving, unpractical, moody, religious, intuitive.

The families are conscious of themselves as images. Denisov in *War and Peace* and Levin in *Anna Karenina* fell in love with the entire set of Rostovs and Shtcherbatskys. They loved the individual members indiscriminately, and with the same emotion; because it was the family life itself that attracted them, the mode of relationship, its tone of spontaneous gaiety, of natural goodness, of vitality and fertility. And the individual members feel the same way. The Rostovs all look silently at Vera every time she speaks—because she spoils their tone. Tolstoy asks us to fall in love with them in a precisely comparable way. And we do, if we respond to the novel at all properly. We want to marry and have a family like that, with the same *degree* of vitality, and, unless we see ourselves as radically different, with the same *kind* of vitality. And just as much he asks us to love his heroes. We feel we have only to open our hearts as Levin's or Bezuhov's is open, and follow its dictates as passionately, as ready as they to fall into absurdity, and we will achieve the same full-blooded, wholehearted innocence, the same salvation. Of course, when we put down the book here and now, we find none of the institutions, the modes of relationship, the modes of being we could deal with in this new role. It remains a great novel, but as an image it fades, becomes distant, romantic.

This was image-making on the grandest scale, and young men growing up in Russia in the same era had perhaps greater opportunities than any comparable group. They were roused and persuaded into life more irresistibly, more richly and melodiously, more deeply and thunderously, than any others I can think of.

And it is interesting for an Englishman to reflect that Russia at that time was in no flourishing condition politically, economically or internationally.

No doubt it was easier for the Russians than for us. They were far enough from, and near enough to, the van of human progress, so that they could see the ways in which they differed, their "picturesqueness," without feeling it an inferiority. But is it impossible we should have the same?

It is clear enough what a phoenix a writer of similar temperament would be, who could create a whole image for Anglo-Saxons, in which people of the greatest intelligence and sensitivity could recognize themselves, and find themselves therein transformed, valuable and beautiful.

I want to suggest that America has such a phoenix in J. D. Salinger.

This is not the place to demonstrate Salinger's purely literary merits, I can only assert that he passes every test the reader's mind imposes, and enters it deeply enough to act upon the faculties of self-creation. The more you read him, the more original you find his meanings; the more he points out to you what you had not seen in your daily life, the finer and more vital his taste and tact are, the more exciting his intelligence and his complex tension of values. With each reading one salutes more perceptions and organizations of perceptions, more penetration; and these salutes act as surrenders of the sensitive mind, the end of resistances and measurings, an opening of those secret areas where one's undirected eagerness and responsiveness lie undefended and indefensible.

But measured by such standards alone Salinger is not a phoenix. We have had as fine writers in our time, and one or two greater. He is no prophet, no D. H. Lawrence. When he approaches that function, in the expositions of Seymour's brand of religion, he becomes less distinguished. He has done nothing to equal the Leopold Bloom part of *Ulysses*. But he is an unparalleled image-maker; because he works essentially through central characters, who live in their own right, independently of the story, and who are beautiful and lovable; Holden Caulfield, Buddy Glass, Zooey Glass. After reading *The Catcher in the Rye*, for instance, one can ask oneself what Holden would say of this and that, what he would do in such a situation, and one can get an answer. Heaven knows how! This is the special miracle of the image-maker. And one rejoices in everything he would say and do, however painful for him, because of the integrity and the sweetness and the vigor of the nature that acts.

When Salinger does not write through such a central character, and the pattern of the writer's sensibility is imprinted on the narrative and action as it were nakedly, his work is much inferior. *Nine Stories*, for example, and even "Franny," seem to me relatively uninteresting. There is a bitterness like a wound in Salinger's mind, an expectation of disaster for anyone sensitive and innocent, which invalidates so much of a story like "Teddy" and "A Perfect Day for Bananafish." But in *The Catcher in the Rye* Holden's own qualities and life-worthiness remain in our mind, contradicting the pattern of failure and meanness; he, after all, cannot be seen through; he is not phony, nor, importantly, defeated. It is this that gives the book much of its poise and integrity.

All the way through *The Catcher in the Rye*, the reader, if he is honest and generous, is becoming aware of Holden's superiority. Each episode, each word in the book, has many "points," but this is the point of each of them, as much as anything else. Holden is taller, handsomer, more lovable, more loving, more intelligent, more honest

—than whom? Than the reader. Than the writer, one can say; it is he who projects this image for us, from this angle, the effect of which is to make us wholeheartedly admire and love his character. At the very beginning, Holden is looking at his school, "trying to feel some kind of a good-by. I mean I've left schools and places I didn't even know I was leaving them. I hate that. I don't care if it's a sad good-by or a bad good-by, but when I leave a place I like to *know* I'm leaving it. If you don't, you feel even worse." The reader must feel that such glimmerings as he had at sixteen of the value of experience as such were never so exactly defined, so unpretentiously phrased, so socially amenable, so completely assimilated into his private language. Next comes the interview with the Spencers, where Holden is so easily aware of all they are thinking and feeling, while they are quite unaware of him, and he so charitably makes the interview easy for them. Again the reader must feel that such social dexterity as he had at sixteen was never so unself-conscious, so unpatronizing, so allied with humor and gaiety and kindness. And so on through the book; Holden's skill at golf, at dancing, at writing, his generosity with money, his enterprise with women, his ability to talk to children— one of the major dimensions by which all these are measured is his superiority in them. The point of them all is that we look up to Holden.

Zooey Glass is even more flamboyantly endowed. A brilliant actor, a very forceful personality, a Greek scholar, a mathematics scholar, unusually beautiful, unusually serious, unusually sardonic and irreverent and impatient; on every side he exceeds and awes us. We feel that were we to meet him, or Holden, we would be overborne. At the same time, we long to meet them. We long to be a part of that complex of interchanges that makes up the Glasses's family life and the Caulfield children's relationships: each member wildly free and independent, and yet deeply devoted to the others: we want to inhabit that world whose every object is so richly significant, every movement or inertia so full of energy. The brilliance of the writing is to be measured by the way it makes acceptable to us something we cannot in the least patronize, makes us love someone before whom we cannot but feel timidity and insecurity about ourselves. This is what the writer is most deliberately making us feel. When he fails, with Seymour, it is precisely because we rebel against the demand for so much reverence, so wholly upward a glance. But when he succeeds, his characters have a natural, unqualified glamour which puts him with Tolstoy, not with Lawrence or Joyce. After *Sons and Lovers*, Lawrence no longer worked importantly in "character," no longer allowed his readers a big emotional relationship with the central figures. Bloom, on the other hand, though a big character, is not one we look upward to; the glamour in *Ulysses* is monopolized by Stephen Dedalus, who is unacceptable on so many other grounds, but who "could have been" much more comparable to Zooey.

So Salinger is definitely an image-maker, a celebrator, not a depicter. But it may seem that the life he celebrates is un-"achieved"; that Zooey and Holden have more problems than solutions, more weaknesses than strengths. This is true only from a point of view unsympathetic to the author; and from such a point of view the same is true of Levin and Bezuhov. Such an attitude can be justified; but only by literary criticism, by proving that Salinger and Tolstoy are not to be taken seriously as writers. From Salinger's point of view, his characters are strongly and vividly alive. So that as long as we acknowledge the value of his insights, his sensibility, they are strong and triumphant for us, too. It is true objectively that his talent is narrow and tortured beside Tolstoy's; the setting, the action, the characters, the problems, the moods—the American writer's total output is only like some of the scenes involving one of the aspects of Bezuhov, who is as a totality only a part of *War and Peace*. Again, however, the objective view is irrelevant. It is the image-maker's privilege that we come to see with his eyes, from inside his work. After all, T. S. Eliot's work has not been notable for breadth or typicality, but it has had a powerful effect.

In Salinger's characters, Wellesley and Harvard undergraduates can recognize themselves transfigured, more intensely alive, more honest, more passionate, more courageous; they are caught up into a mode of being that exhilarates them by its pace and gusto; they reach out into their own routines and difficulties, anxious to achieve something of the same kind for themselves. In other words, they respond to a cultural image. One of the greatest of cultural miracles is taking place.

"WHY THE HELL *NOT* SMASH ALL THE WINDOWS?"

by CHRISTOPHER PARKER

The phenomenal success of the *The Catcher* among college students I think is little more than a kind of myth worship—like Jimmy Dean. Anyway, I knew at least ten Holden Caulfields at IIT. The language is a big part of it—absurd exaggeration and complete vagueness. "One of those little English jobs that can do around 200 miles an hour." "My parents would have about two hemorrhages apiece if I told them. . . ." It's a way of being casual—the use of "or something," "and all," "the thing" in every other sentence. The whole idea about being completely unconcerned about anything—except absurd little things, idiosyncrasies. Like Caulfield's great interest in the ducks in Central Park, and his complete lack of interest in school. Also repetitious, deliberately phony. "I would, I really would, but the thing is, I have to get going. I have to go right to the gym. Thanks, though. Thanks a lot, sir." All this is quite typical.

Also the habit of Caulfield's—deliberate lies and exaggerations just to see if someone else will fall for them. "All you have to do is to say something nobody understands and they'll do practically anything you want them to"—and isn't it true! In fact, that's one of my favorite pastimes; it's a way of making fun of a stupid person without telling him he's stupid.

It's also a sort of fad among us to be very critical of everything and everyone, and those who are most critical are the strongest and most independent from the friendship and aid of us. It's heroic to be lonely, and yet it's considered cool to be suave and diplomatic, so the thing is, to be critical as hell and still keep smiling and tell lies.

I think Caulfield's issue is a very real one—strong—and lets every boy who reads *The Catcher* think he's just like Holden and I think that's one of the reasons for its great success; we can all identify ourselves with his plight. But few of us, myself included, have guts enough to stick with it. There are many who don't even try; they enjoy being phonies because everyone else is and everyone knows it, so it's all a big game. I don't think Salinger is presenting Caulfield as an ideal—he certainly believes in his fight—but I don't think he gives us Caulfield as a solution. It's not a black and white case by any means. For instance, and I don't recall where, someone will say something corny, and Caulfield will remark "witty bastard —all I ever meet is witty bastards" and then on the next page Salinger has Caulfield use exactly the same expression. Isn't he saying there that Caulfield is also phony to a certain extent? Not really phony—but not quite strong enough to break away completely.

Caulfield was looking for pure, unadorned human beauty, pure, innocent friendships. "The Catcher in the Rye" catching little children as they fall off a cliff—it's a motive and an end—pure feeling and probably the most heroic and meaningful existence one could have, and the basis would be love. Of course Salinger has Caulfield find pure feeling with Phoebe, his little sister—watching her as she goes around on the carousel—that's evident; and I think Salinger makes too big a point of Phoebe as the only "innocent" in the book. He puts the sermon into the mouth of Mr. Antolini, who is ironically the crushing blow to Caulfield when he finds out he's a flit—to Caulfield: ". . . I can very clearly see you dying nobly, one way or another, for some highly unworthy cause . . . 'the mark of the mature man is that he wants to live humbly for one'. . . . you'll find that you're not the first person who was ever confused and frightened and even sickened by human behavior. . . ." I think that's Salinger's viewpoint, but again infinitely more interesting because he puts it into the mouth of an Antolini. The great tragedy with Caulfield of course, as with many of Ibsen's characters, is that he has no real ideals of his own to substitute for the phony ideals of society.

But Caulfield is human, ever so human. There are many hints in *The Catcher.* There is the repulsive, pimply-faced fellow named Ackley; everyone shuns him, and Caulfield, though sociable, gives him a pretty hard time. But later, when he tells his sister why he didn't like Pencey, one of the reasons he gives is that nobody would let people like Ackley into their clique—"even the members of the goddam Book-of-the-Month Club stuck together" but everyone ignored Ackley. Caulfield had compassion for him—underneath his criticism and at the root of it, there is compassion. Again, after the episode with Mr. Antolini, Caulfield keeps making excuses that maybe Mr. Antolini "just liked to pat guys' heads," "maybe he was just drunk," "maybe I'll hurt his feelings if I don't go back." His feelings are very deep—Mr. Antolini was one of the only unphony people he knew and then he is disillusioned. It would be quite different, and a far more common reaction, to crack jokes about Antolini, or get mad. Underneath, Caulfield is terribly sincere and human. A friend of mine tried to tell me it was just Caulfield's eagerness to criticize that led him to suspect Antolini and jump to conclusions. I think that attitude illuminates the real meat of the book —it would have meant that Holden was not sincere.

Another thing—when Caulfield's brother Allie dies of tuberculosis, Holden goes out in the garage late at night and smashes all the windows with his fist and even tries to smash the automobile windows. He's sent to the hospital for treatment and observation. But what—what would be more human? Some great force has swallowed up your brother, no reason, he's just gone—why the hell *not* smash all the windows? Is this a time to be reasonable? To me it's a completely natural reaction to something which is beyond comprehension or reason. I think Salinger feels that way too. Like Jimmy Dean in *East of Eden* when he shoves the ice down the trough and bangs his head against the tree. What are you supposed to do—react intelligently and civilized, like the higher animals we are, control your emotions, go to the funeral, put flowers, shed a tear, accept, and bow before Almighty Fate?

Caulfield doesn't belong in the booby-hatch, any more than Hedda Gabler would if she had bungled. Salinger says that in the afterword, "A lot of people, especially this one psychoanalyst guy they have here, keep asking me if I'm going to apply myself when I go back to school next September. It's such a stupid question, in my opinion. I mean how do you know what you're going to do till you *do* it? The answer is, you don't." (If you're true to your emotions.) "I *think* I am, but how do I know? I swear it's a stupid question." This sort of puts forth the question of the role of the psychiatrist and what he judges by, and what is really the norm, and how *we* know it is, and why the hell everyone is unnormal if they don't fit into the pigeonhole. Dad asked me at what point I thought Caulfield was headed for the zoo—it tells you that on the first page, but aside from that, I never thought he deserves to be put away. He would have made out all right—just his nervous hesitant parents and probably Sally's society mother and good old normal Sally were the ones who recommended him.

So what was Caulfield's problem—if he had one. He'd met a dilemma—like all the rest of us; he didn't give in and he didn't ignore (like most of the rest of us). And he couldn't find any other solution except good old Phoebe on the carousel. You could say he was trying to find himself, his identity, and all that; but that's a lot of categorical nonsense—who isn't? It's evident that he was also fed up with hypocrisy—but I think Caulfield's real problem is that he was trying desperately to be sincere in an insincere world, with FUCK YOU signs on the walls of children's corridors, wheezing bald caddy-driving alumni who want to find their initials carved in the door of the can, Antolinis who have the answers but don't use them, and Mr. Vinsons who yell "Digression!" at you every time you become excited enough in an idea you have to forget about the classroom exercise and start talking about the idea. Caulfield was outside of himself looking for others. He wasn't a critical smart-aleck—far, far from it. I'm not trying to say that Caulfield's way is right and society's is wrong—but I do think that Caulfield, the individual, is far more human and right than those of us on the outside asking him if he's going to apply himself or not.

The good thing about Caulfield is that he's trying to do it all by himself—no Beatnik—no Bohemian—no Ivy League—just Holden Caulfield. He knows the others are just as phony as the "American Dream," and he also knows that he's being a bit of a phony; he realizes he's in a bad way but he doesn't know what to do about it.

Why do I like *The Catcher?* Because it puts forth in a fairly good argument the problems which boys of my age face, and also perhaps the inadequacy with which some of us attempt to cope with them. I have great admiration for Caulfield because he didn't compromise. I think he was relatively free of self-worship—his cause was certainly justified, if not just. I think Salinger deals fairly with him—he gives enough grounds to argue either pro or con. Some people condemn Caulfield as "not liking anything," but he does—he likes the only things really worth liking, whereas most of us like all the things that aren't worth liking. Because he is sincere he won't settle for less.

K

I think most fellows who read *The Catcher* don't think about it enough—what's really behind it all. They think he's a cool guy, so they imitate his casual talk and nonchalant attitude. Salinger didn't invent the talk, nor Holden Caulfield for that matter, but it's certainly become much more popular since. I don't even think most fellows notice it's called the "*Catcher* in the Rye" when in the song it's really supposed to be "meet a body," not "catch a body."

I can feel every impulse and emotion that Caulfield experiences— and he's by no means consistent. Sometimes he does exactly what he calls phony in another. That's why I think the book is good—it shows the dilemma of needing people and yet not wanting them. For instance, as Caulfield says after he's asked Sally (whom he despises) to go for a trip and she refuses: "The terrible part, though, is that I *meant* it when I asked her. That's the terrible part. I swear to God I'm a madman." He cannot break completely away from what he knows is phony. Does he make an effort to get along? I certainly think he does, but when it comes to the point of getting along or going phony, he sacrifices the first and ends up with Stradlater's fist in his mouth. The idiot Stradlater stays in school and Caulfield gets the ax—and it's not because he's lazy—he does it deliberately— because he just can't do stupid things like describing a room. Rather he describes his brother Allie's baseball mitt with poetry written on it. If he were unintelligent, there would have been no problem. It is because he was really looking, sincerely, for a pure thing outside himself, that I admire him.

Hope I gave a crazy kid's view of a crazy kid.

XII. Postscripts

Appendix A is a selective catalogue of Salinger's early stories, compiled as part of their pamphlet by Gwynn and Blotner. Appendix B, on "The Language of *The Catcher in the Rye*," shows to what lengths earnest scholarship can go, but it should be of genuine interest to connoisseurs of colloquial English.

APPENDIX A: THE EARLY STORIES
by GWYNN and BLOTNER

Before finishing his "classic period," 1948-51, Salinger had printed twenty tales notably absent from his only collection, *Nine Stories*. Most of them were commercial stories that appeared in *Collier's*, *The Saturday Evening Post* and *Cosmopolitan;* but four of them were more arty sketches published in *Story*. And a half dozen of them introduced sympathetic characters who—under the influence of the same world war experiences that the writer underwent—develop attitudes and relationships and names that end in the fruitful Caulfield and Glass families with whom Salinger is later to feel so much at home. To change classifications, one may note that three of the apprentice works can be written off as short short stories, four as somewhat conventional tales of the Lonely Girl, three Destroyed Artist melodramas, and three as Marriage in Wartime stories. Another six are worth more consideration.

1. The Short Short Stories

The short shorts consist of two of the genuine *Collier's* surprise-ending pieces and one satire of this type in *Esquire*. (1) In "The Hang of It" tough Sergeant Grogan gives up on bumbling Private Pettit, just as he had given up in 1917 on Private Pettit, the boy's father—now *Colonel* Pettit of the regiment. (2) "Personal Notes on an Infantryman" simply reverses this military and family relationship. Lieutenant Lawlor tries to discourage an overage private who insists on making good and turning out to be the Lieutenant's father. (3) *Esquire* printed "The Heart of a Broken Story" as Satire rather than Fiction, since it begins with a Boy about to fall for a Girl he sees on a bus, proceeds to fantasies on how to have Boy meet Girl and ends with Boy taking up with Other Girl, First Girl having been in love with Other Boy all the time. "And that's why I never wrote a boy-meets-girl story for *Collier's*" Salinger concludes. "In a boy-meets-girl story the boy should always meet the girl." Not a very promising start for a writer whose stories would sell a million and a quarter copies.

2. The Lonely Girl Characterizations

Three of the four Lonely Girl tales appeared in *Story* and one in *Mademoiselle*. (1) "The Young Folks," Salinger's first publication, is better done than the others, and indeed, better than anything up to "Once a Week Won't Kill You" four years later. Wallflower Edna, whose pathetic chatter and insinuations are skillfully rendered, fails to impress stupid Bill at a college kids' party, but after retiring, presumably to cry, she reappears to pretend that she's still part of the gaiety. (2) "The Long Debut of Lois Taggett" recounts how long it takes a strange New York debutante (Lois says "ya" and "wanna") to grow up, the process requiring one marriage to a sadist and one to a boor, maternity and the death of the baby. The story's end offers the signal of Lois's maturity: she stops nagging her husband for wearing white socks. (3) "Elaine" represents so marked a regression as almost to suggest that the artist had been reading James T. Farrell a decade too late. Elaine Cooney is a beautiful moron of sixteen, brought up on movies and radio by a moronic mother who whisks her daughter home from her wedding to a movie usher.

That's all. (4) "A Young Girl in 1941 with No Waist at All" is Barbara, a slow-thinking but pleasant eighteen-year-old who finds a new young man proposing to her on a cruise she is taking with her future mother-in-law. Upset by the new proposal but not understanding why, she tells Mrs. Odenhearn that she does not want to get married—much to the latter's relief. The Chorus of the story, the ebullient Mrs. Woodruff, mourns the difficulties in store for the war youth of 1941, and Barbara's situation may be meant as a case in point, but the writer's last words identify Barbara's unresolved crisis merely with "the last minute of her girlhood."

3. The Destroyed Artist Melodramas

Better than any other sequence, the Destroyed Artist trio of stories shows a Salinger struggling with a theme he wants to be able to handle but which he really does not seem to understand. With "The Varioni Brothers," "The Inverted Forest" and "Blue Melody," Salinger never decides who the protagonist really is, what the central conflict really is, or whether or not any of the conflicts really make any difference to any of the possible protagonists.

1. For example, whose story is "The Varioni Brothers"? Is it about Joe Varioni, who fails to finish a wonderful novel because he must write lyrics for brother Sonny's popular songs? Or is it about Sonny, the heel who comes to appreciate Joe's work a dozen years after his sacrificial death? Or could it possibly be about Sarah Daley Smith, from whose point of view the story is told and who understands both the destroyed genius and the reformed heel? Even if the reader chooses, he is reluctant to believe that any one of these persons would ever be mixed up with the others, anyway.

2. "The Inverted Forest," a short novel (24,000 words) complete in one issue of *Cosmopolitan*, is so far from the Salinger of the only other novel, *The Catcher in the Rye*, that its irredeemably fantastic plot should be summarized. In 1918 Corinne von Nordhoffen, eleven-year-old daughter of a German baron and an heiress who committed suicide, is having a birthday party on Long Island. Unhappy because her favorite, a poor boy named Raymond Ford, does not attend, she goes to look for him only to see him being pulled out of town by his tough mother, a waitress. After the baron dies, Corinne goes to Wellesley and becomes six feet tall. She then spends

three years in Europe, liking only a young man who is killed by falling from the running board of her car. Back in New York, she occasionally sees Robert Waner—the narrator of the story up to a point—who loved her unsuccessfully in college, got her a job on a news magazine and watched her rise to be its drama critic.

On Corinne's thirtieth birthday, Waner gives her a book of poems by Ray Ford, now a known poet and an instructor at Columbia. She loves the verse, especially the lines "Not wasteland, but a great inverted forest/ with all foliage underground" (indeed, the best lines in the story), and she uncovers their creator. In ten weeks of talking dates in Chinese restaurants, she gets Ray's life story from him. His mother was alcoholic, and he has never taken a drink or smoked or been in love; he worked in Florida at a racetrack until rescued by a Mrs. Rizzio, who let him use her library and educate himself. Soon Corinne and Ray are married, despite Waner's warning that Ray cannot really love her and that he is "the most gigantic psychotic you'll ever know."

After the honeymoon, Bunny Croft, a literary college girl, enters their lives. (Somewhere in here, Salinger and Waner give up the chore of narration by means of an improbable note from Corinne stating that she will tell the rest of the story in the form of a private detective's log.) Soon Corinne drinks, Ray drinks, and Ray and Bunny run off from New York together. Corinne is consoled and upset by oafish Howie Croft, who, married to Bunny for ten years, reveals her as a shallow, adulterous and alcoholic monster rather than the aesthetic *aficionada* she seemed. Eighteen months later, Corinne finds Ray and Bunny in a Midwestern slum, where Ray sits drunkenly pushing papers around a card table in a pathetic attempt at self-deception and Bunny "work:." on her twelfth "book." Ray explains to Corinne that he can't escape because he is "with the Brain again. . . . *You* saw the original. Think back. Think of somebody pounding on the window of a restaurant on a dark street. *You* know the one I mean"—presumably his own crude mother who has passed alcoholism on to him. The End.

Once again, does all this happen to Corinne or to Ford—or even to Waner? (Surely Bunny is just an agent.) And what *is* significant about what *has* happened? Is it that Corinne has failed to grow up, that Ford has succumbed to a mother-image or even that Waner has been the Jamesian observer who turns out to have lost all by observing? If we care, we can only note finally that the worst things happen to Ray Ford and that it is his forest that is inverted. But the immediate corollary to this is that we have never been able to see this submerged forest for the mass of roots crawling about on the surface.

3. Finally, there is the *Cosmopolitan* Blue Ribbon story, "Blue Melody," another case of triple schizophrenia. Plainly the story wants to be about Lida Jones, a Negro blues singer who (in a situation based on accounts of the tragic end of Bessie Smith) dies from appendicitis because the Southern white hospitals to which she is taken will not admit her. But Lida's story is witnessed and told by a white boy named Rudford, who appreciated blues when he was nine years old, and who taught Peggy Moore to love jazz and him when they were kids, even though she gets married and materialistic a dozen years later. But this is not all. The narrator of the story is not Rudford but *another* person, a man who hears the tale of Rudford and Lida in an army truck in Germany in World War II, who inserts a note of admiration for Lida's records and who then promptly disappears from the reader's ken.

4. The Marriage in Wartime Group

The next three tales, all published in 1944 while the author was undergoing the experiences in the European Theater of Operations that would produce "For Esmé," are polarized between two commercials in *The Saturday Evening Post* and one impressionistic fiction in *Story*.

1. "Both Parties Concerned" are Billy and Ruth, both under twenty when they married, he now bored by war plant work and fatherhood, she worried by his need for diversion. Ruth goes home to mother but returns when Billy becomes understanding and responsible.

2. The "Soft-Boiled Sergeant," Burns, is soft-boiled not about his wife and her love of sentimental war movies but about her appreciation of his appreciation of Sergeant Burke, who befriended the boy rookie Burns in 1922 and who was killed at Pearl Harbor trying to save three buck privates.

3. "Once a Week Won't Kill You" is what Richard, leaving for

war, says to his wife Virginia as he urges her to take his dotty Aunt
Rena to the movies while he's gone. This story could have been
good: the reader can feel empathetically for the husband in his
predicament and the wife in her dilemma, and he can relish the
pathos of Aunt Rena's disoriented but noble response to Richard's
departure. But the tale is unhappily split into two separate scenes,
with Virginia and Aunt Rena never engaged in the dialogue that
would have made the differences between them truly poignant.
And there are mysterious unexploited references to Richard's
mother, who may have drowned with his father in a sailing accident; but Salinger fails to make plain the analogy (if he means it
at all) between the mother who used to whistle "I Can't Behave on
Sundays 'Cause I'm Bad Seven Days a Week" and the wife who
starts to be bad about taking Aunt Rena to the movies *once* a week.
All in all, the most that can be said for these three Husband *vs.*
Wife in Wartime stories is that they point up the same theme's minor
embodiment in "A Perfect Day for Bananafish" and "For Esmé."

5. The Caulfield Stories

The most interesting of the early sequences is the sextet of stories
that do develop five years later into "For Esmé," "Bananafish" and
The Catcher in the Rye.

1. On "The Last Day of the Last Furlough" before going overseas, Sergeant Babe Gladwaller is home reading Tolstoy, Dostoevsky
and Scott Fitzgerald (he incidentally mentions the Father Zossima
whom another sergeant was to quote so movingly). Salinger himself
may have been reading Ernest Hemingway's story "Soldier's Home,"
for Babe, like Harold Krebs, soon gets involved in keeping his
destination secret from his mother and in talking with his ten-year-
old sister, Mattie—who understands him much as Phoebe Caulfield
does Holden in the novel. Babe has two personal problems outside
his family—his love for the disdainful Frances, and his friendship
with the cynical Vincent Caulfield, son of an actor and himself a
writer of soap operas, whose brother Holden has once again run
away from school.

2. "A Boy in France" is Babe again, digging into a foxhole and
reading "for the thirty-oddth time" a loving letter from his sister
containing news of the haughty Frances. Like Esmé's letter to Ser-

geant X and Zooey Glass's phone call to his sister Franny in
"Zooey," the communication relaxes him and he falls asleep.

3. But "This Sandwich Has No Mayonnaise" shifts to Vincent
Caulfield, now seen training in Georgia in the Air Corps, trying to
make G.I. conversation while distracted by the news that his nineteen-year-old brother Holden, who had got through the European
war, is missing in action in the Pacific. Unfortunately for the unity
of the tale, the interest shifts to Vincent's lieutenant, who graciously
arranges for an eighteen-year-old private to go to a dance—a small
sacrificial act that Vincent should have been made to perform if his
feeling for Holden were to be rendered to us by more than wordy
reminiscence.

4. Babe Gladwaller survives the war, but Vincent does not, and
in "The Stranger" Babe takes *his* little sister Mattie to New York
to tell Vincent's girl—now Mrs. Bob Polk—about Vincent's death
in the Hurtgen Forest. Helen is the ideal Salinger girl, with records
and books in her apartment (Fitzgerald again, and the Rilke whose
work Seymour Glass's wife significantly avoids and his sister Franny
espouses). But Helen did not marry Vincent because he was so
cynical: "He didn't believe anything from the time little Kenneth
Caulfield died. His brother." Now, if this report about Vincent is
true, then the story is torpedoed by the very melodrama it seeks to
avoid (seeks to avoid by having Mattie along, by having Helen
happily married and by getting nowhere). On the other hand, if
we recall and utilize the cynical Vincent of "The Last Day of the
Last Furlough," we lose out on the poignancy of Holden-Kenneth's
death. And if we still feel keenly about Holden (because we see the
relation between Babe and his own sister Mattie, and she's still
alive), we are undercut on the poignancy of Vincent's death. Once
again, the writer has not seen it through.

5. Yet three weeks after "The Stranger," *Collier's* also published
"I'm Crazy," which concentrates on Holden at last, and indeed, is
a reasonably complete sketch of the exodus and homecoming of
Holden in *The Catcher in the Rye*, with the profane adolescent
language omitted for the sake of a family readership.

6. A year later, Salinger entered *The New Yorker* for the first
time with the wonderful Holden-Sally Hayes episode in Rockefeller
Center, called here "Slight Rebellion off Madison," which once

again avoided the vulgar phrasing that in *Catcher* allows Holden's climactic opinion of Sally to stamp him as at once neurotic, self-reliant and honest. We are now in the realm of Salinger's great success, and it is dispiriting to note that even a year after this story he could print "The Inverted Forest" in *Cosmopolitan*. Not to mention "A Girl I Knew," a rambling picaresque tale apparently based on the writer's own abortive career as a trainee in a family meat-packing business in Europe in 1937. The comic aspect of an eighteen-year-old American Werther psychoanalyzed in Vienna is delightful, but it hardly jibes with the climax—the narrator's return during World War II to find that his beautiful innocent Leah has been burned up in a Hitler incinerator. Even if Salinger is deliberately contrasting the two periods of his story, the second is simply too deep for tears, let alone for the parody style in which the first is presented.

APPENDIX B: THE LANGUAGE OF THE CATCHER IN THE RYE

by DONALD P. COSTELLO

A study of the language of J. D. Salinger's *The Catcher in the Rye* can be justified not only on the basis of literary interest, but also on the basis of linguistic significance. Today we study *The Adventures of Huckleberry Finn* (with which many critics have compared *The Catcher in the Rye*) not only as a great work of literary art, but as a valuable study in 1884 dialect. In coming decades, *The Catcher in the Rye* will be studied, I feel, not only as a literary work, but also as an example of teenage vernacular in the 1950's. As such, the book will be a significant historical linguistic record of a type of speech rarely made available in permanent form. Its linguistic importance will increase as the American speech it records becomes less current. . . .

In addition to commenting on its authenticity, critics have often remarked—uneasily—the "daring," "obscene," "blasphemous" features of Holden's language. Another commonly noted feature of the book's language has been its comic effect. And yet there has never been an extensive investigation of the language itself. That is what this paper proposes to do.

Even though Holden's language is authentic teenage speech, recording it was certainly not the major intention of Salinger. He was faced with the artistic task of creating an individual character, not with the linguistic task of reproducing the exact speech of teenagers in general. Yet Holden had to speak a recognizable teenage language, and at the same time had to be identifiable as an individual. This difficult task Salinger achieved by giving Holden an extremely trite and typical teenage speech, overlaid with strong personal idiosyncrasies. There are two major speech habits which are Holden's own, which are endlessly repeated throughout the book, and which are, nevertheless, typical enough of teenage speech so that Holden can be both typical and individual in his use of them. It is certainly common for teenagers to end thoughts with a loosely dangling "and all," just as it is common for them to add an insistent "I really did," "It really was." But Holden uses these phrases to such an overpowering degree that they become a clear part of the flavor of the book; they become, more, a part of Holden himself, and actually help to characterize him.

Holden's "and all" and its twins, "or something," "or anything," serve no real, consistent linguistic function. They simply give a sense of looseness of expression and looseness of thought. Often they signify that Holden knows there is more that could be said about the issue at hand, but he is not going to bother going into it:

". . . how my parents were occupied and all before they had me"

". . . they're *nice* and all"

"I'm not going to tell you my whole goddam autobiography or anything"

". . . splendid and clear-thinking and all."

But just as often the use of such expressions is purely arbitrary, with no discernible meaning:

". . . he's my *brother* and all"

". . . was in the Revolutionary War and all"

"It was December and all"

". . . no gloves or anything"

". . . right in the pocket and all."

Donald Barr, writing in *Commonweal*, finds this habit indicative of Holden's tendency to generalize, to find the all in the one:

> Salinger has an ear not only for idiosyncrasies of diction and syntax, but for mental processes. Holden Caulfield's phrase is "and all"—"She looked so damn *nice,* the way she kept going around and around in her blue coat and all"—as if each experience wore a halo. His fallacy is *ab uno disce omnes;* he abstracts and generalizes wildly.

Heiserman and Miller, in the *Western Humanities Review,* comment specifically upon Holden's second most obvious idiosyncrasy: "In a phony world Holden feels compelled to re-enforce his sincerity and truthfulness constantly with, 'It really is' or 'It really did.'" S. N. Behrman, in *The New Yorker,* finds a double function of these "perpetual insistences of Holden's." Behrman thinks they "reveal his age, even when he is thinking much older," and, more important, "he is so aware of the danger of slipping into phoniness himself that he has to repeat over and over 'I really mean it,' 'It really does.'" Holden uses this idiosyncrasy of insistence almost every time that he makes an affirmation.

Allied to Holden's habit of insistence is his "if you want to know the truth." Heiserman and Miller are able to find characterization in this habit too:

> The skepticism inherent in that casual phrase, "if you want to know the truth," suggesting that as a matter of fact in the world of Holden Caulfield very few people do, characterizes this sixteen-year-old "crazy mixed up kid" more sharply and vividly than pages of character "analysis" possibly could.

Holden uses this phrase only after affirmations, just as he uses "It really does," but usually after the personal ones, where he is consciously being frank:

"I have no wind, if you want to know the truth."

"I don't even think that bastard had a handkerchief, if you want to know the truth."

"I'm a pacifist, if you want to know the truth."

"She had quite a lot of sexual appeal, too, if you really want to know."

"I was damn near bawling. I felt so damn happy, if you want to know the truth."

These personal idiosyncrasies of Holden's speech are in keeping with general teenage language. Yet they are so much a part of Holden and of the flavor of the book that they are much of what makes Holden to be Holden. They are the most memorable feature of the book's language. Although always in character, the rest of Holden's speech is more typical than individual. The special quality of this language comes from its triteness, its lack of distinctive qualities.

Holden's informal, schoolboy vernacular is particularly typical in its "vulgarity" and "obscenity." No one familiar with prep-school speech could seriously contend that Salinger overplayed his hand in this respect. On the contrary, Holden's restraints help to characterize him as a sensitive youth who avoids the most strongly forbidden terms, and who never uses vulgarity in a self-conscious or phony way to help him be "one of the boys." *Fuck*, for example, is never used as a part of Holden's speech. The word appears in the novel four times, but only when Holden disapprovingly discusses its wide appearance on walls. The Divine name is used habitually by Holden only in the comparatively weak *for God's sake*, *God*, and *goddam*. The stronger and usually more offensive *for Chrissake* or *Jesus* or *Jesus Christ* are used habitually by Ackley and Stradlater; but Holden uses them only when he feels the need for a strong expression. He almost never uses *for Chrissake* in an unemotional situation. *Goddam* is Holden's favorite adjective. This word is used with no relationship to its original meaning, or to Holden's attitude toward the word to which it is attached. It simply expresses an emotional feeling toward the object: either favorable, as in "goddam hunting cap"; or unfavorable, as in "ya goddam moron"; or indifferent, as in "coming in the goddam windows." *Dam* is used interchangeably with *goddam*; no differentiation in its meaning is detectable.

Other crude words are also often used in Holden's vocabulary. *Ass* keeps a fairly restricted meaning as a part of the human anatomy, but it is used in a variety of ways. It can refer simply to that specific part of the body ("I moved my ass a little"), or be a part of a trite expression ("freezing my ass off"; "in a half-assed way"), or be an expletive ("Game, my ass"). *Hell* is perhaps the most versatile word in Holden's entire vocabulary; it serves most of the meanings and constructions which Mencken lists in his *American Speech* article on "American Profanity." So far is Holden's use of *hell* from its original meaning that he can use the sentence "We had a helluva time" to mean that he and Phoebe had a decidedly pleasant time downtown shopping for shoes. The most common function of *hell* is as the second part of a simile, in which a thing can be either "hot as hell" or, strangely, "cold as hell"; "sad as hell" or "playful as hell"; "old as hell" or "pretty as hell." Like all of these words, *hell* has no close relationship to its original meaning.

Both *bastard* and *sonuvabitch* have also drastically changed in meaning. They no longer, of course, in Holden's vocabulary, have any connection with the accidents of birth. Unless used in a trite simile, *bastard* is a strong word, reserved for things and people Holden particularly dislikes, especially "phonies." *Sonuvabitch* has an even stronger meaning to Holden; he uses it only in the deepest anger. When, for example, Holden is furious with Stradlater over his treatment of Jane Gallagher, Holden repeats again and again that he "kept calling him a moron sonuvabitch."

The use of crude language in *The Catcher in the Rye* increases, as we should expect, when Holden is reporting schoolboy dialogue. When he is directly addressing the reader, Holden's use of such language drops off almost entirely. There is also an increase in this language when any of the characters are excited or angry. Thus, when Holden is apprehensive over Stradlater's treatment of Jane, his *goddams* increase suddenly to seven on a single page.

Holden's speech is also typical in his use of slang. I have catalogued over a hundred slang terms used by Holden, and every one of these is in widespread use. Although Holden's slang is rich and colorful, it, of course, being slang, often fails at precise communication. Thus, Holden's *crap* is used in seven different ways. It can mean foolishness, as "all that David Copperfield kind of crap," or messy matter, as "I spilled some crap all over my gray flannel," or merely miscellaneous matter, as "I was putting on my galoshes and crap." It can also carry its basic meaning, animal excreta, as "there didn't look like there was anything in the park except dog crap," and it can be used as an adjective meaning anything generally unfavorable, as "The show was on the crappy side." Holden uses the phrases *to be a lot of crap* and *to shoot the crap* and *to chuck the crap* all to mean "to be untrue," but he can also use *to shoot the crap* to mean simply "to chat," with no connotation of untruth, as in "I certainly wouldn't have minded shooting the crap with old Phoebe for a while."

Similarly Holden's slang use of *crazy* is both trite and imprecise. "That drives me crazy" means that he violently dislikes something; yet "to be crazy about" something means just the opposite. In the same way, to be "killed" by something can mean that he was emotionally affected either favorably ("That story just about killed me") or unfavorably ("Then she turned her back on me again. It nearly killed me"). This use of *killed* is one of Holden's favorite slang expressions. Heiserman and Miller are, incidentally, certainly incorrect when they conclude: "Holden always lets us know when he has insight into the absurdity of the endlessly absurd situations which make up the life of a sixteen-year-old by exclaiming, 'It killed me.'" Holden often uses this expression with no connection to the absurd; he even uses it for his beloved Phoebe. The expression simply indicates a high degree of emotion—any kind. It is hazardous to conclude that any of Holden's slang has a precise and consistent meaning or function. These same critics fall into the same error when they conclude that Holden's use of the adjective *old* serves as "a term of endearment." Holden appends this word to almost every character, real or fictional, mentioned in the novel, from the hated "old Maurice" to "old Peter Lorre," to "old Phoebe" and even "old Jesus." The only pattern that can be discovered in Holden's use of this term is that he usually uses it only after he has previously mentioned the character; he then feels free to append the familiar *old*. All we can conclude from Holden's slang is that it is typical teenage slang: versatile yet narrow, expressive yet unimaginative, imprecise, often crude and always trite.

Holden has many favorite slang expressions which he overuses. In one place, he admits:

"Boy!" I said. I also say "Boy!" quite a lot. Partly because I have a lousy vocabulary and partly because I act quite young for my age sometimes.

But if Holden's slang shows the typically "lousy vocabulary" of even the educated American teenager, this failing becomes even more obvious when we narrow our view to Holden's choice of adjectives and verbs. The choice is indeed narrow, with a constant repetition of a few favorite words: *lousy, pretty, crumby, terrific, quite, old, stupid*—all used, as is the habit of teenage vernacular, with little regard to specific meaning. Thus, most of the nouns which are called "stupid" could not in any logical framework be called "ignorant," and, as we have seen, *old* before a proper noun has nothing to do with age.

Another respect in which Holden was correct in accusing himself of having a "lousy vocabulary" is discovered in the ease with which he falls into trite figures of speech. We have already seen that Holden's most common simile is the worn and meaningless "as hell"; but his often-repeated "like a madman" and "like a bastard" are just about as unrelated to a literal meaning and are easily as unimaginative. Even Holden's nonhabitual figures of speech are usually trite: "sharp as a tack"; "hot as a firecracker"; "laughed like a hyena"; "I know old Jane like a book"; "drove off like a bat out of hell"; "I began to feel like a horse's ass"; "blind as a bat"; "I know Central Park like the back of my hand."

Repetitious and trite as Holden's vocabulary may be, it can, nevertheless, become highly effective. For example, when Holden piles one trite adjective upon another, a strong power of invective is often the result:

"He was a goddam stupid moron."

"Get your dirty stinking moron knees off my chest."

"You're a dirty stupid sonuvabitch of a moron."

And his limited vocabulary can also be used for good comic effect. Holden's constant repetition of identical expressions in countless widely different situations is often hilariously funny.

But all of the humor in Holden's vocabulary does not come from its unimaginative quality. Quite the contrary, some of his figures of speech are entirely original; and these are inspired, dramatically effective and terribly funny. As always, Salinger's Holden is basically typical, with a strong overlay of the individual:

"He started handling my exam paper like it was a turd or something."

"He put my goddam paper down then and looked at me like he'd just beaten the hell out of me in ping-pong or something."

"That guy Morrow was about as sensitive as a goddam toilet seat."

"Old Marty was like dragging the Statue of Liberty around the floor."

Another aspect in which Holden's language is typical is that it shows the general American characteristic of adaptability—apparently strengthened by his teenage lack of restraint. It is very easy for Holden to turn nouns into adjectives, with the simple addition of a -*y*: "perverty," "Christmasy," "vomity-looking," "whory-looking," "hoodlumy-looking," "show-offy," "flitty-looking," "dumpy-looking," "pimpy," "snobby," "fisty." Like all of English, Holden's language shows a versatile combining ability: "They gave Sally this little blue butt-twitcher of a dress to wear" and "That magazine was some little cheerer-upper." Perhaps the most interesting aspect of the adaptability of Holden's language is his ability to use nouns as adverbs: "She sings it very Dixieland and whorehouse, and it doesn't sound at all mush."

As we have seen, Holden shares, in general, the trite repetitive vocabulary which is the typical lot of his age group. But as there are exceptions in his figures of speech, so are there exceptions in his vocabulary itself, in his word stock. An intelligent, well-read ("I'm quite illiterate, but I read a lot") and educated boy, Holden possesses, and can use when he wants to, many words which are many a cut above basic English, including "ostracized," "exhibitionist," "unscrupulous," "conversationalist," "psychic," "bourgeois." Often Holden seems to choose his words consciously, in an effort to communicate to his adult reader clearly and properly, as in such terms as "lose my virginity," "relieve himself," "an alcoholic"; for upon occasion, he also uses the more vulgar terms "to give someone the time," "to take a leak," "booze hound." Much of the humor arises, in fact, from Holden's habit of writing on more than one level at the same time. Thus, we have such phrases as "They give guys the ax quite frequently at Pencey" and "It has a very good academic rating, Pencey." Both sentences show a colloquial idiom with an overlay of consciously selected words.

Such a conscious choice of words seems to indicate that Salinger, in his attempt to create a realistic character in Holden, wanted to make him aware of his speech, as, indeed, a real teenager would be when communicating to the outside world. Another piece of evidence that Holden is conscious of his speech and, more, realizes a difficulty in communication, is found in his habit of direct repetition: "She likes me a lot, I mean she's quite fond of me," and "She can be very snotty sometimes. She can be quite snotty." Sometimes the repetition is exact: "He was a very nervous guy—I mean he was a very nervous guy," and "I sort of missed them. I mean sort of missed them." Sometimes Holden stops specifically to interpret slang terms, as when he wants to communicate the fact that Allie liked Phoebe: "She killed Allie, too. I mean he liked her, too."

There is still more direct evidence that Holden was conscious of his speech. Many of his comments to the reader are concerned with language. He was aware, for example, of the "phony" quality of many words and phrases, such as "grand," "prince," "traveling incognito," "little girls' room," "licorice stick" and "angels." Holden is also conscious, of course, of the existence of "taboo words." He makes a point of mentioning that the girl from Seattle repeatedly asked him to "watch your language, if you don't mind," and that his mother told Phoebe not to say "lousy." When the prostitute says, "Like fun you are," Holden comments:

> It was a funny thing to say. It sounded like a real kid. You'd think a prostitute and all would say "Like hell you are" or "Cut the crap" instead of "Like fun you are."

In grammar, too, as in vocabulary, Holden possesses a certain self-consciousness. (It is, of course, impossible to imagine a student getting through today's schools without a self-consciousness with regard to grammar rules.) Holden is, in fact, not only aware of the existence of "grammatical errors," but knows the social taboos that accompany them. He is disturbed by a schoolmate who is ashamed of his parents' grammar, and he reports that his former teacher, Mr. Antolini, warned him about picking up "just enough education to hate people who say, 'It's a secret between he and I.'"

Holden is a typical enough teenager to violate the grammar rules, even though he knows of their social importance. His most common rule violation is the misuse of *lie* and *lay*, but he also is careless about relative pronouns ("about a traffic cop that falls in love"), the double negative ("hardly didn't even know I was doing it"), the perfect tenses ("I'd woke him up"), extra words ("like as if all you ever did at Pencey was play polo all the time"), pronoun number ("it's pretty disgusting to watch somebody picking their nose") and pronouns' position ("I and this friend of mine, Mal Brossard"). More remarkable, however, than the instances of grammar rule violations is Holden's relative "correctness." Holden is always intelligible, and is even "correct" in many usually difficult constructions. Grammatically speaking, Holden's language seems to point up the fact that English was the only subject in which he was not failing. It is interesting to note how much more "correct" Holden's speech is than that of Huck Finn. But then Holden is educated, and since the time of Huck there have been sixty-seven years of authoritarian schoolmarms working on the likes of Holden. He has, in fact, been overtaught, so that he uses many "hyper" forms:

"I used to play tennis with he and Mrs. Antolini quite frequently."
"She'd give Allie or I a push."
"I and Allie used to take her to the park with us."
"I think I probably woke he and his wife up."

Now that we have examined several aspects of Holden's vocabulary and grammar, it would be well to look at a few examples of how he puts these elements together into sentences. The structure of Holden's sentences indicates that Salinger thinks of the book more in terms of spoken speech than written speech. Holden's faulty structure is quite common and typical in vocal expression; I doubt if a student who is "good in English" would ever create such sentence structure in writing. A student who showed the self-consciousness of Holden would not *write* so many fragments, such afterthoughts (*e.g.*, "It has a very good academic rating, Pencey"), or such repetitions (*e.g.*, "Where I lived at Pencey, I lived in the Ossenburger Memorial Wing of the new dorms").

There are other indications that Holden's speech is vocal. In many places Salinger mildly imitates spoken speech. Sentences such as "You could tell old Spencer'd got a big bang out of buying it" and "I'd've killed him" are repeated throughout the book. Yet it is impossible to imagine Holden taking pen in hand and actually writing "Spencer'd" or "I'd've." Sometimes, too, emphasized words, or even parts of words, are italicized, as in "Now *shut up*, Holden, God damn it—I'm *warning* ya." This is often done with good effect, imitating quite perfectly the rhythms of speech, as in the typical:

> I practically sat down on her *lap*, as a matter of fact. Then she *really* started to cry, and the next thing I knew, I was kissing her all over—*any*where—her eyes, her *nose*, her forehead, her eyebrows and all, her *ears*—her whole face except her mouth and all.

The language of *The Catcher in the Rye*, is, as we have seen, an authentic artistic rendering of a type of informal, colloquial, teenage American spoken speech. It is strongly typical and trite, yet often somewhat individual; it is crude and slangy and imprecise, imitative yet occasionally imaginative, and affected toward standardization by the strong efforts of schools. But authentic and interesting as this language may be, it must be remembered that it exists in *The Catcher in the Rye* as only one part of an artistic achievement. The language was not written for itself, but as a part of a greater whole. Like the great Twain work with which it is often compared, a study of *The Catcher in the Rye* repays both the linguist and the literary critic; for as one critic has said, "In them, 1884 and 1951 speak to us in the idiom and accent of two youthful travelers who have earned their passports to literary immortality."

NOTES ON THE CONTRIBUTORS

In order of their appearance in this volume:

JOHN SKOW, "Sonny: An Introduction," first published in *Time*, September 15, 1961.

Mr. Skow, born in South Bend, Indiana, 1932, is a contributing editor of *Time*.

ARTHUR MIZENER, "The Love Song of J. D. Salinger," *Harper's Magazine*, February, 1959.

Mr. Mizener, born in Erie, Pennsylvania, 1907, is professor of English at Cornell University; author of *The Far Side of Paradise: A Biography of F. Scott Fitzgerald;* editor of *Afternoon of an Author.*

DAVID STEVENSON, "J. D. Salinger: The Mirror of Crisis," *The Nation*, March 9, 1957.

Mr. Stevenson, born in Escondido, California, 1910, is professor of English at Western Reserve University and coordinator of graduate studies there; author of *The Love-Game Comedy.*

ALFRED KAZIN, "J. D. Salinger: Everybody's Favorite," *The Atlantic*, August, 1961.

Mr. Kazin, born in Brooklyn, New York, 1915, is a teacher at the New School for Social Research; critic; author of *On Native Grounds, A Walker in the City*, contemporaries; editor of *The Viking Portable William Blake, Moby-Dick, F. Scott Fitzgerald, the Man and His Work.*

JOHN UPDIKE, "Franny and Zooey" (originally titled "Anxious Days for the Glass Family"), *The New York Times Book Review*, September 17, 1961.

Mr. Updike, born in Shillington, Pennsylvania, 1932, is the author of *The Poorhouse Fair, The Same Door, Rabbit, Run* and *Pigeon Feathers and Other Stories.*

LESLIE FIEDLER, "Up from Adolescence," *Partisan Review*, Winter, 1962, and "The Eye of Innocence" (abridged), from *No! in Thunder*, Beacon Press.

277

Mr. Fiedler, born in Newark, New Jersey, 1917, is chairman of the department of English at Montana State University; author of *An End to Innocence* and *Love and Death in the American Novel.*

SEYMOUR KRIM, "Surface and Substance in a Major Talent," *The Commonweal,* April 24, 1953, and "Stung by an Exquisite Gadfly," *Washington Post,* September 17, 1961.

Mr. Krim, born in New York City, 1922, is a critic and editorial director of *Nugget Magazine;* author of *Views of a Nearsighted Cannoneer;* editor of *Manhattan* and *The Beats.*

DAVID LEITCH, "The Salinger Myth," *Twentieth Century,* November, 1960.

Mr. Leitch, born in England, 1937, is on the staff of *The Times* (London).

JOAN DIDION, "Finally (Fashionably) Spurious," *The National Review,* November 18, 1961.

Miss Didion, born in Sacramento, California, is associate feature editor of *Vogue* magazine; author of a forthcoming novel, *Harvest Home.*

ISA KAPP, "Salinger's Easy Victory," *The New Leader,* January 8, 1962.

Miss Kapp, born in Brest-Litovsk, Poland, is a free-lance critic.

GEORGE STEINER, "The Salinger Industry" (abridged), *The Nation,* November 14, 1959.

Mr. Steiner, born in Paris, 1929, is a Fellow at Churchill College, Cambridge; author of *Tolstoy or Dostoevsky* and *The Death of Tragedy.*

MAXWELL GEISMAR, "The Wise Child and the *New Yorker* School of Fiction," from *American Moderns,* Hill and Wang.

Mr. Geismar, born in New York City, 1909, is a critic and essayist; author of *Writers in Crisis: The American Novel, 1925-1940; The Last of the Provincials: The American Novel, 1915-1925;* and *Rebels and Ancestors: The American Novel, 1890-1915.*

FREDERICK L. GWYNN and JOSEPH L. BLOTNER, "One Hand Clapping," (abridged), from *The Fiction of J. D. Salinger,* University of Pittsburgh Press.

Mr. Gwynn, born in Tampa, Florida, 1916, is chairman of the department of English at Trinity College; author of *Sturge Moore* and *The Life of Art;* co-editor with Joseph Blotner of *Faulkner in the University* and co-editor of *The Case for Poetry.*

Mr. Blotner, born in Plainville, New Jersey, 1923, is associate professor of English at the University of Virginia; author of *The Political Novel.*

WILLIAM WIEGAND, "The Knighthood of J. D. Salinger," *The New Republic*, October 19, 1959, and "J. D. Salinger, Seventy-Eight Bananas," *The Chicago Review*, Winter, 1958.

Mr. Wiegand, born in Detroit, Michigan, in 1928, is Briggs-Copeland Instructor in English at Harvard University; author of *The Treatment Man* and *At Last, Mr. Tolliver*.

IHAB HASSAN, "J. D. Salinger: Rare Quixotic Gesture," from *Radical Innocence*, Princeton University Press, originally published in *Western Review*, Summer, 1957.

Mr. Hassan, born in Cairo, Egypt, 1925, is professor of English at Wesleyan University; author of the forthcoming *Aspects du Héros Americain*.

JOSEPHINE JACOBSEN, "Beatific Signals: The Felicity of J. D. Salinger," *The Commonweal*, February 26, 1960.

Mrs. Jacobsen, born in Canada, is poetry critic of the *Baltimore Evening Sun*—author of *Let Each Man Remember, For the Unlost* and *The Human Climate*.

DONALD BARR, "Saints, Pilgrims and Artists," *The Commonweal*, October 25, 1957.

Mr. Barr, born in New York City, 1921, is assistant dean of the faculty of engineering of Columbia University, a literary critic and author of two children's books on science. His article on Salinger will be part of a forthcoming book on American writers to be published by Doubleday.

DAN WAKEFIELD, "Salinger and the Search for Love," *New World Writing #14*, 1958.

Mr. Wakefield, born in Indianapolis, Indiana, 1932, is a free-lance writer and critic, author of *Island in the City*.

GRANVILLE HICKS, "J. D. Salinger: Search for Wisdom," *Saturday Review*, July 25, 1959.

Mr. Hicks, born in Exeter, New Hampshire, 1901, is contributing editor for *The Saturday Review;* author of *The Great Tradition—an Interpretation of American Literature Since the Civil War, Figures of Transition, Small Town, Where We Came Out;* editor of *The Living Novel*.

ARTHUR HEISERMAN, and JAMES E. MILLER, JR., "J. D. Salinger: Some Crazy Cliff," *Western Humanities Review*, Spring 1956.

Mr. Heiserman, born in Evansville, Indiana, 1929, is assistant professor of English at the University of Chicago; author of *Skelton and Satire* and various short stories.

Mr. Miller, born in Bartlettsville, Oklahoma, 1920, is Charles J. Mach Regents Professor of English at the University of Nebraska, and editor of *College English;* author of *Start with the Sun, The Fictional Technique of Scott Fitzgerald;* editor of *Myth and Method: Modern Theories of Fiction.*

EDGAR BRANCH, "Mark Twain and J. D. Salinger: A Study in Literary Continuity" (abridged), *American Quarterly,* Summer, 1957.

Mr. Branch, born in Chicago, Illinois, 1913, is chairman of the department of English of Miami University; author of *The Literary Apprenticeship of Mark Twain* and *A Bibliography of James T. Farrell's Writings, 1921-1957.*

MARTIN GREEN, "The Image-Maker" (abridged). (Originally titled "Cultural Images in England and America.") From *A Mirror for Anglo-Saxons,* Harper & Brothers.

Mr. Green, born in London, 1927, is a critic, now at Peterhouse College, Cambridge.

CHRISTOPHER PARKER, "Why the Hell *Not* Smash All the Windows?" (previously unpublished).

Mr. Parker, born in 1942, in Hornell, New York, is a philosophy student at Oberlin.

DONALD P. COSTELLO, "The Language of *The Catcher in the Rye,*" *American Speech,* October, 1959.

Mr. Costello, born in Chicago, Illinois, 1931, is assistant professor of English at the University of Notre Dame.

UNIVERSITY OF
EXTRA-
MURAL
LIBRARY
LONDON

INDEX

281